Amateur Armies

Amateur Armies

Militias and Volunteers in War and Peace, 1797-1961

Stephen M. Cullen

Pen & Sword

MILITARY

First published in Great Britain in 2020 by
PEN & SWORD MILITARY

An imprint of
Pen & Sword Books Ltd
Yorkshire – Philadelphia

ISBN 978-1-52673-443-3

Typeset in 11/15 by Ehrhardt

Printed and bound by TJ International Ltd

Pen & Sword Books Ltd incorporates the imprints of Pen & Sword Archaeology, Atlas, Aviation,
Battleground, Discovery, Family History, History, Maritime, Military, Naval, Politics, Social
History, Transport, True Crime, Claymore Press, Frontline Books, Praetorian Press, Seaforth
Publishing and White Owl

For a complete list of Pen & Sword titles please contact

PEN & SWORD BOOKS LTD
47 Church Street, Barnsley, South Yorkshire, S70 2AS, England
E-mail: enquiries@pen-and-sword.co.uk
Website: www.pen-and-sword.co.uk

Or

PEN AND SWORD BOOKS
1950 Lawrence Rd, Havertown, PA 19083, USA
E-mail: Uspen-and-sword@casematepublishers.com
Website: www.penandswordbooks.com

Contents

For my grandson,
Toby,
a budding historian and writer.

List of Illustrations

Acknowledgements

My thanks go to Rupert Harding at Pen and Sword, for his patience and always welcome feedback and encouragement. Also, to my erstwhile classmate at primary school, Katharine Ball, now Librarian of the Leddy Library, University of Windsor, Ontario, Canada, for hunting down a difficult-to-find history of the War of 1812. To my wife, Mairi Ann, whose encouragement enabled me to keep writing. Finally, to my late parents, who, many years ago, bought me a little desk at which I copied out favourite passages from Ladybird Books, a process that taught me that writing was not just something one did at school.

Chapter 1

From Wales to Cuba, 1797–1961

The Roman Legionary is one of the most recognised figures from history, and the general perception of the Legions as an extraordinarily effective military force is common. That commonplace view is built upon the Roman army as it developed in the second and first centuries BC as Rome began to spread beyond the Mediterranean, beginning the process that Scipio Africanus called, in his pre-battle speech to the Legions at the Battle of Zama in 202 BC, 'the conquest of the world'. That rise to pre-eminence was enabled by the professional legionaries of Marius, the general credited with the creation of a new type of legionary 'for whom military service was a career rather than a temporary interlude'.[1] These professionals became the model of military organisation that, following the collapse of the Empire in the west, princes and kings dreamt of recreating, and it is a model that still, today, defines the western military tradition. Yet, the very term *legio*, or legion, meant a mass levy of citizens, and the temporary call-out of able-bodied male citizens which formed the basis of Rome's first half millennia of existence. The change from a citizen army to a professional army brought with it political as well as military change, as 'the army ceased to represent the whole Roman people under arms and became more and more separate from the rest of society, their loyalty focusing more on their legion than on Rome'.[2] It was a change that enabled the continued growth of the Empire, but could not, in the end, prevent Imperial collapse in the West. Even though the habits and practices of Rome faded, the creation of a permanently embodied professional army had established a formula that survived, and returned fully in Europe during the eighteenth century. But, just as the model of the professional soldier survived through the centuries of war bands, knights, retainers, and the armed peasant, so, too, did the amateur soldier survive in the world of the professional army.

This book examines the role of the amateur soldier in the modern period, the period when warfare, at least in the Western world, has been characterised by the dominance of the professional soldier and the standing army. Despite that dominance, the amateur soldier, the part-timer, men embodied for local defence, and the volunteer, have played a constant role in military history, and, sometimes, a key role. Further, just as Rome's original levy, its part-time legionaries, had a political and social role, so, too, have many amateur soldiers and their units. For example, Chapter 7 in this book examines the vital role of amateur soldiers in the age of nuclear war, in Cuba in 1961. That year, the Cuban National Revolutionary Militia (MNR) played a crucial role in defending Castro's communist revolution on the island from invading Cuban exiles at the Bay of Pigs. The MNR not only had a military role, but also had political and social functions related to securing the revolution, and repressing any opposition. These were quite deliberately part of the role of these amateur soldiers (both men and women), but other amateur soldiers, who were not the creation of any government or revolution, also took on political and social roles. An example is discussed in Chapter 4, with the history of the Rifle Volunteer Movement in Victorian Britain. It was not until almost the end of the Volunteer Movement's existence that any of these amateur soldiers saw active service, but they had a noted place in Victorian society and culture. They were, in effect, an important part of one of the great projects of the long Victorian century, the creation of an orderly, stable civil society out of the social chaos of the Industrial Revolution. But, they also stood ready to face the French invasion which, at various times up until the defeat of France in 1871, seemed imminent.

Amateurs and Professionals

Almost fifty years ago, the prolific military historian, Major C.J.D. 'Jock' Haswell, turned his attention to the amateur soldier in his book *Citizen Armies*.[3] In his history, Haswell attempted the tricky task of defining what is meant by the terms 'amateur soldier' and 'citizen army', and arrived at a four-part definition:

> Firstly, it should have come into being as the result of a supreme national crisis arising from an actual or threatened attack on a country's territory and, or, its "freedom". Its original motives were therefore primarily defensive: to protect a "way of life". Secondly, the army thus raised must have had, from the beginning, the approval and support of the recognized local government within the country concerned. Thirdly, it must have developed into a properly constituted field force; and fourthly, the majority of its soldiers and officers

must have been volunteers whose lives and interests, certainly for several years before the war began, were not associated with soldiering, and who, when the war was over, returned to the lives they had been leading.[4]

This definition has only partial applicability to the amateur soldiers and armies examined here. It applies in the case of the various amateur military units that came together to frustrate the last French attempt at invading Britain, at Fishguard in 1797, but does not really match with the various volunteer units that rallied to the Stars and Stripes in 1898 to fight in Cuba against the Spanish; while the Rifle Volunteers persisted over long periods when there was no real threat to Britain from France, and, in fact, only saw action in 1899 against the Boer Republics. Further, the military structures that the various Canadian and US volunteers rallied to during the War of 1812 were already in place before any 'supreme national crisis' transpired. In addition, there is the case of the astonishing range of militias that prosecuted the Spanish Civil War, especially in the crucial initial stages when the outcome hung in the balance. In Spain in 1936, the regular army, split between those loyal to the Republic and those who rallied to the nationalist rebels, formed only part of the fighting forces of both sides, with anarchists, socialists, communists, Falangists, and Carlists putting large numbers of militia into the field. It was militia from these opposing political groups which determined the fate of the Alcázar in 1936, which is examined here in Chapter 6. The other strongly political militia and volunteer example in this book is that of the Castroist MNR, but this was a very large force organised by the new Cuban regime, as opposed to the Spanish Civil War where the political militias represented bottom-up creations at a time when there was no effective government which controlled all of Spain.

Considering the amateur armies covered in this book, it is possible to modify Jock Haswell's definition of what constitutes the amateur soldier and the citizen army. There is a difference of focus in that Haswell's approach was to consider amateur armies, his 'citizen armies', as emergency creations of established governments and existing states. The impetus for the rallying of Haswell's amateur soldiers came from the top, even if, in the case of the American and French Revolutions, the governments were very new creations. Interestingly, these two cases differ, in that the American revolutionaries were drawing, at first, on an established and inherited tradition of the English militia to create the revolutionary 'Minuteman', ready at a moment's notice to leave his place of work, pick up his musket and face the professionals of the British Army, while the French revolutionaries, although inspired by the example of America, turned instead to mass levies, organised from above, and rallied as the 'nation in arms'. The latter went on to act as a model for the armies of continental Europe, while the former, Anglo-Saxon tradition, continued to dominate in North America, Britain, and its Empire, right up until the First World War, which Britain, initially, tried to fight on the basis of the volunteer alone. The examples in this book represent both the top-down amateur army and the bottom-up creation, with some, particularly in North America, representing a combination of the two, with existing, but usually semi-moribund, militia structures being rapidly filled with enthusiastic volunteer soldiers at some time of need.

The amateur armies considered here cover a long time span, from the French Wars of the late eighteenth century to the Cold War, but there are constants that can be identified throughout. For an army, or any military unit to successfully take the field there are two basic requirements which relate to organisation and motive. The first reflects the fact that 'the essence of an army is that it should be organised',[5] and that even an almost totally amateur force still needs, if it hopes to be effective, discipline and some leadership by either professional soldiers, or those with prior military experience. This is best illustrated here by the case of the Defence of the Alcázar in 1936, where a large force of Republican militias failed to take the fortress and barracks of the Alcázar in Toledo. The Republican militias, largely anarchist and socialist in composition, lacked discipline and were quick to reject the leadership of regular Spanish officers. This contrasted with the defending nationalists, composed of regular officers, Falangist and other militia volunteers, and police, all of whom accepted the discipline and leadership of professional soldiers and officers, and, as a result, triumphed despite what was, apparently, a hopeless position. In a similar vein, the great explosion of amateur enthusiasm that created, in the face of government opposition, the British Rifle Volunteer Movement was, once it became apparent that it represented an unstoppable popular movement, provided with professional adjutants and non-commissioned officers who were responsible for organisation and training.

In addition to the demands of organisation and discipline, the amateur soldier is, more than the professional, a soldier motivated by idealism, by a cause. Jock Haswell's citizen armies, created by governments to defend their immediate

interests at times of national crisis, stressed the mercurial idea of 'freedom' as
the core motivator for the newly embodied amateur soldier:

> Invariably, the 'cause' was Freedom, or one of its synonyms: liberty,
> independence, emancipation or immunity, and nearly always the free-
> dom for which much blood was shed turned out in the end to be noth-
> ing of the sort … Yet Freedom, the cause which has no substance, has
> been the inspiration of most citizen armies.[6]

There is a good deal in this, which applies to many of those amateur soldiers
who fought, or prepared to fight, in the cases examined in this book. But there
was, in many cases, more than this. When the USA found that it was on a path
to war with Spain in 1898, there was no threat to the freedoms of ordinary
Americans, and, until the sinking of the USS *Maine*, the generalised hostility
(fed by the US press) towards Spanish rule in Cuba had not been transformed in
any concrete fashion in terms of volunteering for the life of a soldier. However,
once the *Maine* had been sunk, war fever took hold of a sizeable proportion of
American manhood, and, eventually, a very large volunteer movement forced
itself on the planning of the US War Department and the professional military
men. In this case, the motive was more akin to national pride and the determination to prove the superiority of American manhood over the 'Dons' and
the 'Garlics' (as the American soldiers termed the Spanish) than a desire to
defend American freedoms. Those motivations enabled ordinary Americans to
insist that the political decision-making of their country take into account their
demands, and, in that, showed that another constant of the amateur soldier, and
his armies, is the link with politics.

Amateur soldiers and politics

Clausewitz's famous reflections on war included the statement that 'war is a mere
continuation of policy [politics] by other means', and that 'war is not merely
a political act, but also a real political instrument, a continuation of political
commerce, a carrying out of the same by other means'.[7] However, Clausewitz's
central concern was war between nations, and the politics he was concerned
with was high politics, diplomacy and war on the grand scale. That concern is
present in a number of the cases examined here, but there is also a pronounced
current of internal national politics that, frequently, arises when one examines
the activities of amateur soldiers and their armies. Even in the examples where
amateur soldiers rallied to defend their homelands against invaders, such as in

Britain during the French Wars, or in British North America in 1812, internal politics were involved to a greater or lesser degree. The more that the amateur armies were the product of popular initiative (as opposed to government-led), the more, it seems, that politics featured. That tendency was not always welcomed by governments or by professional soldiers and regular armies. It was, for example, enthusiastic, patriotic Britons who created the Rifle Volunteers in the face of official opposition. This was a pattern that re-emerged in Britain again during the First and Second World Wars, when the popular instinct to defend the country was ahead of official policy in the creation of the Volunteer Training Corps (VTC) in 1914, and the Local Defence Volunteers (LDV) in 1940. In cases where existing military structures existed, such as militias or reserve forces, they were often neglected by governments and when times of crises did occur, the sudden rallying of amateurs to their flag also involved internal politics. This was the case, in particular, when the public commitment to national defence could often enhance the personal political ambitions of those who saw themselves as the officer corps of newly raised armies. Perhaps the best example in this book is that of 'Teddy' Roosevelt, a New York-based politician, whose heroic role as second-in-command of the US Volunteers 1st Cavalry, the famed 'Rough Riders', in the Spanish-American War helped, with judicious press coverage, propel Roosevelt to the White House.

If internal politicking was an aspect of the amateur military story, then revolutionary politics also played a part. In this book, the Spanish Civil War provides an example of the para-militarisation of politics of all types, and the pursuit of internal political goals through organised violence on a large scale. Interestingly, the various militias of the Republic and the nationalist rebels soon found themselves being corralled into more formal armies by their respective governments, before they were finally forced to conform to the political diktats of the Communists on the one side, and of the personal rule of General Franco on the other. The Cuban episode of the Bay of Pigs invasion in 1961 offers a different case of the amateur army and politics. To some degree the invading Cuban exiles, supported and armed by the CIA, were an amateur force, but the core of Brigade 2506, as it was known, was made up of men who were well trained and led by experienced fighters. More in keeping with the amateur tradition were the militia of the new Castro government, and it is this amateur army that is the focus of the account in Chapter 7. These examples are, of course, only two of many in the modern military history.

Two other good examples can be found in Ireland before the First World War, and in Germany after that war. The history of Ireland was effectively determined by two opposing amateur armies which emerged during the period of the UK Liberal government, 1906–14. One of the great constitutional issues of that time was that of the status of Ireland as a part of the United Kingdom; in particular, whether the island would be granted Home Rule by the Westminster government. In response to that possibility, the largely Unionist and Protestant north of Ireland created a popular army in the shape of the Ulster Volunteer Force (UVF). This force, founded in 1912, was able to put up to 100,000 men into the field, and claimed to be 'the first to use motorcycle despatch riders and motor transport on a large scale and the first to use armoured lorries for street patrols'.[8] This dramatic move by Loyalists brought a similar response from Irish nationalists, who created the Irish Volunteers (*Óglaigh na hÉireann*) from a range of nationalist and Republican groups. The Irish Volunteers, who, like the UVF, were partly armed by Germany, reached 200,000 by September 1914, when the First World War brought a very temporary end to both forces. Large numbers of men from the rival armies then volunteered for the British Army, forming both the National Volunteers, some of whose members fought in the 10 and 16 (Irish) Division, and the Ulster Volunteers who formed the 36 (Ulster) Division. While both varieties of Irishmen fought on the Western Front, a smaller, Republican amateur force of a few thousand, under Patrick Pearse, carried out the Easter rebellion, largely centred in Dublin in 1916, an event that led to the war of independence, the partition of Ireland, and civil war in the newly founded Éire.

Just as the formation of amateur forces transformed the history of Ireland between 1914 and 1922, so did another amateur army alter the course of German and European history. The collapse of Imperial Germany in November 1918 was rapid, with the emergent Republic facing a Bolshevik revolution, separatism, and, on its eastern borders, the appearance of new nation-states. The latter sought to seize and hold as much territory as possible, fearing that the victorious Allies might impose a settlement, something that, in fact, did not occur. Faced by a disintegrating army, a mutinous navy with pronounced Bolshevik sympathies, and a host of Slavic and Baltic nationalists, the German government was unable to organise the defence of the country. What emerged in this period of national crisis were numerous private armies who, together, were known as the *Freikorps*. Typically of battalion strength, but in a few cases of divisional strength, while others were merely enlarged companies, the *Freikorps* won a fearsome reputation in their destruction of Bolshevik amateur forces, and in their defence of Germany's eastern borders. Their savagery and fighting prowess came from the fact that the majority of their men were veterans of the First World War, joined in many cases by enthusiastic youngsters, particularly students, who had just missed fighting in the world war. Insofar as the *Freikorps* had a uniting political stance, it was nationalist, anti-Bolshevik, and strangely nihilistic.[9] The latter characteristic may well have been a product of the response of so many 'front fighters' who had fought, and lost, a war that brought their country to its knees. It was the fact that most of the *Freikorps* were veterans that puts their 'amateur army' in a different category from those discussed in this book, which were typically armies of amateurs with a leavening of veterans. It was also an inheritance that helped this type of 'amateur army', filled with demobilised soldiers, make the interwar period in Europe one that was, in part, shaped by politicised fighters. These were men like Ferruccio Vecchi, a demobilised *Ardito* (an Italian storm-trooper) who, in late 1918, wrote, 'With the end of the [First World] war, we are precisely those who have no direction any more, those surrounded by the abyss, those without bread ... where shall I go? What shall I do?'.[10] The answer for many of these men was to form the hard core of Mussolini's Blackshirt squads, and, in the case of ex-*Freikorps*, Hitler's *Sturmabteilung* (SA), both of which had a profound impact on their respective countries.

Soldiers and society

While the professional soldier may play a noted and sometimes pivotal role in society, the amateur is, by nature, an integral part of society as his 'soldiering' is sporadic and temporary. The amateur soldier's normal state is civilian, and the impact of that type of soldiering was often greater on society than that of the professional soldier and regular armies. In different contexts, amateur military service was sometimes seen as a burden to be avoided, while at other times it was seen to be a patriotic duty, a way of avoiding other military service, a source of interesting vacations, or an extra weapon in the arsenal of the socially and politically ambitious. All of these feature in the amateur armies discussed here, with the long-lived Rifle Volunteer Movement providing perhaps the best example of the inter-relation between the amateur soldier and the society he lived in. The British Army of the period was largely stationed abroad, in Britain's growing empire, and the professional soldier had little domestic social status.

The Rifle Volunteers, in contrast, acted as a focus for patriotic pride, a butt of popular humour, and the only way in which large numbers of men could learn something of military science in a country that refused to countenance compulsory conscription. Like the volunteer units of the French Wars, who were derided as having 'never charged anything but their glasses',[11] the Rifle Volunteers were sometimes dismissed as 'the dog potters', in memory of an incident involving an enthusiastic volunteer and an angry dog in Hyde Park. Yet, in the early years of the Rifle Volunteer Movement, vast crowds came out to watch the volunteers at their field day manoeuvres, and they received the accolades of Queen Victoria herself, who was particularly interested in these loyal subjects' part-time efforts. As the movement grew, so it changed, and by the end of the Victorian period it had taken on a decidedly working-class tone, with working men valuing the yearly camps, which were as much social as military. The amateur soldier was an established part of Victoria society, in a way that represented the ordinary subject's investment in Britain. In a different vein, the amateur soldiers of Castro's Cuba represented the state's mobilisation of that part of the Cuban population that Castro favoured as the recipients of the coming largesse of the communist regime. But it is also the case that the Castroist supporters in the MNR saw themselves as being involved not only in the defence of the regime against counter-revolutionary subversion and invasion, but also as playing a key role in the re-casting of Cuban society.

Soldiers and war

For perhaps the majority of volunteer and militia soldiers, war was a rare experience, yet in all the cases discussed in this book, amateur soldiers saw combat, and many died on active service. Further, in at least three of the examples, in the War of 1812, the Spanish Civil War, and Cuba in 1961, amateur armies made all the difference, and changed the course of their countries' history. More typically, the amateur soldier stood ready to defend, as the various amateur forces did in Britain during the French Wars – the Militiamen and Fencibles, who in time of war were integrated into the regular establishment, and were joined by the Volunteers, all tasked to provide home defence of the British Isles. This was a vital role, and enabled the professionals to take the war to the enemy overseas. This important function was, in Britain, still played by amateurs during the Second World War, when, by June 1944, around one and a half million Home Guards took on the main responsibility for the defence of the UK. The Home

Guards' role in anti-aircraft defence alone enabled 100,000 Royal Artillery to be released for the invasion of Europe.[12] At that point, around one out of every five men in Britain, and quite a few women, were members of the Home Guard,[13] and the UK's defence would have been much less secure without them. The Second World War saw amateur armies, police and security forces created in all combatant nations, and the final battles in Berlin, for example, witnessed the dying Nazi regime reduced to defending itself with *ad hoc* forces that included the desperate amateurs of the *Volkssturm*. Interestingly, there was also a Second World War connection with one of the amateur forces covered here, as a remnant of the Rifle Volunteer Movement, in the form of the Hong Kong Volunteers, put 1,662 officers and men, including an armoured car detachment, into the heroic defence of that city against the murderous Japanese assault in December 1941.[14]

The last example of an amateur army playing a significant role covered in this book is that of the Cuban militia in 1961, and it remains to be seen whether the enthusiasm of the amateur, and the needs of governments, will see such forces emerging in the future. In the past, professional and amateur soldiers have fought side-by-side, and paid the same price, as did the British regulars and Canadian militia at the Battle of Crysler's Farm in 1813. After the battle, burial pits were quickly filled with both types of men:

> Into the pits went the bodies of Sergeant William Bell, Drummer John Coppin and others of the 49th Foot, including Private John Torrance, who would never see Kerry again, Corporal John Murphy and Private Michel Janvin of the Canadian Fencibles, Corporal James Kain from Morton Salop in England and Private George Rose from Cork in Ireland.[15]

Chapter 2

Fishguard, 1797: Militia, Fencibles, and Volunteers

France, revolution, insurrection and war

The outbreak of the French Revolution in 1789 brought all the confusion and horror of societal collapse, regicide, the Terror, and for the rest of Europe the threat of a revolutionary infection. The prospect was of a 'vast, tremendous, unformed spectre'[1] spreading across the Continent, and a spectre whose proximity to the great monarchies of Europe made it far more of a danger than the American Revolution, the support of which had helped drain the French monarchy's coffers and prepared the way for its own demise. The chaos that ensued in France after the Revolution included eight years of fighting in the west of France, where anti-Republican forces fought a guerrilla war – the *Chouannerie* – characterised by atrocities on both sides, and the mass killing, verging on genocide, of the rebel population in the Vendée. That futile attempt to roll back the revolution, supported by French exiles from Britain, did not stop revolutionary France declaring war on both Britain and Holland at the beginning of 1793. Now the threat was of an ideologically-driven France attempting to export its revolution, while reasserting itself as a great power. Britain had entered a new phase in its long-time rivalry with its nearest continental neighbour, and one that, the brief Peace of Amiens aside, meant two decades of war.

French planning to invade Britain and Ireland

France sought to capitalise on its status as a new, revolutionary force, believing that an invasion of Britain would be aided by disaffected Britons eager to overthrow the monarchy and the established order. The primary obstacle in the way of an invasion of Britain was the Royal Navy, and French planning to overcome this obstacle moved away from a full-scale assault to the idea of landing comparatively small numbers of men at numerous points on Britain's coastline. The intention was to provide a catalyst for local revolutionary guerrilla bands to emerge in Britain, to be supported and armed by French invaders; in other words to 'establishing *Chouannerie* in England, a guerrilla movement made up of small but dedicated armed groups, like the pro–royalist *Chouans* of Brittany'.[2] The major flaw in this plan was the French assessment of the economic and social conditions, and the nature of unrest in Britain. While it was the case that the economic stresses of war, including high and rising food prices, had led to disaffection among elements of the urban and rural poor, 'all of which seriously concerned the authorities'[3], it did not amount to anything approaching a revolutionary situation – especially one led by France. Nonetheless, planning for French-led guerrilla war on British soil continued.

In December 1795, General Hoche, commander of the Revolutionary Army of the Atlantic coast, was tasked with launching the guerrilla campaign against Britain. The tactical planning was delegated to General Jean Joseph Humbert, who prepared two expeditions, one involving a landing in Cornwall, the second in Wales. Humbert planned to land 1,600 French regulars in Cornwall with additional weapons and equipment which, it was hoped, would be used to arm supposedly radical Cornish tin miners ready to support the forces of revolution. At the same time, a similar-sized force would be landed in South Wales, also provisioned on a scale that would permit the arming of potential Welsh revolutionaries, who, like the supposed revolutionaries of Cornwall, existed largely in the imagination of French commanders. Both French expeditionary forces were readied at Saint Malo in Brittany, and were due to embark at the end of June 1796. However, shortly before the invasions were launched, Humbert was ordered by Paris to begin fresh planning which involved an invasion of Ireland.

The last-minute change in the French invasion plans was a result of lobbying in Paris by the Irish nationalist, Theobald Wolfe Tone, who saw in the desire of the new French Republic to export its revolution a chance to free Ireland from British control. Wolfe Tone was joined in his efforts in Paris by other Irish patriots like Lord Edward Fitzgerald, arguing strongly that an invasion of Ireland by French forces would lead to a general uprising, and one that British forces, largely the Irish Militia, would be unable to quash. There appeared to be a good deal in the arguments put forward by Wolfe Tone and his compatriots, as the main Irish nationalist group, the United Irishmen, claimed to be in a position to put up to 20,000 into the field. In addition, in south Ulster, the midlands and the west of Ireland, a secret society, the Defenders, was engaged in a tit-for-tat low-level war with Protestant organizations that had appeared in response to the Defenders' activity, which largely involved attacking Protestant homes and seizing weapons. All of this activity and disorder gave credence to the Paris-based Irish patriots in their appeal to the Revolutionary French government.

Wolfe Tone's plan for 'the invasion involved 15,000 French troops being landed near Dublin, with another 5,000 in the north, plus 100,000 stand of arms and money sufficient to pay 40,000 men for three months'.[4] This was an ambitious and costly plan, and Wolfe Tone was passed from one government department to another for most of the summer of 1796. Worse, the picture that the Irish were giving the French government of the support they could expect was overblown, and the United Irishmen, in particular, 'sometimes appear to have been the most inept, and irresponsible conspirators in Irish history'.[5] However, in one respect, the situation in Ireland did appear to be in both the nationalists' and French favour, and that was the paucity of the defences. The Irish military establishment was independent from that of the British establishment, and in 1793, the total of Irish regulars was only 9,000 men, out of an establishment of 15,000. Further, 4,000 of the supposed 'effectives' were actually on leave of absence, leaving only 5,000 to defend the entire country.[6] As a result, a new Militia Act of March 1793 was passed, creating thirty-eight Militia regiments to defend Ireland. Their ranks were filled by ballot and by volunteers, and the men were called out once a year for 28 days' training, but served full-time when embodied. The introduction of the new Militia Act led to riots during the spring and early summer of 1793, with over 100 deaths, mostly in areas that were already affected by Defender violence. Despite this, the Irish Militia played the central role in the defeat of the 1798 rebellion, particularly 'for the defeat of the rebellion and of the French at Ballinamuck in September 1798'.[7]

The Battle of Ballinamuck marked the effective end of the French invasion that Wolfe Tone had lobbied so hard for in Paris, and which had led to the cancellation of General Hoche's plan to invade Cornwall and Wales. Following the last-minute cancellation of that plan, the French, influenced strongly by their Irish allies, drew up a new invasion plan which envisaged Ireland as the main target, with a landing in Wales as a diversion designed to prevent reinforcements from Britain being moved to Ireland. The main force set sail from Brest on 15 December 1796. On the face of it, the task force was strong enough for the task that lay ahead of it in Ireland, with forty-five ships, and around 15,000 men. The invasion fleet's objective was Bantry Bay, one of the longest inlets on the west coast of Ireland, and a fine natural harbour. The French fleet, however, faced a westerly wind that prevented some of the ships entering the bay, and made progress painfully slow up the inlet for those that did manage to enter. The weather worsened, ships dragged their anchors, French leadership was confused, and, eventually even Wolfe Tone agreed that the expedition be abandoned. Harassed by both the weather and the rather tardy Royal Navy, the remains of the French force returned to Brest by mid-January 1797, having lost at sea about 4,000 men and ten ships. The Bantry Bay expedition had failed, but the diversion landing in Wales was still open.

Invasion at Fishguard

The leader of the intended attack on Wales was a friend of Wolfe Tone, and another exile in France. He was an American in his forties, Colonel William Tate, a veteran of the American Revolution, but one who had been cashiered from Patriot forces, and who bore a strong personal as well as a political grudge against the British. He had arrived in Paris in the summer of 1795, met Tone the following year, and like his Irish colleague, petitioned the Revolutionary government to equip him to lead an attempt against Britain. Tate was taken up by General Hoche, who thought him the ideal commander to lead a small force – the *Légion Noire* – tasked with raising rebellion and destroying key installations, while spreading panic among the British. The original plan envisaged Tate landing near Bristol, marching on that city's docks to destroy shipping and the docks themselves, before marching north towards Chester, with the final goal being the destruction of shipping at Liverpool. This somewhat ambitious plan was to be carried through by the small force using the tactics of revolutionary terror; Hoche's orders included the advice that:

> The success of the expedition will likewise be materially forwarded ... by the terror which the success of the legion and the progress of the insurrection will carry into the bosoms of the unwarlike citizens ... Subsistence is to be seized wherever it can be found; if any town or village refuse it in the moment [i.e. immediately] it is to be given up to immediate pillage ... the inhabitants must be obliged to serve as guides, and any who refuse are to be punished on the spot ... All denunciations against those who join the legion must be punished by death.[8]

Tate was given the rank of *Chef de Brigade*, and his force of around 1,400 men scraped together from prisons under Hoche's coastal command, and from convicts, in irons, released from galleys. The military effectiveness of such men was clearly doubtful, but perhaps Hoche thought he had provided Tate with the right men to spread terror. Wolfe Tone's view, however, was that Tate's men were '*banditti*' and 'sad blackguards', and expected little from them.[9]

Tate and his Legion left Brest in four ships, two large frigates, a corvette and a lugger. Hoping to reach their landfall near Bristol without being spotted, the small force was sighted on 21 February by a customs cutter and a sloop from St Ives, and the alarm was raised. Worse, the wind prevented Tate from sailing up to Bristol. Tate and the navy commander, Jean Castagnier, argued over what step to take next, and, in fact, it is unclear whether or not they attempted to approach Ilfracombe. However, after various sightings of the small force, by 4pm on Wednesday 22 February it had anchored off Carreg Wastad Point, two miles west of Fishguard Bay. The last invasion of Britain had begun.

As darkness fell, the French force began its landing with small boats ferrying men and equipment to shore. One boat capsized, and eight men, plus the force's field pieces, were lost. Nonetheless, by the early hours of Thursday 23 February around 1,400 men had been landed, along with 2,000 stand of arms for the revolutionaries that were expected to flock to join the French. They had faced no opposition during the landing, and there were no British regular forces in the field anywhere near the invaders' bridgehead. Defence relied entirely on temporary and amateur soldiers. A scratch force was hastily assembled by Lord Cawdor, officer in command of the Yeomanry cavalry, who had been informed of the landing around midnight on 22/23 February. He assembled 'the Castlemartin Yeomanry, some local militiamen, some sailors from a man-o-war then in Fishguard harbour, and various other parties'.[10] The 'other parties' that would soon be deployed included the Pembroke Fencibles, the Fishguard Fencibles, and a troop around fifty mounted Yeomanry, some 500 men in all.[11] The Fishguard Fencibles were under the command of Thomas Knox (whose father had been responsible for raising the unit), a young man with no prior military experience. He had been informed of the presence of the French ships before any landing had begun, but failed to attack the invaders before they gained a foothold. Instead, with the men he had on hand, he set out pickets and sent for reinforcements. Other defenders, however, were more proactive. The officer commanding of the Pembrokeshire Militia, Lieutenant Colonel Colby, ordered up his men, along with the Pembroke Fencibles and the Castlemartin Yeomanry. All this activity took time, and it was not until noon on the 23rd that the various elements of the defending force were in place.

Having established their bridgehead, the invaders then appear to have lost all the initiative, and Colonel Tate seems to have abandoned any intention of leading a devastating raid through enemy country. Nonetheless, members of the Legion went out on foraging expeditions, taking cattle and sheep, and raiding homes that had been abandoned by locals. In the face of this activity, and the alarmist reports it generated, Thomas Knox, at his headquarters at Fishguard Fort with around 150 men, realised that the invaders outnumbered his Fencibles, and he decided to abandon Fishguard and retire to Haverfordwest. He ordered the guns in Fishguard Fort to be spiked, but the three professional gunners (from an invalid unit) refused to do so, and Knox led his men away. The small force of retreating Fencibles under Knox met up with Lord Cawdor, Lieutenant Colonel Colby and their mixed force. Cawdor took command, and the combined force of Yeomanry, Fencibles and Militia finally began an advance on the French. They and Tate had, meanwhile, had a commanders' conference, with Tate agreeing with Castagnier that the French ships should return to France, leaving the expedition to its task. In fact Colonel Tate appears to have lost heart altogether, later saying that 'he had been often in battle over his shoes in blood, but he had never felt such a sensation as when he put his foot on British soil – that his heart had altogether failed him'.[12] That, of course, was unknown to the forces advancing towards the French, many of whom, in keeping with their criminal background, were roaming around engaging in fighting with local people that left at least two dead, as well as a number of the invaders. In fact, it was the resistance of local civilians that entered the folk history of the invasion, particularly the famous actions of the women of the area:

> Campbell [i.e. Lord Cawdor] ordered all the women of the country-
> side ... to be wrapped in the long red cloaks then universally worn
> by Welshwomen, and supplying [them] as he could with real muskets
> and bayonets, and others with stakes, pokers, and the old-fashioned
> roasting spits, lined the stone walls from Bryn-y-Mor to Manorowen,
> with those brave lasses in their tall, steeple-crowed hats to make the
> French ... believe they were in face of overwhelming force.[13]

There appears to have been a good deal of truth in this story, but, whatever the details, Lord Cawdor's force of some 600 men were in striking distance of the French by the early evening of 23 February. Darkness was falling, however, and Cawdor decided to wait until first light to attack the invaders. In the French camp, matters had deteriorated rapidly. Not only had Colonel Tate lost heart, but so had many of the men who watched the French ships sail away. Further, the officers had little control over their men, whose indiscipline was heightened by drunkenness and shortage of food, while the general view among them was that they faced thousands of regular line infantry of the British Army. By late evening, Tate and his officers had decided that their only option was surrender. Tate sent a message to Lord Cawdor, headquartered in the centre of Fishguard:

> The circumstances under which the body of French troops under my command were landed at this place renders it unnecessary to attempt any military operations, as they would tend only to bloodshed and pillage. The officers of the whole corps have therefore intimated their desire of entering into a negotiation upon principles of humanity for surrender.[14]

By 9am on the morning of 24 February, it was all over, and the 'Black Legion' marched into captivity at 2pm, reportedly singing and laughing, with the exception of those that were too drunk and had to be moved by cart.

The French invasion at Fishguard was, in the event, little more than a chaotic farce. However, from the British point of view it was both a morale boost, and proof of the efficiency of the country's defence plans, particularly those involving temporary, part-time and volunteer soldiers. The Fencibles, Militia, Yeomanry and volunteers had all moved quickly to meet the invaders:

> there had been an effective 'closing up' of forces from as far away as Hereford and Gloucester, and some impressive performances by individual units. The New Romney Fencible Cavalry covered 61 miles [97km] from Worcester to Brecon in 5 hours, the Brecon Volunteers marched 20 miles [32km] to Llandovery in four[15]

All this seemed to support the reliance of the country on its amateur soldiery of one type and another, from the permanently mobilised, or embodied, Militia, to the enthusiastic Volunteer.

The Militia
Creating a new home defence force
In England, the Militia was a long-standing, much formed, disbanded, and reformed force. Originating after the Civil Wars when the 'trained bands' were supposedly replaced by the Militia in 1649, it was disbanded following the flight

and exile of Charles II following the Battle of Worcester. But on the Restoration of the monarchy in 1660, the Militia was re-established as a way of creating a defence force that was acceptable in a country tired of soldiery and unwilling to countenance a standing army of any size. Instead, the Militia, 'satisfied a populace who were content that these men should appear occasionally for drills, and not be always in evidence as representatives of oppression and discipline'.[16] This model also informed the defence of the colonies in North America in wars against the French, native Americans, and, eventually the British.[17] Nonetheless, the subsequent history of the Militia was characterised by periods of vitality, usually associated with invasion fears and panics, and periods of dormancy when the threats, both real and imagined, were few.

The Militia Act 1757 made substantial changes to the formation of what was the country's main home defence force, one that once embodied in time of war was regarded as being a regular force, and part of the standing army. As such, it then ceased to be an 'amateur' army – 'the militia was designed to form the home garrison in time of war in co-operation with the army, and indeed under army command. Long embodiments away from the counties made the militia semi-professional under officers who had often see service in the army'.[18] However, given the part-time nature of its peacetime training, in the initial stages of wartime embodiment the Militia exhibited many of the characteristics of an amateur force. The 1757 Act abandoned the property qualifications that had underpinned the Militia of Charles II, introducing the ballot. Each parish had to provide lists of all able-bodied men between the ages of seventeen and fifty (later, between the ages of eighteen and forty-five), and from those lists men were chosen, by ballot, to be eligible for military service. This only meant that a small proportion of men were, in fact, eligible for service; for example, in the East Riding of Yorkshire in 1757 only 12,339 men were eligible, or one man in every thirty-one.[19] Further, men could pay others to act as their substitutes, which increased the likelihood of service being carried out by the poor and the desperate. In effect, the Act was widely regarded as having introduced a general levy of all men, with the poorest being expected to give as much as wealthy men. The result was widespread rioting, just as occurred in Ireland once the Irish version of the legislation, the 1793 Militia Act came into force.[20] But rioting against the introduction of the Act was just a foretaste of localised, but worrying, problems with some Militia regiments once the entire English Militia was embodied in March 1778 and revolutionary France emerged as a new threat.

The Militia mutinies of 1795

With the outbreak of war with revolutionary France, the perennial problem of manpower reappeared. The Royal Navy and the Army struggled to fill their ranks, as service overseas, and aboard ship, was unpopular. Being posted to British territory in the West Indies was particularly feared, with very high death rates due to disease meaning that for many such a posting was a death sentence. One way of avoiding naval or regular army service was to enlist as a volunteer in the Militia, which meant no service abroad, and the Militia rose from 30,000 men in 1794 to 42,000 in 1796. The majority of these men were stationed on England's southern and eastern coastlines, being the most obvious, though not necessarily, as Fishguard showed, the only invasion area. The concentrations of troops in these coastal areas created billeting problems, with the barrack-building programme being inadequate and behind schedule. This meant that the options were tented camps, or billeting on civilians. Both came with problems, and the authorities were particularly concerned by fraternisation between Militiamen and locals, along with drunkenness and disorder. The concern around fraternisation focused on fears of revolutionary ideas spreading from elements in the population to the Militia. This was worsened by food shortages in the winter of 1794–95, when a very bad harvest and the exigencies of war led to price rises of basic foodstuffs. It was price rises and food shortages, rather than revolutionary ideology, that triggered localised, but serious, Militia disturbances in 1795.

In addition to its primary role as an army embodied for home defence, the Militia had a secondary role in respect of maintaining public order. However, the shortages of bread and meat, and the associated price rises, affected the Militia as well as the civilian population, from which they had so recently been drawn. Both Militiamen and much of the civilian population still had a strong belief in what was a 'fair price' for food, as opposed to the more recent concept of the 'market price'. This was the backdrop to Militia units seizing bread and meat and selling it at 'fair prices' both to themselves and to the civilian population. In early April 1795, the Northamptonshire Militia, stationed in the key naval towns of Plymouth and Devonport, seized foodstuffs and imposed maximum prices on bread, meat, potatoes and other basics. Other Militia in the south carried out similar actions, for example the Glamorganshire Militia at Bideford, the Exeter Fusiliers also at Bideford, and the Regulars of the 122 Foot at Wells in Somerset.[21] But the worst disorder was yet to come.

On 17 April 1795, 400 men of the Oxfordshire Militia, stationed at the unfinished barracks at Seaford, one of the Cinque Ports in East Sussex, fixed bayonets and entered the town, where they seized all the meat from butchers and sold it for 4d a pound. They then reduced prices at all other food shops in line with the concept of the fair price, before repairing to inns where they demanded ale at a 'fair price'. However, the unit's commanding officer appeared and got the men to leave the pubs. But the Oxfordshire Militia were far from finished. They seized a flour mill, took control of nearby Newhaven by 1pm on 18 April, where they boarded a sloop, carrying flour, in the estuary. In Newhaven, many men went to demand 'fair price' ale, while others went looking for ammunition. They approached a cliff-top battery of guns, but were foiled by a unit of Volunteers. Meanwhile, the authorities had begun to react, sending Royal Horse Artillery to the town. The Militia formed a line facing the artillerymen, but they were low on ammunition and eventually agreed to return to barracks under their own officers. But around sixty of the men left the returning column and returned to the White Hart, where they spent most of the night drinking with civilians, both groups taking the opportunity to indulge 'in their inevitable drunken orgy'.[22] The Militiamen were found all around the town the next morning by the Royal Horse Artillery, the Lancashire Fencibles, and the local Volunteers. Eventually, after much fighting, all the Militiamen were arrested. News of this reached the men's comrades who had returned to barracks, and 160 of them marched on Newhaven. Conflict was inevitable:

> The Artillery stationed cannons in support of the Lancashires who advanced on the approaching Militia. The mutineers plunged into a cornfield, which offered some protection, and faced up to the cavalry. They were fired on by the Artillery and when one ball struck a militiaman's musket and carried away the butt end, their resistance as a body ended and they fled, pursued by the Fencibles. Even so some men refused to give up without a fight and an hour passed before they were all taken. Two Fencibles were wounded, one seriously, but several militiamen were severely wounded by the Fencibles.[23]

The mutinous Oxfordshire Militia had been suppressed, but their example spread, with similar, though less serious, disturbances at Guildford, Petersfield, and Porchester Castle, along with rumours of potential disturbances elsewhere.

In the minds of the army and government, the Oxfordshire Militia suggested that there was a problem with sedition and revolutionary sentiment, and 'it [was] hardly possible to exaggerate the alarm felt in government circles over the Militia mutinies'.[24]

The aftermath of the Oxfordshire Militia mutiny saw improvements in rations, extensive efforts to discover how far sedition, particularly sedition carried out by civilian radicals, was responsible, and, of course, retribution. Twenty-two Militiamen were tried, two by regimental Court Martial, fourteen by General Court Martial (which could impose the death penalty), and six by civil courts. Four were acquitted, one was not tried, three were sentenced to be shot by firing squad, and the remaining six were sentenced to between 500 and 1,500 lashes. In the event, one of the death sentences was commuted, with the man agreeing to serve in New South Wales, one of those to be flogged was pardoned, and the others had the numbers of lashing reduced. The floggings and executions were carried out near Brighton Camp, with all the awful ceremony the army could muster. The High Sherriff reported that the floggings were carried out first, then:

> The men capitally convicted were then marched up between the two lines of the army accompanied by a clergyman, and escorted by pickets from the different regiments of horse and foot; at the upper end of the line, after a short time spent with the clergyman, they were shot by a party of the Oxfordshire Militia who had been very active in the … riots, but had been pardoned … the awful ceremony was concluded, by the marching of all regiments round the bodies … laid upon the ground.[25]

The firing squad then took the bodies away in coffins that leaked, covering the Militiamen with the blood of their comrades.

Militia life, training and service

On embodiment, the Militia became part of the regular army, but for service at home only. The Militia's wartime role was to provide home defence, release regulars for service abroad, undertake garrison duties, and, increasingly as the French wars continued, provide a pool of trained men that the regular army could draw upon to replace losses. The training undertaken by the Militia followed the handbook, *Rules and regulations for the formation, field exercise, and movements of HM Forces*, by David Dundas, which became the army's official manual in 1793. Militia recruits first learned to wear, clean and maintain their uniform and equipment, and were then introduced to foot drill, followed by arms drill. The key to this was the central importance of volley fire: 'accuracy was not at a premium – a battalion of Norfolk Militia in 1779, fired two volleys at a target 70 yards distant, which measured about eight feet by two feet. They fired 632 rounds and scored 126 hits on the target – a score of twenty per cent, which was considered good'.[26] Once trained to work at platoon level, recruits then had to master battalion training, involving forming up for line of battle, and the important skill of firing by platoon along the whole battle line. These skills mastered, training advanced to moving from line to column, and advancing and retiring. All of this took time, anywhere between two and three years. It is clear, therefore, that the embodied Militia, not to mention many new recruits to the regular army, were far from fully trained men.

The memoir of Militia and regular army life by Sergeant Thomas Jackson of the King's Own Staffordshire Regiment of Militia, and the Coldstream Guards, provides a detailed account of Militia service during the Napoleonic Wars.[27] Jackson's family were badly affected by wartime depression in his father's business, and, as a result, Jackson joined the Staffordshire Militia in 1803, 'under the delusion held out to young men that the calling-out would only be for twenty-eight days training and then home again'.[28] In fact, on completion of the basic training, Jackson and his new comrades learnt that they were to march south to garrison Windsor Castle. King George III had a particular interest in the Staffordshire Militia which dated back to 1797, 'when the monarch, impressed by the regiment's fine appearance and fervently expressed loyalty to the Crown, invited the corps to take up royal duties a Windsor Castle, his main residence'.[29] There, in addition to garrison duties, the Militia continued to undertake training, but their 28 days' basic training compares unfavourably with the two to three years that a regular soldier needed to become fully proficient. It was this disparity, and the fact that few of the Militia had seen the face of battle, that led them to being derided by some of their compatriots. Jackson, however, argued that on defence duties, and especially at the beginning of any war, the Militia were little different from the regular counterparts, who made the militiamen, 'the subject of taunt and ridicule of the soldier of the line, who gives him the soft and easy title of the "feather bed soldier" '.[30] Jackson's argument was that on home defence there was no difference between what was required of the Militia and the regulars, and, in his opinion, there were areas in which the Militia, or at least his own regiment, excelled:

> If taken from such a regiment as I was trained in, 'The King's Own, Stafford,' the militia soldier is, in every point of order and discipline, not only his [the regular soldier] equal, but, perhaps, his superior. For instance, marching regiments are so frequently on the move, to and from foreign quarters – having no settled place long together, even at home – so that they have not the mean of being made very perfect in their discipline. While the militia regiments are usually located in one spot for years together, and kept in constant drill and field practice till the attain the highest degree of discipline: hence the more probable superiority. And, farther, it may be observed, that in the first several years of the late French War, our troops made but few conquests, but oftener sustained defeat, owing, in all probability, to want of well-trained men; it being, to my knowledge, the custom to raise recruits as fast as possible, and, with scarcely any drill at the home depot, send them off to fight when they must be defective. But observe, again, the difference after the militias had been out and practised all sorts of duties for seven or eight years, and encouraged by large bounties to volunteer by thousands into the line, then we heard scarcely of anything but victories, down to the close of the war. So now where is the boast over the militia man?.[31]

The Militia was, as Jackson said, an invaluable source of trained men for the regular army to draw upon to replace its losses abroad, and Jackson himself eventually volunteered for the line, and entered the Coldstream Guards in May 1812. He subsequently took part in the storming of the fortified town of Bergen-op-Zoom on 8 March 1814, when he was severely wounded in the leg, which was later amputated, a process described in detail by Jackson in his book.[32]

The experience of Napoleonic warfare was not the only horror that Jackson witnessed in his service, and he has left us an account of the extremes of discipline that militiamen and regulars faced. Jackson wrote of the 'incorrigibly bad characters' in his Militia regiment, 'which nothing but strong coercion could restrain'; that was forthcoming from the 'lieutenant-colonel [who] was an old soldier, and very severe, determined to have discipline to the height'.[33]

That discipline was enforced by men being sentenced to 'three or four weeks in the black hole, some the "porcupine drill", as it is called, others to flogging, and, in some instances, to transportation'.[34] All of these measures seem to modern eyes to be extreme, yet were normal, even in the civilian sphere. That is not to say that they were not without a terrible shock value, as was most dramatically the case with flogging. Jackson gave a graphic account of floggings, and made a point of describing the impact on the watching soldiery: 'the first man I saw flogged was at Windsor barracks; the sight made me turn sick; I nearly dropped down. Many of the youths fainted and fell flat down'.[35] Men were typically sentenced to 300 lashes, although far more could be given:

> The culprit is finally arraigned for flogging, and to receive, probably, three hundred lashes with the cat-o'-nine-tails. The doctor stands by; the commanding officer then gives order to the drummer to go on. The drummer, with his shirt sleeves turned up, strikes on one spot – the shoulder blade – with all his might; if he does not, the drum-major at his back beats him with his cane until he strikes harder. Each drummer gives five-and-twenty lashes in turn. The first round generally brings a stream of blood to the waist; and as each proceeds to strike on the same spot, the mangled flesh will adhere to the lash, steeped in blood; some of the drum-boys being short trail the bloody cat in the gravel of the yard, which adds to the cut of every stroke. The poor victim, writhing in inconceivable agony, cries for mercy, but the answer is generally, 'No,' and, as I have heard added, 'If I forgive you God will not forgive me: go on, drummer.' The main faints; the doctor examines him, gives him water, and if he revives, 'Go on again,' till he is exhausted.[36]

Jackson went on to note that after 'a few years of these severities', discipline improved, unsurprisingly, and 'the regiment became perfected in the highest state of discipline'.[37]

The king took great interest in the Staffordshire Militia, and in 1805 he awarded them the title of 'The King's Own Staffordshire Militia', and they were then entitled to change their facings on their red coats from yellow to the blue of a royal regiment. The regiment accompanied the king on his annual summer stay near Weymouth on the Dorsetshire coast in August 1804. There they added to units already providing coastal defence. Those units included the

King's German Legion (KGL), made up of former Hanoverian soldiers allied to the British Crown. These men, along with the Militia, volunteers and Fencibles guarded the coast. The Militia also had another role, that of reinforcing the regular army. Between 1807 and 1814, more than 94,000 men transferred from the Militia to the regular army, compared with just over 100,000 direct entry recruits into the army.[38] Thomas Jackson was one of the men who took the bounty and transferred to the Coldstream Guards on 4 May 1812. His long Militia service was over, and a new and difficult chapter of his life was about to begin. As for the Militia, after the final defeat of Napoleon in 1815 it withered on the vine, 'its permanent staff was cut to the bone, musters were few, and in 1831 it ceased altogether. Though officers continued to be appointed'.[39] In 1852 the Militia was partly revived, though enlistment was voluntary, and, finally, in the great reforms of 1908 it officially disappeared, becoming a special reserve to the new Territorials.

Fencible Men

Two of the units which were involved in the response to the French landings at Fishguard were the Pembroke Fencibles, and the Fishguard Fencibles. There were similarities between the Militia and the Fencibles in that both were embodied during times of war when the regular army was largely committed overseas. However, whereas the Militia were embodied in peacetime for train-ing, the Fencibles were not. Further, all Fencible men were volunteers, whereas, in theory at least, Militia men were raised from balloting; although, in reality many, like Thomas Jackson, were volunteers. The term 'fencible' was originally a Scots word for 'a militiaman or more precisely someone capable of carrying arms "defencible" '.[40] Fencible regiments were raised at the time of the Seven Years' War, 1756–63, and during the American Revolution. They were again raised during the war with revolutionary France, disbanded following the Peace of Amiens and raised once more with the resumption of war with France.

In 1793, Fencible regiments were raised in numbers first in Scotland and on the Isle of Man, and then in England, Wales and Ireland. Although the orig-inal terms of service stipulated that the area of a Fencible regiments' service was within its country of origin, that changed under the pressures of war. For example, one of the first Fencible regiments raised in Scotland was the Earl of Hopetoun's Regiment. Recruited in the Edinburgh area, they were told that they could not be marched out of Scotland, except in the event of a French invasion. This proved not to be the case, and there was much opposition among Scots Fencibles to being ordered to England. The Hopetoun men, however, were sent to Banff in the north of Scotland. The resistance to being deployed beyond Scotland led to a change in terms of service, and 'subsequent letters of service stipulated that Fencible regiments could be employed anywhere in the British Isles. Eventually this was widened still further to take in service anywhere in Europe'.[41] Far more typically, however, fencible men served in Britain, and added to the mix of units which provided home defence. In the East Riding of Yorkshire, for example, from 1792–1801, three regiments of Militia were raised, two of foot and one of horse, totalling some 1,711 men, while only one Fencible regiment was raised, the Loyal York Fencibles, with an establishment of ten companies. These men, in fact, served in Ireland until 1801 before being disbanded in 1802, after the Peace of Amiens.[42] In the same period, the defence of the Isle of Man was largely in the hands of two corps (i.e., regiments) of the 'Fencible Corps in the Isle of Man', later the Royal Manx Fencibles. The first corps was raised in 1793, and by June 1798, consisted of:

> Two majors, three lieutenants, two ensign, twenty-six sergeants, ten drummers and 464 rank and file at Castletown; one captain, one ensign, two sergeants, two drummers and fifty-nine privates at Douglas; one captain-lieutenant, one lieutenant, one sergeant, one drummer and thirty-two rank and file at Ramsey; at Peel there were one lieutenant, one sergeant, one drummer and thirty-three privates.[43]

These 644 Fencible men, and a small number of artillery pieces defending the island's four ports, represented the main wartime defence of the island.

Fencible regiments were not the only type of Fencibles raised, as the Royal Navy raised 'Sea Fencibles' for operations in coastal waters. The government authorised the raising of Sea Fencibles in May 1798. Volunteers for this coastal defence force were exempt from being press-ganged into the Royal Navy, which acted as a strong incentive to men living on the coast and engaged in maritime activities to join the Sea Fencibles. Captain Edwards, RN, was appointed commander of the Sea Fencibles on the Humber, and quickly raised enough men from merchant sailors, pilots, fishermen and bargees, to put 'a sloop with eight guns, and eight smaller craft, each equipped with two long 9-pounder guns and one 32-pounder carronade'[44] to sea to guard the approaches to the River Humber. The important port of Hull was defended by five 24-pounder guns, thirteen 18-pounder guns and four 9-pounder guns, plus two 24-pounders and two 18-pounders outside the citadel. These were augmented by six more 24-pounders, which at first were crewed by Sea Fencibles, then by regulars who trained militiamen to man the pieces.[45]

As with their land-based Fencible counterparts, the men of the Humber force were disbanded following the Peace of Amiens. But that short-lived peace soon ended, and a major recruiting effort to the Sea Fencibles was undertaken to help defend Hull, the Humber and the coastline from the River Ouse to Flamborough Head:

> By the middle of July [1803] no fewer than 3,000 men had been enrolled in the Sea Fencibles in East Yorkshire, exercising each Sunday and receiving 1/- a day if called out for duty. In Hull several vessels were converted for use as gun boats on the Humber, principally the Trinity House yacht and six pilot boats which ranged in size from 20 to 42 tons, and also a number of sloops armed with 24-pounder guns.[46]

In the period of the struggle against Napoleon, the Sea Fencibles on the Humber represented the largest coastal force immediately available in the area. Similarly, on land, it was Militia forces, the Yeomanry and the Volunteers which provided the core of the defence of this part of England, with five Militia battalions (approximately 4,000 men), supported by three Yeomanry Cavalry regiments totalling around 390 men, and eleven Volunteer infantry regiments and one Volunteer artillery unit with around 1,750 men.[47] The embodied, war-time Militia was, of course, regarded as 'regular', but the Fencible, Yeomanry, and Volunteer units were all temporary and volunteer men.

The Volunteers

The Volunteers of the French Wars represent a recurring theme in the defence of Britain – that of the spontaneous and popular emergence of local defence, typically in the face of initial official disapproval and obstruction. The widespread belief at the start of the war with France was that neither the regular army nor the Militia provided a sufficient force with which Britain could be defended, which led to concerned citizens forming their own Volunteer units. The initial impetus was that French revolutionary ideas were present in Britain and might spread, creating an internal opposition that would aid any attempt by France to invade; a belief that did, indeed, influence French invasion planning. The first

Volunteer Association was formed in March 1794 for the parish of St George's, Hanover Square, in west London. Unlike the Militia, the Association had no formal or statutory basis, and was not under any legal control of the authorities. There was fear in government circles that the appearance of such Associations might represent some kind of politicised popular militia of the sort that had characterised the early days of the American Revolution. However, although the large number of Volunteer units which eventually appeared were far from being uniform in outlook or politics, the overwhelming stance of the Volunteers was loyal and, 'dedicated to resist French ideas and to defend the British constitution and the existing social order'.[48] That focus on combatting any spread of French revolutionary ideas in Britain changed, particularly after the failed invasion attempts at Bantry Bay and Fishguard, which led to an increase in the numbers of patriotic volunteers coming forward infused with 'a patriotism ... that invoked defence and survival of the nation in the face of threatened conquest, or, if not that, French world hegemony'.[49] In the face of the spontaneous organisation of Volunteer associations, the government put its fears aside and, within a few weeks of the St George's Association being formed, passed a new Act, in April, 'for encouraging and disciplining such corps or companies of men as shall voluntarily enrol themselves for the defence of their counties, towns, or coasts, or for the general defence of the Kingdom during the present war'.[50] Not for the last time was a tardy British government pushed by patriots into accepting and recognising the role of volunteers in the defence of Britain. The same process was repeated again in the First World War, when popular pressure helped create the Volunteer Training Corps, and, yet again, in 1940, when public pressure led to the formation of the Local Defence Volunteers, later the Home Guard.[51]

The Act of 1794 led to the rapid establishment of Volunteer units of foot and horse, to add to the thirty-two already existing mounted Volunteer units – the Yeomanry – and seventy-two Volunteer companies of foot and guns. A second Act was passed later in the year that gave Volunteers exemption from service in the Militia provided they could show attendance at unit drills and training. In addition, the Act offered counties the option of deciding whether their forces would be raised by Militia ballot or by service in Volunteer units. This created an opening for leading members of local society to raise and support the creation of Volunteer regiments, and the movement continued to grow. Following the Fishguard invasion, the government put forward the idea that in addition to the Volunteers, parishes should establish Armed Associations for local defence.

The next year saw the threat of invasion reach a new level, and the authorities pushed for even greater levels of local defence by Volunteers. A further Act enabled the creation of more Armed Associations, while popular enthusiasm led to even more Volunteer units being formed:

> By 1 June 1798, the strength of the Yeomanry and other Volunteer cavalry corps in Great Britain was claimed to be 19,190. By the end of 1800 the total was 24,000, with another 87,000 (all ranks) serving in Volunteer infantry and artillery corps. These totals did not include those men enrolled in the parish Armed Associations.[52]

During the short lull in hostilities following the Peace of Amiens, the government sought to keep the Volunteer movement alive, especially the Yeomanry, as the latter were seen as having a dual role, that of guarding against invasion but also of helping to keep the peace and, if necessary, suppress outbreaks of radicalism. A new Act was passed in June 1802, which allowed Yeomanry and Volunteers to continue on the understanding that no financial support would be forthcoming from the government. In the event, some subvention was deemed necessary, and the majority of Yeomanry corps continued in existence.

With the resumption of war with France, the Militia was embodied once more, and the government offered pay for Volunteers. New Volunteer units were formed, and old ones reformed until some 380,000 men could be mustered by the Volunteer infantry, artillery, and the Yeomanry. But the enthusiasm of the Volunteers, while welcomed when it was feared that the French were on the point of descending on Britain (especially in the period from 1803–05, when Napoleon's 'Army of England' was encamped near Boulogne), it was less so when that threat waned. The particular issue was that Volunteers were exempt from service in the regular army or the Militia, and were therefore seen as a limit on the numbers of men that could be recruited into these forces. This issue came to the fore after William Windham became Secretary for War and the Colonies in February 1806. Windham was an opponent of the Volunteers, believing them to be ineffective as soldiers, expensive, and a barrier to recruiting for the army. His 'reforms' of the Volunteers impacted on their morale and training, and led to some 90,000 men resigning from their units by the end of 1807. A new administration, under Castlereagh, saw a new approach to the question of home defence, with a Local Militia force being established. The Local Militia was designed to form permanent local forces, drawn from men aged between eighteen and forty. Service was for four years, decided by ballot, with no substitution allowed. The men were only to serve in their local area, and the training obligation was the same as that of the Volunteers, some twenty days per year. It was possible to pay a fine, which depended on annual income, to avoid service in the Local Militia, and that fine system was also extended to those men balloted but already serving in the Volunteers, albeit at half rates. The latter 'encouragement', when added to the abolition of the bounty and uniform allowances, dealt a heavy blow to the Volunteers. By early 1810, some 125,000 Volunteers had transferred to the Local Militia, which, in total, numbered 195,161 men. By contrast, the Volunteers continued to decline, falling to 68,643 men by March 1812.[53] A year later, almost all Volunteer units were disbanded, with the exception of the Yeomanry, of nearly 20,000, who were deemed to have a useful public order role, officered as they were by the aristocracy and gentry, who frequently filled their ranks with their own servants, tenant farmers and employees.

Volunteers had been raised before in the eighteenth century, in 1745 to face the Jacobite threat, in 1759 and in 1779, but the Volunteers of the French Wars, 'not only came out in unprecedented numbers but also remained ready for active service for a much longer period of time'.[54] Military service reached high levels during the French Wars, with around twenty per cent of British men seeing service, the greater number of whom served in the Volunteers. Although the Volunteers saw no action, they played an important role in the defence of Britain, and the memory of the Volunteer movement at that time lived on, helping to inspire the much more long-lived, and significant, Rifle Volunteer movement of the Victorian period.[55] The Militia, the Fencibles and Volunteers who formed ranks to defend their country against revolutionary then imperial France, also had counterparts across the Atlantic in British North America, who were, in the War of 1812, central to the successful defence of their homeland against an expansionist United States.[56]

Chapter 3

The War of 1812: War, Society and Politics – Militias in the United States and Canada, 1812–15

Militias in North America – the British and French traditions

Militia forces have an important political and military place in North American history. From the outset of English, then British colonisation, local militias were essential to the survival of the tiny outposts that eventually grew into the United States. Similarly, the combination of distance from the home country, manpower shortages, the imperatives of agriculture and fur trapping, also gave militias a central role in the development of 'New France'. In the struggle for supremacy in North America, militias not only protected British and French colonists from attacks by increasingly displaced Indians,* but were also key to the two rival European powers in their attempts to dominate North America. The importance of militias to the survival and expansion of the colonies led to them playing a role in the political and social life of both British and French North America that was long-lasting. In fact, the British militia tradition, given new life in the Americas, went on to be one of the vital foundation myths of the victory of the new American Republic over its parent nation. The fame of the 'Minuteman', the heroic, democratic citizen, ready at a moment's notice to fight the might of the British Empire, and its famous Redcoats, meant that a generation after the American Revolution, US militiamen were 'the overwhelming majority of the soldiers employed during this war [of 1812]'.[1] In New France, the small settler and pioneer population relied as much, if not more, on the militia system for the defence, consolidation and expansion of French Canada. However, whereas the English and British model of militia organisation in North America helped grow a democratic form of defence and politics, New France was the product of an absolutist system that relied much more on an aristocratic form of part-time military

---

* The term 'Indian' has been used throughout this chapter to refer to First Nation, or indigenous peoples, as the contemporary usage.

organisation. By the War of 1812, both traditions were in play, with important military implications, especially for the United States, which rediscovered that militias alone were far from the answer to European-style warfare, even in the significantly different geographic and climatic conditions of North America.

The origins of militia forces in North America – three traditions
The English inheritance

By the seventeenth century, the ancient system of militia defence, dating back to the Anglo-Saxon *fyrd*, was moribund in England. However, the nature of English colonisation of the New World gave that system new life, and the conditions of North America brought changes to the militia as a form of military organisation. A mixture of inherited distrust of standing armies, the civilian-led nature of English colonisation, the threats the colonists faced (from other European powers and indigenous tribes), limited manpower resources, and the geography of the new colonies, all combined to create an English-origin, American adaptation of militia warfare.

The early colonists were not soldiers, although they counted veterans of the near genocidal wars in Ireland, and of the Dutch Wars, among their numbers. These veterans provided a degree of military expertise, but the combination of a deep-seated distrust of standing armies, along with the very limited manpower resources that the colonists possessed, meant that the defence of the colonies lay in the hands of numerous militias. The original organisation of those militias was based on universal male service (including, at first, indentured servants and slaves), but the basic structure of the town or county militia unit provided only for local defence. This was very much in line with the older, English tradition, but the circumstances of the colonists meant that by itself, reactive defence was not sufficient. Instead, the town or county militia formed the recruiting pool for the younger men who gave the militias a vital offensive capability. Faced by enemies who held the initiative in terms of choosing when and where they would raid, the colonists developed their own counter-offensive militia forces:

> Astute colonial leaders quickly learned to concede the first blows
> to Indians and rely on the militia primarily as an offensive, or more
> accurately counteroffensive weapon. During the half-dozen major
> Indian wars of the seventeenth century, it was not unusual for pow-
> erful colonial expeditions of up to a thousand men to attack and lay

waste Indian towns and fields … Again and again, the militia seized
the initiative and relieved pressure on beleaguered colonial farms and
villages along the frontier. Reliance on the offensive was one of the
key differences between the English and American militias; since
Anglo-Saxon times the militia in England had served as a shield, but
in America it functioned as a sword as well.[2]

In effect, a dual militia system grew up, with the most active elements typically
being younger men, and those with fighting experience. These men were part of
the general muster of militia, but were usually volunteers who came forward for
offensive operations, effectively volunteering for a campaign, which often meant
a season. The skills and effectiveness of volunteer militia gave them a role fighting alongside British regulars, as well as providing much of the raw material for
the Provincial Corps. These men, raised for a single campaign against Indian or
French raiders, or for wars against Spain or France, became a valuable adjunct
to the regular British forces, whose numbers rose and fell depending on the state
of relations between the European powers at any one time. At the same time, the
growth of the British North American colonies, and the increasingly settled and
secure nature of most towns and villages, meant that the general militia fell further into disuse. Additionally, many townsmen had few, if any skills that applied
to the sort wilderness fighting that characterised warfare along the frontiers.
Musters of general militias became fewer, and membership of a militia often had
more important social or political than military implications. When needed, the
volunteer militiamen, often non-property owners who were excluded from the
general militia, were there to do the fighting.

British North American militia were, from the outset, an example of civilian control of the military. All of the early, male colonists were expected to
muster to defend their villages and towns, but not as a regular force, organised
and differentiated from their fellow citizens. Seventeenth-century 'colonial
magistrates, by tightly controlling the purse strings, made subordination of the
military fundamental to the colonial way of war'.[3] Even with the later rise to
importance of the volunteer militiaman, and hence the decline of the idea of
all citizens as soldiers, the concept of a military that was led, organised, and
legitimised by civilian authority remained strong. This ideal would come into its
own with the American Revolution, bringing with it popular support, but also
military headaches for General Washington.

The militia of New France

In contrast to the Anglo-American militia tradition, the militia of 'New France' had different social and political functions, even if its military use paralleled, to a large degree, that of the colonists in British territory. French colonisation of territories that would eventually be known as Lower Canada took on a different form in respect of military organisation. As with the English colonists further south, one of the initial problems facing the French was the very small numbers of colonists. By 1648, over a decade since the founding of what would become the city of Quebec, there were only around 600 French settlers in New France. This figure would grow, but never as quickly as the population of British North America. Much of the French growth was the result of high birth rates among French colonists, whereas the British colonies grew through increased settlement as well as by reproduction. By 1776, the population of the province of Quebec was around 100,000, compared to the 2.5 million of British North America. This continued demographic constraint, allied to the autocratic and absolutist nature of the French political system, meant that the militia system that emerged in French North America was different in many respects to that created by and in the Anglo-American tradition.

In 1648, Governor d'Ailleboust took charge of the tiny French settler population. He was a soldier, and quickly organised a militia unit of around fifty men to protect the colony from the Indian population, in particular from attacks by the Iroquois. It was not until 1665, by which time the French settler population had grown to around 3,000, that France sent a regiment of regulars to attempt to end the Iroquois threat. The regulars were supported by some independent companies of militia, and together they effectively cleared the St Lawrence of Iroquois warriors. That success led to the withdrawal of the regulars, who were in permanent demand in France. Not for the first time, the defence of New France was left to the militia. A new governor, the Comte de Frontenac et de Pallau, was appointed in 1672. An experienced soldier, bearing disabling wounds from his service in the Thirty Years' War, he proved to be a divisive figure and managed to antagonise most of the main interest groups, both clergy and laity, in New France. He was recalled to France in 1682, but was reappointed governor in 1689, at the start of 'King William's War' (1689–97) between France and England. In this war, Frontenac would redeem himself by his use of militia and American Indian allies. Believing British colonists in North America to be tradesmen not warriors, Frontenac launched an offensive that saw the burning of New York and attacks on Maine and New Hampshire. This led to a major expedition by the British-Americans (known to the French as the '*Bostonnais*') with the aim of taking Quebec, which, through poor logistics planning and mis-timing, was defeated. Frontenac was hailed a hero, and New France was saved from absorption into British North America.

Frontenac's successes were built upon his reorganisation of the French Canadian militia, and the development of alliances with American Indian tribes that enabled joint raiding parties and columns against the British and their allies, including the Iroquois who had sworn allegiance to the British Crown. Frontenac correctly assessed the demands and constraints placed on military organisation by geography, demography and the wider European focus of the French monarchy:

> Knowing what was required in a wild country like Canada, he [Frontenac] planned neither the formation of a regiment, nor a bat-talion, nor even companies [of militia]; but he based his system upon the instruction of squads at home, with a view to training scouts, skir-mishers, the lightest sort of infantry – the very men indispensable for an Indian war. ... The whole country was a military establishment; and no man or grown boy remained outside the organization, unless excused for some good cause.[4]

This gave the French an offensive capability attuned to the wilderness and distances that enhanced any provision of regular troops in war with England and its colonists.

Although there were military parallels between the militias of the English and French-speaking populations of North America, there were clear social and political differences. The French model was firmly top-down, and captains of militia not only had a military role, but also wider administrative and political roles, unlike militia officers in the British colonies. In New France:

> The captain of militia was not only a military personage; he was five or six other personages, all in the same man. He was recorder, and he was superintendent of roads. No government case before a tribunal was examined without his being present, notwithstanding that the official attorney was there also. Any dealings between the *seignior* or the *curé* and the civil authorities passed through him. If an accident

happened somewhere, it was the captain of the place who wrote the report, and any action taken subsequently was under his management. If a farmer wished to approach the government or the judge, the captain took the affair into his hand.[5]

This was not a role that the colonists of New England would recognise, or accept, and reflected the differing traditions that had been brought to the New World by French and English-speakers.

The French and Indian War and the defeat of French Canada
In English-speaking North America, the history-changing Seven Years War, 1756–63, is known as the French and Indian War. The war altered the direction of world history, making Britain the pre-eminent power, and confirming the Royal Navy as the dominant sea power. In North America it saw the eventual triumph of the English-speaking colonists, and, ironically, opened the way for the American Revolution and the expulsion of the British Crown from the Thirteen Colonies. It was therefore fitting that the first shots in this world war were fired by Anglo-American militiamen, and that the man who led them, Major George Washington, would in a few more decades go on to be the commander-in-chief of the new American republic.

By the 1750s tension between the Anglo-Americans and the French Canadians centred on French attempts to prevent further American expansion in the north-west, with the French building a series of forts along the banks of the Ohio. Diplomatic efforts to resolve the frontier question dragged on, but on 28 May 1754, Major Washington's combined Virginia militia and Mingo Indian column's action at Great Meadows, on the Ohio, sparked what became the French and Indian War. Washington's ambush of a small French force was followed by his retreat and surrender. Although the French permitted the Virginian militia to return home, and despite initial British and French reluctance to declare war, events were underway. As so often with Britain's wars, the initial stages of the French and Indian War saw a succession of defeats, with the French colonists and their militia, supporting a well-acclimatised and professional French regular force, the *Compagnies Franches de la Marine*, repeatedly gaining the better of British regulars, Provincials, and American militia units.

The French and Indian War showed both the strengths and weaknesses of militia forces on both sides. The initial successes of the French resulted from the deployment of militia and Indian forces in support of the regulars, in a fashion that maximised their potential in fighting against British and American forces that were less acclimatised, and less capable in wilderness and frontier warfare. However, the final victory of the British and Americans in the war also exposed the weakness of militia units at the famous Battle of the Plains of Abraham on 13 September 1759, which led to the fall of Quebec city, and the immortalisation of the British and French commanders, General James Wolfe and the Marquis de Montcalm. The battle was fought on open ground in the European fashion, and the 'perfect volley' that the British line delivered drove the French from the field in short order. Defeated French officers were unanimous in blaming the defeat on the mixing of regulars with militiamen, claiming, that the latter's 'lack of training and discipline were directly responsible for the poor performance of some units'.[6] Whatever the value of that claim, the defeat led to a renewed emphasis among the French on using their Canadian militia in a way that max-imised their tactical effectiveness:

> The most effective of the Canadian militia had been those employed as skirmishers, and [there was] a renewed emphasis on moving and fighting in column rather than line, the militia contingents assigned to each regiment appear to have been attached to them rather than integrated within their ranks. The intention was that the irregulars would act as *tirailleurs* or sharpshooters, screening and providing fire for the columns.[7]

In the event, the French were to lose their North American possessions, as the pressure of British sea power, and the strength and increasing effec-tiveness of British and American land forces, finally removed the French threat to the Thirteen Colonies, and thereby opened the way to an eventual American Revolution.

Minutemen and the American Revolution
Central to the myth of the American Revolution is the belief that the British and Loyalist forces were defeated by rebellious armed citizens, militiamen, who at a moment's notice picked up their muskets, left their farms and workplaces and took to the field of battle. In fact, the revolutionary militiamen provided some 164,087 of the total of 395,858 Americans who served in the war,[8] but their effectiveness was highly varied, not to say problematic. One of Washington's great challenges

centred on the belief that the militias of the various states were sufficient to prosecute a war against regular British forces, and their Loyalist volunteers and militiamen.[9] The Revolutionary militias were an expression of the political will of the emergent republic, but they were not the guarantor of its success:

> During the Revolutionary War numerous problems arose in the use of militia. Short enlistments limited their availability; they lacked discipline and training; and they were poorly armed and led. Early in the war General George Washington confessed that he felt a 'want of confidence, in the generality of the Troops.' His experience confirmed him in his opinion, and his famous statement regarding the militiamen was often repeated: '[They] come in, you cannot tell how; go, you cannot tell when, and act, you cannot tell where, consume your provisions, exhaust your stores, and leave you at last in a critical moment.' So many problems arose that the Continental Congress moved cautiously to create a regular army, which played an important part in winning independence.[10]

Despite this, the image of militia driving British regulars back into Boston in the Battles of Lexington and Concord in April 1775 overshadowed the victorious reality of Washington's Continental Army and its French allies. The myth of the triumph of the citizen soldier, of the militiaman as much as the long-distrusted idea of regular army, would impact on the United States' efforts in the War of 1812, when Washington's observations would, once again, prove to be valid.

The road to the War of 1812

With the exception of two brief periods, Britain was at war with France from 1798 until the final defeat of Napoleon in 1815. The 'French Wars' would end with Britain being confirmed in its global mastery of the seas, a state of affairs that lasted for nearly a century. But the path to that victory was uncertain, and, it appeared to Britain's enemies in the United States, provided an opportunity to finish the expulsion of the Crown from North America. From Britain's standpoint, its possessions in North America became vital, as the creation of Napoleon's 'Continental System' under the Berlin Decree of 21 November 1806 cut Britain off from raw materials, particularly the timber which was essential to the maintenance and expansion of the Royal Navy. Her naval prowess was also threatened by a shortage of seamen, a shortage that even the assiduous application of the press gang system in Britain's ports could not offset. Both these pressures would add to the mix of pre-existing American resentments and enable the drive to war in 1812.

The commonly accepted first step on the road to war was the Chesapeake affair of 1807. Napoleon's decree creating the Continental System led to a response from Britain, forbidding trade with France. This counter-thrust was enforced by the Royal Navy, which claimed the right to stop and search vessels at sea, despite the objections of neutral countries such as the United States. On 22 June 1807, HMS *Leopard* attempted to stop the USS *Chesapeake* to search for British citizens and deserters. The *Chesapeake* refused, and HMS *Leopard* responded with a broadside that killed and injured US personnel, followed by boarding. The incident caused outrage in the US, and marked the beginning of the decline in US–British relations. There was already a 'war party' in US politics and society, and the *Chesapeake* incident simply added another motivation for war.

Those in the United States who argued for war did so on a number of grounds. At root, it was a case of unfinished business. American rebels had attempted to spread their revolution to Canada as early as December 1775, with an heroic, but ill-fated assault on Quebec. The American failure to spread their revolution to Canada meant that Britain still had a very substantial presence in North America. For those who wanted war, it was not just a case of unfinished business. It was also the pursuit of what would eventually be known as America's 'manifest destiny' – that the United States was destined, indeed, ordained, to spread across the entirety of the North American landmass. Behind such grand ideological claims, however, lay straightforward economic self-interest for some Americans. Canada was seen to be a barrier to US expansion in the north-west, as well as a rival in the export of key raw materials. Further, Britain's support of Indian tribes was also seen as a threat to US expansion, particularly as the British had forged important, long-term alliances with the majority of the Indians in the north-west. War between the United States and the Confederacy of Tippecanoe led by the Shawnee chief, Tecumseh, broke out in November 1811. Although it was ultimately a setback for the Indians, the limited US victory intensified American calls for war with Britain which was blamed for supporting and provisioning its Indian allies.

All these varied US grievances, both real and imagined, were given extra potency by the political concerns of James Madison, president since 1809. Madison was fearful that he would lose the presidential election of 1812, faced

opposition from within his own Democratic– Republican party, and was widely
regarded as weak in his handling of international affairs. Madison hoped that
he could retrieve his situation by preparing for a showdown with a Britain dis-
tracted by its continuing struggles with France, and he called Congress into an
early session for November 1811 to prepare for war: 'his objectives were to unite
his supporters and increase the pressure on the British to relent'.[11] He was to be
more successful in his first objective than the second. Nonetheless, believing that
Britain would be unable to reinforce its limited regular forces of only 7,000 men
in Canada, and convinced of the capabilities of the US citizen in arms, Madison
and the war party believed that the half million British subjects in Canada
would collapse in the face of the might of the United States, with a population
of seven and a half million. The United States declared war on 18 June 1812 and,
expected, in the words of Thomas Jefferson, that: 'the acquisition of Canada
this year [1812] as far as the neighbourhood of Quebec, will be a mere matter of
marching and will give us experience for the attack on Halifax the next [year],
and the final expulsion of England from the American continent'.[12] The reality
would prove to be quite different, not least because of the failure of the US
militia system, and the comparative effectiveness of the Canadian system.

Opposing forces, opposing militias
The US militia – disorganisation and neglect
In the summer of 1812, the United States' government believed that it could field
a regular army of 35,000 men, along with 100,000 militiamen, which Congress
had called, on 10 April, to be readied for war.[13] Against this supposedly formidable array, the position of the British-Canadians was feeble, with only 7,000 regulars in the whole of British North America; most of whom needed to be held in
the defence of Montreal, Quebec and Halifax. For the crucial region of Upper
Canada, where any US offensive would hit, there were only 1,600 British regulars available, and very little chance of reinforcement from a Britain embroiled
in the continuing war with France. Worse, the militia system in Canada, both
English and French-speaking, could put only a fraction of the equivalent US
militia numbers in the field, with just 10,000 men available to the Crown.[14]
It was little wonder that many Americans agreed with Thomas Jefferson that
the conquest of British North America would be a 'mere matter of marching'.

However, the paper strength of the US concealed the reality of what was a
woefully inadequate US regular and militia force. In terms of numbers, the US
Army had at most 13,000 men, and perhaps as few as 6,000,[15] while the militias,

dependent on the individual states of the USA for their organisation, support and mobilisation, were in a parlous situation. While many individual militiamen, especially volunteers, were ready to fight, others were only willing to fight in a defensive war, or to defend their own state, while the overall picture was of militias that were poorly trained and even more inadequately supplied. Added to these problems were inter-state rivalries, and economic and fiscal arguments that had led to decades of neglect for state militias. In the years following independence, the US Congress had made attempts to set the militias on some sort of stable foundation. In 1792, Congress passed the Uniform Militia Act, under which, 'all able-bodied white male citizens between eighteen and forty-five were required to enroll and to furnish their own stand of arms (a musket and accoutrements: bayonet, cartridge box and pouch, cartridges, powder, lead, priming wire and brush, and flints)'.[16] This was seen by many as being a universal tax applied to all able-bodied men. Worse, simply requiring these citizens to enroll, with equipment, did nothing to guarantee training, which was left entirely in the hands of the states, as was the organisation and provisioning of the militias. In addition, there was no structure in place that would enable Congress to impose any national framework on the militias. This was the American revolutionary ideal in action, for both good and ill; an ideal that might have sufficed for a defensive war, but not for an invasion of British North America. There were, unsurprisingly, voices that warned of the limitations of the system, not least that of President Washington. He was acutely aware of the inadequacy of the small US Army and its supporting militia, especially in its expansionist war with the Indian Confederacy on the north-west frontier.

One of the handicaps which the US militia laboured under was a lack of clarity about their role in case of an offensive war. It was generally accepted that militias could not be compelled to cross a territorial border. This included, for many, state borders as well as international borders. Given this, it was unrealistic to imagine that in a war with Britain, tens of thousands of militiamen would accompany the small US Army into Upper Canada. Certainly, a general call-up of militias – the embodiment of militias – would not provide the numbers needed for an offensive war. Yet at the very outset of the war this fundamental issue appears to have been ignored by many policymakers, as was the reality of poor training, equipment and organisation. But there were some observers and policymakers who were able to see this reality. The day after the US declared war, Senator Obadiah German watched as 1,600 New York militiamen mustered. The men had no hats, blankets, or any camp equipment, and the muster was, he said, 'a spectacle that would wound the feelings of the most callous man', and he went on to note that the militia would not perform well: 'the evils attending upon calling upon a large proportion of the militia into actual service for any considerable time, is almost incalculable. After a short time, sickness, death, and many other evils will teach you the impropriety of relying on them for carrying on the war'.[17] Senator German's observations proved prophetic, but it was not until after the collapse of the initial US thrusts into British territory that Congress would be forced to reconsider its approach, not least in terms of the need to raise volunteer militia forces.

Canadian militias on the eve of war

If the US believed that it possessed regulars and militia in more than sufficient numbers to conquer Canada, it was clear that, in terms of numbers, the British and Canadians were in a poor position in the summer of 1812. However, what they lacked in numbers they made up for in determination, and the militia system of British North America proved adapted to its role in the defence of the territory. The heart of the defence of Canada was the small force of British regulars, especially the 41 and 49 Foot. Both regiments had been stationed in Canada for some time, the 41 since 1799, and the 49 since 1802, and were destined to remain throughout the war. This established link with the people and conditions of Canada may explain the success of the two regiments, as 'they gave outstanding service during the War of 1812 against the Americans, possibly because of increased familiarity with the country and its peoples'.[18] The British regulars in Canada would not receive substantial reinforcement until 1814 and the end of the war in Europe.[19] Instead, it would be militiamen and Provincial regiments that stepped into the line in defence of their homeland.

Lower Canada militias

Unlike the peacetime US militias, the British–Canadian militias were organised in a fashion that was task-orientated, and, from the beginning of 1812, incorporated an embodied force placed on a wartime footing in anticipation of war. This force, of some 6,500 men, was raised from February 1812, under the title of 'Lower Canada Select Embodied Militia Battalions'. It was chosen by lots from men aged between eighteen and thirty, who were called up to serve not less than two years; they were trained as front-line troops, and, in effect, were a regular, provincial force, an elite among the militia. One of the most famous Select Embodied battalions was the 'Canadian Voltigeurs', also known as the *Voltigeurs canadiens*. This highly effective unit was listed as part of the British regular forces in the Army Returns, and at the battle of Châteauguay on 25 October 1813, the Voltigeurs made up the largest part of a Canadian force which defeated a much larger column of US Regulars, stopping in its tracks an American offensive aimed at taking Montreal.

Supporting the Select Embodied militias in Lower Canada were other French and English-speaking militias. The Select Embodied units could be reinforced quickly by volunteer militiamen, and, within a few days, by a general embodiment of the 'Sedentary Militia', who provided an additional area defence force. In Lower Canada, this represented a reserve of 54,000 men, from both main communities. The French-speaking units were organised, as in the days of New France, on the basis of parish companies under their captains. Although some English-speaking contemporaries were dismissive of their capabilities, they were also described as 'rural militiamen [who] were usually very sturdy fellows and often excellent shots'.[20] The English-speaking militias in Lower Canada, largely displaced American Loyalists and their sons, were organised as a county militia regiment with six battalions and a troop of cavalry. Their French-speaking counterparts were organised in 'divisions' which belonged to one of the three districts of Montreal, Trois-Rivières, and Quebec. The Sedentary Militia from these areas wore Canadian civilian clothing, and the Canadian *toque*, a woollen cap, in a different colour for each district – blue for Montreal, white for Trois-Rivières, and red for Quebec. A surgeon of the 89 Foot has left us a memorable description of the Montreal Sedentary Militia on the march:

> We came up with several regiments of militia on their line of march. They all had a serviceable appearance – all had been pretty well drilled, and had their arms being direct from the tower, were in perfectly good order, nor had they the mobbish appearance that such a levy in any other country would have had. Their capots and trousers of home-spun stuff, and their blue tuques (night caps) were all of the same cut and color, which gave them an air of uniformity that added much to their military look … They marched merrily along to the music of their voyageur songs, and as they perceived our uniform as we came up, they set up the Indian War-whoop, followed by a shout of *Vive le Roi* along the whole line …[21]

This description provides a snapshot of Lower Canada militiamen called out to defend their homes, wearing the clothes and displaying the attitude and royalist sentiments of their forebears who founded New France.

Upper Canada militia

Following the American Revolution, change had also come to the administration of the remainder of British North America, with the Constitutional Act of 1791 splitting Canada into Lower and Upper Canada. The latter was largely settled by Loyalists who had served the Crown during the American war, many of whom had seen active service with famous Provincial regiments such as the Queen's Rangers. These Loyalists were subsequently joined by many new American settlers, something that caused some concern for the British authorities, concern that, it would transpire, was ill-founded, as American-born settlers went on to fight loyally in the War of 1812. In the mid-1790s, these communities saw the establishment of new militia forces with county regiments as the basic unit of organisation. As with militia in the USA, the militia of Upper Canada waxed and waned in the years between the American Revolution and 1812.

The example of the New Brunswick militia, founded in 1787, shows how despite the provincial legislature of New Brunswick establishing such a force and legislating for its mustering and training twice a year, little was routinely done. Instead, the New Brunswick militia remained poorly trained and only part-formed until the beginning of the French wars in 1793. Then the fear of French attack led to a major improvement in the standing of the militia, and a new militia act of 1794: 'discipline was tightened and training periods, now under the direction of paid regimental adjutants, were extended from two to four days a year and subject to inspection by senior regimental officers'.[22] The following year the newly reformed New Brunswick militia proved their worth by repulsing two assaults by pro-French Americans:

> in 1795, a raid on the isolated settlements around Passamaquoddy Bay
> by pro-French Americans was thwarted by the local authorities and a
> well-prepared detachment of the Charlotte County Militia. A second
> raid, later that year, resulted in the capture of the would-be invaders
> by alert local militiamen.[23]

Yet despite these successes, the state of readiness of the militias continued to change in relation to the perceived level of threat. So, for example, the Peace of Amiens (1802), which brought a temporary end to the French Wars, led to a falling-off in militia preparedness, whereas following the *Chesapeake* affair in 1807, and heightened US-British tensions, the militias were strengthened, with New Brunswick's militia rising to the level of 2,000 effectives. But the very next year this force was first disbanded, then reinstated and reinvigorated by a new military governor of New Brunswick, Major General Hunter. He instituted new organisation, brought in new personnel, retired the older Loyalist officers, and put the whole force on a firmer legal footing. Hunter brought in practical organisational and training reforms to the militia, was supported by New Brunswick's assembly, and as a result improved the effectiveness, morale and popular support for the force:

> The province's militia was completely restructured and major efforts were made to improve leadership and training. The eight county regiments were reorganized into 14 battalions making it easier for militiamen to attend musters in more convenient locations. The older generation of Loyalist officers was retired and their places taken by younger men better able to carry out the responsibilities of command. ... Revised legislation in 1808 made provision for paid provision of additional training for the militia under the direction of the newly appointed inspecting field officer, who was also responsible for reporting back to Fredericton on the state of the provincial militia. Although shortages of weapons were a major problem, within two years sufficient progress had been made for Hunter to dispense with the extra days of drill. His final act was a major rewriting of the province's militia legislation in 1810 which tightened discipline and improved training under paid instructors, recruited from among regular force, non-commissioned officers stationed in the province. Much of Hunter's success was due to a renewal of tensions between Britain and the United States, which was accompanied by the provision of some financial support for the militia and by a revival of patriotic sentiment in New Brunswick. ... When Hunter stepped down in June 1812 he handed over to his successor, Major-General Stracey Smith, a militia force better trained and organized than previously and once again enjoying a wide measure of public support.[24]

The new commander almost immediately faced wartime conditions, and 500 militiamen were embodied (a shortage of weapons preventing more being called up), to help defend key coastal sites. Other volunteers were mobilised to build fortifications around Saint John, and Martello towers and blockhouses. In the event, however, British naval supremacy kept the seaborne threat at bay, and New Brunswick did not become embroiled in the fighting, while the New Brunswick militia's role was replaced by a newly raised regiment of Fencibles.

The New Brunswick example illustrated the difficulties facing Upper Canada militias, and the variable levels of preparedness. Too often, too little was taken in hand until the threat of war galvanised the authorities and enabled military governors to take action to improve training, leadership and effectiveness. And it was the threat of US aggression that led to the embodiment of the militias, the creation of volunteer militia units, and the raising of full-time militiamen for the duration of the coming war. In March 1812, the government ordered all militia battalions to form two 'Flank Companies' of men under forty years of age. They would be called out for six days' training per month, and would be embodied for six months' fulltime service should war break out. The Flank Companies would take to the field, and, as their title suggests, take up position on the flanks of the battle line, with the centre being taken by Regulars and Provincials. In addition, militias were called upon to form volunteer militia companies, and several volunteer corps were created as the country moved to a war footing. Together, the Flank Companies and the volunteer militia were able to put 4,000 men in the field in the summer of 1812. As a result of these moves 'when the Americans did attack in July, many hundreds of adequately trained militiamen were mobilised and fought effectively with the small regular garrison [in Upper Canada] during the summer and autumn of 1812'.[25] But these men were still only obliged to serve for six months, and in early 1813 the militias provided more men for the Volunteer Incorporated Militia Battalion, who were embodied to serve, fulltime, throughout the war. Companies were embodied at Prescott, Kingston, York and Niagara in the spring of 1813. Thirteen companies were raised, trained as a ten company battalion at York and saw extensive active service on the Niagara front from the spring of 1814 until the war's end.[26]

In the early summer of 1812, the stage was set for the US invasion of Canada. On paper, the United Sates possessed overwhelming superiority in numbers, including up to 100,000 militiamen. By contrast, small British regular forces, supported by French and English-speaking militias, and allied Indians, were thin on the ground, and unlikely to receive much in the way of reinforcement from Britain, embroiled in the war against the French in Europe.

The campaign of 1812, US failure

The War of 1812 would eventually involve actions all along the eastern seaboard of the USA, down to the Gulf of Mexico, while naval warfare ranged across the Atlantic and Pacific oceans. But the main fighting throughout was centred on the Great Lakes – lakes Huron, Erie and Ontario – and the St Lawrence River, with raids, battles, sieges and skirmishes ranging across Upper and Lower Canada, Michigan Territory, Ohio, and New York state. With the advantage of the initiative and numbers, the US planned a three or four-pronged invasion of Canada. The aim was to divide the already outnumbered British and Canadian forces, quickly defeat them in the field and march to take Montreal, thereby taking control of Upper Canada. The conquest and occupation of British territory was the primary US war aim. Success would push the Crown out of most of its remaining possessions in North America, while isolating the western Indian tribes, and opening them to US depredations. The US armies would cross the Detroit River in the west, the Niagara, and the St Lawrence in the east. But such simultaneous action on differing fronts was beyond the organisational abilities of US commanders, and instead the simultaneous attacks became a series of piecemeal assaults. The failure of the 1812 campaign was the first of eight attempted US invasions of Canada during the war, and only one saw the temporary occupation of British territory. The US military, both its regulars and militia forces, were taught some hard lessons by the defending British, Canadians and Indians.

On 12 July 1812, the US General William Hull, Governor of Michigan Territory since 1805, and a veteran of the Revolutionary War, led three regiments of Ohio militia and a regular US Army regiment into Canada, with the initial aim of taking the town of Amhertsburg. Hull had been reluctant to accept command, but there were few other options, and despite his age he had the status of a successful Revolutionary War veteran. Almost immediately it became clear that the Ohio militia regiments were ill-equipped and ill-provisioned, while discipline among Hull's small army depended on the 300 or so men of the 4 US Infantry. Hull was unsure how to proceed, was fearful of Indian attacks on his flanks, and lost baggage, supplies and, crucially, orders and plans to the British when they captured a US vessel on Lake Erie. To make matters worse, the British commander in Upper Canada, Major General Isaac Brock, was determined to take the initiative from the Americans, and on 17 July his men took the US fort on Mackinac Island in a bloodless *coup de main*. This was just the development that Indians in the upper lakes region were waiting for, and they began to rally to the British. Hull's fears concerning a British–Indian assault on his ill-equipped, fractious, and ill-trained force led him to withdraw to Detroit, then a US outpost of less than a thousand people. Detroit was, however, also a key jumping-off and supply post for any invasion of Canada from Michigan Territory or Ohio. Hull completed his withdrawal to Detroit by 11 August, and with 2,200 men, arms, equipment and supplies awaited the British. Brock approached with some 1,300 regulars from the 41 Foot, militia, and, crucially for the state of Hull's already shaken morale, Indians under their renowned leader, Tecumseh. It was not only the American commander who was suffering from a lack of morale, as militia under his command now began to desert to the British, and 'at the critical moment of siege of Detroit … at least two companies of the Michigan militia deserted to the enemy',[27] while Colonel Elijah Brush, the commander of the 1st Michigan militia, exclaimed that, " 'By God, he believed his men would have run away to a man'".[28]

Brock played on the Americans' fears of Indian massacre, and in his surrender demand to Hull stressed:

> The force at my disposal authorizes me to require of you the immediate surrender of Fort Detroit. It is far from my intention to join in a war of extermination, but you must be aware, that the numerous body of Indians who have attached themselves to my troops, will be beyond control the moment the contest commences.[29]

Tecumseh also convinced the Americans that he had brought thousands of warriors with him, rather than the several hundred he had, by a *ruse de guerre* in which his warriors rapidly appeared and reappeared in the forests around Detroit. Hull surrendered Detroit and the elated British and their allies entered to take possession of arms, munitions, supplies and the only American armed vessel on the upper Great Lakes, the USS *Adams*. It was a major victory for Brock and the British, who in one move had secured their western flank, ensured continuing Indian support for their cause, captured enough supplies to re-equip Brock's militia, and defeated the first American thrust into Canada.

The surrender of Detroit now placed the US in a dangerous position in Michigan. The way was open for the British to advance down the coastline, rolling up the small American outposts as they went. The US militia from

Frenchtown, thirty-five miles from Detroit, had surrendered and there was no immediate obstacle to a further British advance. While further attempted US attacks on Canada on the Niagara and Montreal fronts continued, the scene in the Michigan Territory was set for what would be some of the worst losses experienced by the US militia during the war.

The Battles of Frenchtown and Disaster on the River Raisin

The new American commander for the 'Army of the Northwest' was Brigadier General James Winchester, but he was quickly replaced by Major General Henry Harrison, with Winchester becoming the new commanding officer's second-in-command. Harrison's plan was to retake Detroit, dividing his command into two columns, one led by Winchester. His orders were to advance north to support Harrison's march on Detroit. Winchester's column consisted largely of volunteer militiamen from Kentucky. Three regiments of Kentucky militia – the 1, under Colonel John Smith; the 5, under Colonel William Lewis; and the 1 Rifle Regiment, under Colonel John Allen – had been in the field since August 1812, and had been on their way to Detroit when news came of its fall.[30] Both the militiamen and the regulars had been engaged in skirmishing with Indians, as well as destroying Indian crops and villages. However, the militia were poorly supplied and clothed, with one of their number, Elias Darnell, recording the state of provisioning in journal entries for 29 and 30 December 1812, a few weeks before they marched north towards Detroit:

> *29th*: We are now about commencing one of the most serious marches ever performed by the Americans. Destitute, in a measure of clothes, shoes and provisions, the most essential articles necessary for the existence and preservation of the human species in this world, and more particularly in this cold climate. Three sleds are prepared for each company, each to be pulled by a pack-horse which has been without food for two weeks, except brush, and will not be better fed while in our service; probably the most of these horses never had harness on, but the presumption is they will be too tame; we have prepared harness out of green hides.
>
> *30th*: After nearly three months preparation for this expedition, we commenced our march in great splendour; our elegant equipage cast a brilliant lustre on the surrounding objects as it passed! Our clothes

and blankets looked as if they had never acquainted with water, but intimately with dirt, smoke and soot; in fact we have become much acquainted with one much despised in Kentucky, under whose government we are obliged to live, whose name is *Poverty*.[31]

The situation that Darnell described in his journal came *after* the Kentucky militia had been resupplied. This was in the depths of winter, and not only were clothing and shoes in short supply, but rations varied, with a pattern of glut and famine being the usual situation for these men. Unsurprisingly, sickness and disease had depleted the numbers in the American camp, with a comrade of Darnell's later remembering that 'there comes up before the mind the many times the dead march was heard in camp, and the solemn procession that carried our fellow sufferers to the grave'.[32] Some relief was forthcoming when supplies of winter clothing reached the militia after they had begun their march, sent by voluntary effort of the 'daughters of Kentucky'.

The first objective of the column was Frenchtown, which the Americans intended to retake prior to an attack on Detroit. Under the command of Colonel Lewis some 660 Kentuckians, supported by a small contingent of French-speaking militia from Michigan Territory, attacked the Canadian-Indian camp across the frozen River Raisin on 18 January. There some sixty men from the Essex militia, with a small howitzer, and around 200 Potawatomi Indians staged a fighting retreat. The Canadian militiamen used the same tactics as their Indian allies. The fighting lasted from three o'clock in the afternoon until darkness, and the defenders contested the American advance throughout. The Kentucky militia proved deficient in the type of light-infantry/Indian fighting that their opponents were skilled at. The Kentucky militiaman, William Atherton, wrote:

Very few of our men were killed or wounded until we reached the woods; here we fought under great disadvantages, not being acquainted with the ground, and most of us being unacquainted with the Indian mode of warfare. Thus our want of experience and eagerness to overtake the enemy, gave them a decided advantage over us. Their method was to retreat rapidly until they were out of sight, (which was soon the case in the brushy woods,) and while we were advancing they were preparing to give us another fire; so we were generally under the necessity of firing upon them as they were retreating. During the charge, I saw several of our brave boys lying upon the snow wallowing in the agonies of death. But none could stop even to help his brother, for our situation required the utmost exertion of every man as long as he could render any service.[33]

When night came, the Canadian militia and the Indians broke contact, and the Americans held Frenchtown after the hard fight which, Atherton's comrades believed had been against 100 British and 400 Indians. The Kentuckians settled themselves in Frenchtown, and reinforced its defences. General Winchester, with 250 men, arrived two days later taking the combined force to around 1,100 men. However, the newly enlarged encampment was not further fortified. Although a breastwork and palisade had been constructed by the men who had retaken Frenchtown, the officers decided that the reinforcements did not need to extend that defensive structure, or, indeed, strengthen it:

> The officers having viewed and laid off a piece of ground for a camp and breastworks, resolved that it was too late to remove and erect fortifications that evening; farther, as they resolved to remove early next day, it was not thought worthwhile, though materials were at hand, to fortify the right wing, which therefore encamped in the open field.[34]

Given that it had been the Canadians and Indians who broken contact, and had not been routed, the expectation should have been of a counter-attack, but inexperience and lack of training on the part of the Americans led to this disastrous decision, which, as Darnell tersely commented, 'this want of precaution was a great cause of our mournful defeat'.[35]

Later still on the 21st, the Americans received intelligence from a French speaker who entered their camp that a large force of 3,000 British and Indians, with artillery, were on the way to attack the Americans. Opinions were divided as to the veracity of this information, but nothing was done to prepare for a possible attack. In fact, the officer commanding British forces in the Detroit area, Brigadier-General Henry Procter,[36] had reacted quickly as soon as news came in that the Americans had retaken Frenchtown. Nearly 600 regulars from the 41 Foot and the Royal Newfoundland Fencibles, along with some 800 Indians from ten tribes, and a battery of six light artillery of the Canadian Provincial Marine (a Provincial regular unit dating back to the French and Indian War), were despatched to deal with the American threat. As the British approached Frenchtown, they were joined by the Canadians from the 1 and 2 Essex militia, who were still in the field around the town. The stage was set for one of the worst disasters faced by the Americans during the war, and the brunt of the disaster would be taken by the three regiments of Kentucky militia.

At daybreak on 22 January, the British attacked the encamped Americans, who had not even put out pickets much beyond their camp. The attack was a complete surprise, and opened with artillery fire and volleys from the British and Provincial regulars. The Kentuckian militiaman, William Atherton, described the opening attack:

> every circumstance attending this awful scene, conspired to make it more alarming – the time and manner in which it was commenced – for they approached in the dark with profound silence – not a breath was heard until all was ready, then, sudden as a flash of powder, the bloody work began'.[37]

The American regulars and militia formed battle lines and fought back. The Kentucky militia took up position behind their breastwork, topped with a palisade, and threw back the initial British attack. But on the totally unprotected right-wing, the Americans were overwhelmed, and retreated in confusion, with the Indians wreaking havoc on the broken US line. The shattered American unit was the 17 US Infantry, largely recent recruits, who, in the face of the British and Indian onslaught collapsed. The Kentucky militia were unable to support them, and the US regulars' fled the field, hunted down by the Indians. Americans outside the defences of Frenchtown fared very badly, but the Kentuckians continued to resist from behind their defences, the Kentucky riflemen in particular, successfully targeting the Canadian artillerymen.

Unable to break into Frenchtown, Procter was concerned that the Americans might be reinforced. Procter demanded of the captured Winchester that he order his men to surrender, and a written surrender order from the US commander was delivered to the remaining defenders. Procter told Winchester that if there was no unconditional surrender, then Frenchtown would be burnt and that he would not be able to guarantee the lives of captured Americans at the hands of the Indians.

The Kentucky militiamen were concerned that they would be massacred by the Indians if they surrendered, and an American major negotiated with Procter that 'all private property should be respected – that sleds should be sent next to remove the sick and wounded to Amhertsburg – and that in the mean time they [American prisoners] should be protected [from the Indians] by a guard'.[38] The Kentuckians surrendered, and the American defeat was complete, with 397 dead and missing, and some 526 captured, twenty-five of whom were wounded. The numbers of American captives exceeded Procter's effective regulars, as he had lost twenty-four killed and 158 wounded in the fighting – two-fifths of the British and Canadians engaged.[39] The Americans had expected the wounded to be evacuated by sled by their captors, but, the following morning, Procter ordered a rapid withdrawal from Frenchtown, and, in the confusion, the Indians set about killing American captives, particularly those who could not walk. They also set fire to buildings containing American wounded. The entire event became known as the 'River Raisin Massacre', with anything up to 100 American prisoners killed. Many of the dead were Kentuckians, and once news of the massacre spread, more of their compatriots rallied to the Kentucky militia. The final American tally of dead and missing, both in the battle and the subsequent killing, was:

> 17th United States Infantry – one surgeon, two captains, three lieutenants, two ensigns, 112 NCO and privates.
>
> 1st Regiment Kentucky Militia – one major, one captain, one surgeons mate, one ensign, 36 NCO and privates.
>
> 1st Kentucky Rifles – one lieutenant-colonel, one surgeon, four captains, one ensign, 154 NCO and privates.
>
> 5th Regiment Kentucky Militia – one major, one captain, one lieutenant, 73 NCO and privates.[40]

The British continued to hold the area, and Detroit, until September 1813, when a changed strategic situation forced withdrawal back into Canada.

The Battles of Frenchtown showed the strengths and weaknesses of the American forces in 1812. Poorly supplied, and affected by the harsh conditions of winter, the Kentucky militiamen nevertheless performed well in the taking of Frenchtown, and in its defence. They had difficulties in facing what were effectively light infantry tactics used by the Indians and Canadian militia in woodlands, 'which were very brushy and suited to their mode of fighting'.[41] By contrast, they drove off three assaults by artillery-supported British and Canadian regulars on 22 January, ensconced as the Kentucky militia were behind defensive breastworks and palisades. The failure on the part of the American command was in not fortifying the encampment of the newly arrived regulars on the evening of the second battle of Frenchtown, an error that left the untried regulars in the open the next morning when the British battle line put them to flight within twenty minutes.

The American defeat at Queenston

The failure of the US offensive in the north-west, which resulted in the capture of Detroit and the disaster of Frenchtown, was not the only defeat the British, Canadians and Indians inflicted on the invading Americans in 1812. Following the Detroit debacle, the Americans next planned a major thrust on the north-ern front across the Niagara River for a second attempted invasion of Upper Canada. The US assembled some 900 regulars and 2,500 New York militia, and, unlike their Kentucky counterparts at Frenchtown, many of the New York militia would perform far from creditably in the coming battle. It was on the northern front, the Niagara region, where the most fighting would take place, and where, 'more than in any other area of the country, the mettle of the militia was tested. Sadly, the performance of the militia reflected in microcosm its gen-eral lack of effectiveness throughout the war, weak discipline, poor leadership, and lack of supplies'.[42]

The US-Canadian border on the Niagara peninsular ran for over 42 miles along the Niagara River, with forts on both sides of the border guarding access to the river from Lake Ontario in the north, and Lake Erie in the south. To the west was Upper Canada, to the east, the state of New York. That state was expected to be able to embody 13,500 militiamen, but in the summer of 1812 there were neither enough weapons, camp equipment, blankets or many other essentials to supply such a number. There was also a need to recruit volunteer militia who would be expected to stay in the field for longer than embodied mili-tiamen. As soon as the USA declared war, some 2,500 New York militia flocked to support 300 US regulars on the northern front. However, a thousand of the militiamen were only ready to remain for a short time before they needed to return to homes and crops. The officer-commanding, Brigadier General Hall, noted that not only could he not supply these men, but the militia were also lack-ing in basic discipline – 'the disorders incident to camps thus formed of citizens will prove more fatal in one season that [sic] two campaigns of hard fighting'.[43]

The command of the Niagara front was taken over by Major General Stephen Van Rensselaer, a senior officer in the New York militia, in mid-July, and he at once began preparations for an invasion of Upper Canada. He was aware of the poor state of his troops, lacking in supplies and beginning to suffer disease and illness, in part due to poor camp discipline. To make matters worse, there were serious divisions between Rensselaer and Major General Alexander Smyth of the US Army, divisions that would impact on the coming battle. Van Rensselaer appreciated that time was not on his side, as 'while we are thus growing daily weaker, our enemy is growing stronger'.[44] Finally, the governor of New York pressed Rensselaer, for political reasons, to mount an offensive as soon as possible, and the decision was made to attack across the Niagara River and take Queenston Heights and the town of Queenston.

During the night of 12/13 October, American artillery opened a bombardment against Queenston, covering boats crossing with American militia and regulars. The defending British opened a determined fire against the attackers, but, despite losses, the Americans made the Canadian shore and took Queenston Heights which overlooked the town. The British commander, General Brock, realised the danger and personally led British and Canadian troops up the slope to attack the Americans. In the exchange of fire, Brock was mortally wounded, and the attack faltered. Major-General Sheaffe took command of British forces, and called in more men from outlying areas, including Iroquois. All the time, defenders were firing on American boats crossing the river, with some boats taking heavy casualties. When the Iroquois arrived, the Americans found that they were unable to effectively counter Indian tactics, just as in the fighting for Frenchtown. Accurate and sustained fire from Iroquois hidden in the edge of brush and woods overlooking the American landing ground beneath Queenston Heights unnerved the Americans who were running low on ammunition. Worse, many of their compatriots across the river, seeing the heavy casualties in the boats and on the shore, began to refuse to cross to their aid. The men who refused to move were New York militia. Arguments broke out between men and their officers about the legal question of asking militiamen to leave their state, and to be involved in an offensive against another country. Some militia did agree to cross, but, by now the situation had become critical. The British formed a battle line, gave the Americans a volley, and charged. Within minutes, it was over, and 960 Americans were taken prisoner (of whom 378 were New York militia), while some 500 were dead or wounded. The British and their allies had only 104 killed and wounded. The defeat at Queenston further affected American morale, and 'within a week, another 1,000 dismayed American fighting men had deserted their camps on the New York side of the border and headed for home'.[45]

The fiasco at Queenston was blamed by Van Rensselaer on the New York militia who refused to cross the river, with Van Rensselaer reporting the day after the stunning defeat of American arms that, 'I can only add that victory was really won; but lost for the want of a small reinforcement. One third part of the idle men might have saved all'.[46] But that was not all, as the deep divisions between the US Army's Major General Smyth and Van Rensselaer meant that few of Smyth's 1,500 regulars crossed the river to support the efforts of their countrymen. They, in turn, were lacking in the training they needed in order to combat the tactics of the Indians; neither were they able to withstand a charge from British and Canadian regulars. In the immediate aftermath of Queenston, Smyth took command of American forces on the Niagara front, but they were the 'same undisciplined and discontented militia' along with regulars who were, in truth, 'little better than raw militiamen'.[47] Matters deteriorated further, with a mutiny by some militia, continued desertions, and little in the way of resupply of essential equipment. Further militia reinforcements arrived, from Pennsylvania, but despite rumours of another assault on Canada, nothing happened. The fact was that US forces were simply unprepared in terms of command experience, training, equipment, supply and morale to undertake successful offensives against Canada. By the end of 1812, the United States was 'reeling from unanticipated military failure ... The militia, which was to be the primary force for waging the war, was simply not organized, trained, disciplined, equipped, armed or ready'.[48]

The 1813 campaign – the defence of Lower Canada

By the beginning of the campaigning season in 1813, the Americans had come to realise that they could no longer rely on a comparatively small regular army supported by large numbers of militia. But neither the regulars nor the militia were in a strong position in 1813. The rapid expansion of the regulars meant that few were well trained, or experienced, while militia units continued to be poorly equipped and supplied, and the political and constitutional questions that impacted upon their effectiveness had still not been resolved. Further, after the defeats of all the US attempts to invade Canada in 1812, it was becoming difficult to draw upon volunteers for the militias. In Kentucky, for example, from where the hard-fighting militia of the disaster of Frenchtown had been drawn, there was difficulty in replacing all the losses and the state had to resort to drafting militiamen. Perhaps worst of all, the US lacked good military leadership, something that would doom the 1813 campaign, especially the American attempt to invade Lower Canada, where French-speaking militiamen and volunteers would play a part in the defeat of the invaders.

Throughout the summer and early autumn of 1813, Canadian militia maintained a campaign of raiding across the border in the northern New York, Lake Champlain region. These frequent raids had to be dealt with by New York militia, as the American officer commanding for the front, Major General Wade Hampton, was planning a major offensive against Montreal with an army of over 11,000 men. Hampton's plan was to mount a two-pronged assault along the Châteauguay River. His intelligence was that the British could only field some 2,100 men in total, 700 of whom were militiamen. This small force was all that stood between his army and Montreal. Further, most of the enemy's troops were French-speaking Canadians, and, just as some British officers were far from sure about the loyalty of the *Canadiens*, so Hampton and the Americans hoped that the French-speaking soldiers and militia would offer little resistance. In this, they were to be disabused.

By the beginning of October, Hampton's army was starting to feel the effects of the oncoming winter, and the inactivity of camp life. If Hampton was to mount a successful invasion of Lower Canada, then he had to move soon. On 18 October, a deserter brought the Americans news that only 1,600 men, including nearly 800 militia, were defending the lower Châteauguay. By 25 October, Hampton decided to attack, 'he was confident as he had four thousand men and also accurate information that the enemy's entire force" immediately in front of him "did not exceed three hundred and fifty combatants altogether, [French] Canadian and Indian" commanded by some "militia colonel" named de Salaberry'.[49] In dismissing de Salaberry as a mere 'militia colonel', Hampton was making a grave mistake. Lieutenant Colonel Charles-Michel d'Irumberry de Salaberry was a highly experienced, professional soldier at the forefront of military science in the very field, that of the light infantryman, that counted for so much in the wooded, close country of the region. De Salaberry was from a long-established *Canadien* family, whose grandfather had fought the British in the Seven Years War, and whose father had served the Crown during the American Revolution. The younger de Salaberry joined the 60 Foot as a sixteen-year-old ensign in 1794, and saw active service against the French in the Caribbean for a decade. He had then been posted, as captain, to England in the 5 Battalion of the 60 Foot, commanded by Francis de Rottenburg, who was training the battalion to become the first regular light infantry battalion in the British Army. De Rottenburg was a leading authority on light infantry training and tactics, and took his battalion, along with de Salaberry, to fight in the Walcheren campaign of 1809, before both officers were posted to Lower Canada the following year. De Salaberry was then asked by Sir George Prevost, the governor of British North America, to raise a *Canadien* light infantry regiment. That regiment, the Canadian Voltigeurs, or *Voltigeurs canadiens*, would earn a formidable fighting reputation during the war. This, then, was the mere 'militia colonel' who was officer in charge of the border defences of Lower Canada from the autumn of 1812.

The Battle of Châteauguay

The Americans had begun their advance along the Châteauguay River on 21 October, having taken three days to concentrate their army. The weather had begun to turn, and it was very cold with snow on the ground. Hampton's force was headed by an advance guard of 700 light infantry drawn from all the regular regiments and some dragoons. They had before them woodland, broken by occasional cleared farmers' fields. Following up, the main body of the army made slow progress, constructing a log road on the cart track that they were following, and clearing obstructions left by the British. By 25 October, Hampton's entire force was 'concentrated at Spear's, about nineteen miles from their first objective, Caughnawaga, across the St. Lawrence for Montreal.'[50] All this while, de Salaberry and his small force had been preparing extensive defensive positions in the woodland along the river. The Canadian force consisted of a light company of Canadian Fencibles, two companies of Voltigeurs, and a company of the Select Embodied Militia, and one of the Sedentary Militia, supported by a number of Abenaki and Nipissing warriors. As a reserve, de Salaberry had 600 Select Embodied Militia led by a veteran light infantryman, and loyal subordinate, Lieutenant Colonel George Macdonell. These militiamen had just completed a move, by river and land, of 210 miles in three days to reinforce the Châteauguay position, a remarkable feat in which not one man dropped out.[51] In all, militiamen made up a significant element in the defending force. All the bridges around the area were destroyed, and the defenders built four defence lines across the road that ran to the north, and parallel with, the river. Each line was around 200 yards from the next, with the final line being half a mile to the rear, protecting a ford that represented a potentially vulnerable flank if the Americans advanced south of the river as well as along the northern bank. In front of the entire position, an extensive *abatis* of sharpened timber stretched for over 100 yards from the river bank into the woods.

Hampton planned to take advantage of his intelligence on the Canadian positions by advancing on both sides of the river. The Second Brigade, under the command of Brigadier-General George Izard, would assault the enemy's positions in the woods along the north of the river, while the First Brigade, under Colonel Robert Purdy, would push down the right bank of the river with the aim of outflanking the defenders by crossing the ford at the rear of the Canadians' position. In all, some 3,564 Americans would take part, faced by 339 Canadians and Indians.[52]

As soon as the Americans made contact at around 10am, de Salaberry moved most of his men forward to the *abatis* line, with twenty-two Indians being dispersed into the woodlands to cover the approach to the flank of the position. The Fencibles and one company of Voltigeurs were deployed in a skirmish line in front of the *abatis*, while the second company of Voltigeurs and a company of sedentary militia from Beauharnois faced the river to put under fire any attempt by the Americans to advance along the opposite bank. The attitude of the *Canadiens* to the coming battle, and the nature of their loyalties, was symbolised by an incident recounted by a Voltigeur, Michael O'Sullivan:

> Having given his orders, de Salaberry 'placed himself in the centre of the front line' as Captain Joseph-Marie Longtin, commanding the company of Beauharnois militia knelt down with his men and 'said a short prayer in his own good way.' This necessary prelude to battle observed, Longtin told his company that, as 'they had done their duty to their God,' he now 'expected they would also do their duty to their King.'[53]

Americans began to appear in force, led by dragoons and the light infantrymen from Izard's advance guard, and Izard, acting on instructions from Hampton, advanced 250 regulars of the US 10 Infantry. An inconclusive firefight commenced, which lasted around 20 minutes before the American regulars began to run short on ammunition. The sound of the volleys and individual shooting enabled the Purdy's 1 Brigade on the right bank to orientate themselves and begin their advance with two companies. However, as de Salaberry had intended, this move was countered by a company of Sedentary Militia under

Captain Jean-Baptiste Brugière, and a company of Select Embodied Militia under Captain Charles Daly, with some Indians, who advanced to meet the Americans on that bank. The action became confused, with signs of panic setting in among both the sedentary militia and the American regulars. A Canadian eyewitness remembered that the 'sedentary militia and some Indians [were] running away … blue toques of the former flying in the wind'.[54] However, the American regulars, fearing that the woods around them were full of Indians, fell back towards the main column. This respite enabled Brugière to rally his men and form on the Select Embodied Militia under Daly. Together, they then shadowed the withdrawing Americans. Despite the momentary wavering on the part of some of the Sedentary Militia, the two militia companies had stopped the Americans' attempt to outflank the main body of Canadians via the ford.

The firing died down as more of Izard's brigade moved up to join the 10 US Infantry. Now complete, with the combined 11/29 and 30/31 Infantry, the second brigade advanced down the cart track. Hampton was aware by now that Purdy's attempt to reach the ford had failed, and he sent an order for Purdy to withdraw and cross the river to the left bank. Hampton then ordered Izard to attack once more, and, at 2pm, the three regiments of US infantry advanced in line to the cleared ground in front of the *abatis* and began volley firing. Inexperienced as most of the men were, they fired too high, while the Canadians replied with aimed shots – 'the *Canadiens*' fire was much more effective: they were behind cover and they took their time, making each round count'.[55] Nonetheless, in the face of the weight of American fire, the defenders fell back on the *abatis*, which the Americans took to be the beginnings of a retreat. American cheering was returned by the Canadians, while de Salaberry's buglers sounded the advance, which was the signal for Macdonell to bring up the reserve of his Select Embodied Militia, while 'war-whooping' Indians advanced through the trees. At the same time, the militiamen of Brugière and Daly, advanced on the right bank, unleashed a volley on Purdy's men and attacked. The militiamen there numbered only seventy or eighty men, while Purdy's force numbered at least 1,500, but the thick brush meant that the American regulars had no real idea of how many they faced. Worse, American officers began to abandon their men, throwing away their swords and plunging into the river to escape the small force of attacking Canadians and Indians. Some of the Americans rallied, and the Canadians fell back, only to attack again, with the bayonet, but both Brugière and Daly were wounded, and the Canadians fell back, pursued by the

Americans. But the riverside flank of the American line then came under fire from across the river, which the Voltigeur O'Sullivan remembered as being 'a heavy and well-directed fire, which suddenly checked their career, and threw them back in the greatest confusion'.[56] That marked the end for Purdy's brigade, which retreated back down the river, hoping to cross to Izard's brigade under their protection. However, Izard had already withdrawn his men under orders from Hampton. Three miles back from the battle site, the Second Brigade encamped, while Purdy's First Brigade withdrew two to three miles to a bend in the river. Night fell, and the miseries of the defeated Americans were added to by sniping Indians and heavy rain.

The Canadians had won a significant victory with little loss to themselves, with only two dead, sixteen wounded and four taken prisoner. American losses are unclear, but de Salaberry's men buried nearly forty American dead, while Purdy's brigade lost twenty dead and forty wounded on the right bank. Perhaps some 100 Americans were casualties in total. The bigger loss was a defeat that once more showed the inadequacy of American leadership, of senior and junior officers, along with the poor training of its regulars. As for the defenders, not only had a small force defeated a vastly superior force in terms of numbers, but the British and *Canadien* officers had proved more than a match for their opposite numbers. In addition to the professionalism of de Salaberry and Macdonell, there was the aggressive leadership of the Select Embodied and Sedentary militia officers, Brugière and Daly. Worse was to follow for their defeated opponents when, less than a month later on 11 November, the second prong of America's thrust aimed at Montreal also came spectacularly undone. On open fields at Crysler's Farm on the St Lawrence, 1,169 British and Canadians, under Lieutenant Colonel Joseph Morrison, defeated over 3,000 Americans. The two battles of Chateauguay and Crysler's Farm marked the disastrous end of the United States' most dangerous offensives against Lower Canada during the war.

By the end of 1813, the Americans had realised that even greater efforts were going to be needed if their war aims, of ridding North America of the Crown and invading and occupying Canada, were going to be achieved. Yet even after a year and a half of war, the US still 'faced the prospect of the next campaign [in 1814] relying on militias to bear a large part of the burden of military action'.[57] For example, at the Battle of Plattsburgh in September 1814, which marked the last British counterattack into the US, nearly half of the victorious defenders were militia – 2,200 Vermont militia, and 700 New York militia, from a total American force of over 6,000. Despite the ebb and flow of the frontier war during 1814, the strategic position changed in Britain's favour with the defeat of Napoleon, and the resultant release of thousands of regulars who could be sent to reinforce Canada. The US knew that it had little time left to win the war, and during the summer of 1814 put in its last major offensive, launched with 5,600 men from the town of Buffalo. The resulting battles of Chippawa and Lundy's Lane were both characterised by the sort of linear fighting, albeit on a smaller scale, that typified war on the European field of battle. Fought largely between well-disciplined regulars, casualties were high and the outcome was stalemate. By the time the US and Britain signed their peace in Ghent on 24 December, the position was little changed from that which had pertained at the outset of the war – 'despite most people's predictions in 1812, with the exception of a small portion of south-western Canada lost in 1813 Canada had survived'.[58]

Final militia actions

From the first to the last, militiamen in both armies had performed key roles. The performance of the militias had been variable, but in many instances they represented most of the forces that could be fielded. The Americans, in particular, found that their faith in the militia system, a faith resting as much on historical necessity, myth and political preference for the armed citizen over the regular soldier, was misplaced. Whatever the merits of the state-based militia systems, they did not provide armies capable of sustaining an aggressive war of conquest. For the British, the French and English-speaking militias more often than not proved their worth in the defence of their country, as well as providing a source of recruits for wartime Provincial regiments. But the reality was that the longer the war went on, the more its continued pursuit required regulars. By late 1814, well-trained, disciplined and experienced regulars were predominant on the field of battle, and two examples provide evidence of this.

On 24 August 1814 a small force of 2,600 British regulars, marines and disembarked sailors faced some 6,500 militia from Maryland and the District of Columbia, supported by around 450 regulars and marines. In short order, the British swept the Americans from the field, despite sustaining heavy casualties inflicted by American artillery. In the words of the American officer, Joseph Sterett, 'we were outflanked and defeated in as short a time as such an operation could well be performed'.[59] The victorious British then marched the eight or so miles to Washington DC, and burned the American capital in retaliation for the earlier American firing of Niagara and York.

The very last battle of the war on Canadian soil took place on 6 November, and it was, on the Canadian side, an affair solely of the militia. The defeat of the British and the Indians at Thamesville (known to the Americans as the Battle of Moraviantown) on 5 October 1813 was an important US victory. During the battle the Indian leader Tecumseh was killed, resulting in the effective collapse of the confederacy that he led and inspired. The victory also opened up the Thames area of Upper Canada to further American incursions, and in the summer of 1814 the US Secretary of State for War ordered General McArthur to plan for 'the destruction of all settlements on the Thames and eastward [to...] quiet the frontier and break the chain that bound the Indian allies to the British cause'.[60] McArthur put together a substantial raiding force, in the knowledge that the British were in no position to reinforce this region quickly. The American raiding column was a mix of regulars and militia, including fifty US Rangers, 344 volunteers of the Kentucky militia, 145 volunteers of the Ohio militia, and seventy Indians. They left Detroit (back in American hands since September 1813) on 22 October 1814 and took a circuitous route into Canada.

On the Canadian side, four militia units had been in the field for months, guarding against the possibility of just such a despoiling raid by the Americans. Altogether, there were some 400 Canadian militiamen under arms from the 1 Norfolks, 2 Norfolks, 1 Oxfords, and the 1 Middlesex, under the command of Lieutenant Colonel Ryerson of the 1 Norfolks. Aware that they were heavily outnumbered by the Americans, most of whom were mounted infantry, and that they were unlikely to receive reinforcement, the Canadian militia set about building a field fortification across the road that ran south from the hamlet of Perth towards Sovereign's Mills. Ryerson chose a strong position on which to build a breastworks, with *abatis*. An American at the battle explained that it was a 'fortified camp on a hill, before which there was a deep and rapid creek about 120 yards from their breastwork. The millpond [of Malcolm's Mills] secured their left and in front the only chance to cross was on the frame of a narrow bridge from which the planks had been torn'.[61] Behind the 200 yards of breastwork, the four militia units were arrayed in line, in a strong defensive position against a frontal assault.

McArthur had only one real option, and that was to occupy the defenders with a frontal attack, while throwing more mounted men and Indians out into two wide, flanking attacks to turn the entire Canadian position. The process was intended to end with a simultaneous attack from the front and both flanks. Kentucky militia undertook the frontal assault on the breastwork, but the flank attacks hit the Canadians first, as Ohio militia and Indians began firing before the Kentucky men were within range. The Canadians were under attack on three sides, and some militia began to run back into the woods behind. However, the majority did not, and the fire fight continued for nearly an hour before, at last, the Americans overran the defenders. One Canadian officer had been killed, along with seventeen privates, while nine other men were wounded, and three captains, five subalterns and 103 privates were captured.[62] The Americans admitted to the loss of one killed and six wounded. In the aftermath of this final battle on Canadian soil in the War of 1812, the Americans burned the mills and destroyed stores of grain. The American column then headed for home, some 200 miles away, pursued by British and Canadian forces. On 18 November the Americans reached Detroit, and the Kentucky and Ohio militiamen were discharged. The Battle of Malcolm's Mills had been largely fought by militia of both sides, helping to draw to a close the fighting which had been so often sustained by men like themselves.

Chapter 4

The Rifle Volunteers: The 'Wonder of the Age', the Victorian Amateur Soldier

Invasion scares, patriotic citizens and government
The French Wars, 1793–1815, and the Volunteer model

Volunteer forces have often had a notable presence in Britain in the modern period. The combination of reliance on naval power, government parsimony, and a long-standing distrust of standing armies, have underpinned the phenomena of rapidly raised volunteer forces at moments of crisis. Periodic invasion panics drove government reforms of the Militia system, but also popular demand for, and creation of, volunteer defence. This was the case in 1745, 1759 and 1779, when a mix of Jacobite insurrection and French intervention brought volunteers out for short periods of time. However, the long struggle with France, from the founding of the French Republic in 1793 until the final defeat of Napoleon in 1815, brought repeated fears of the French invasion of Britain and Ireland. The territorial defence of the country was supposed, in large part, to be in the hands of the Militia, which had, yet again, been reformed and supposedly revitalised by the Militia Acts of 1782–83. Although the Militia had an important role in Britain's military organisation, most notably as a reserve pool from which the regular army drew new recruits,[1] its usefulness for widespread territorial defence was limited. It was popular concern about the weakness of that defence that led to volunteers forming Associations in the spring of 1794 to help defend the country from external threat, as well as from those Britons deemed sympathetic to the French Revolution. As with later iterations of this volunteer movement, the government at first resisted the demands of patriotic citizens to form Volunteer units. However, the Volunteer movement of the French Wars was outstandingly successful, with 'unprecedented numbers [who] also remained ready for active service for a much longer period of time' than hitherto.[2] That success would not be forgotten at the time of the next French invasion scare, which saw the emergence of the longest-lived volunteer movement in British defence history – the Rifle Volunteer Movement.

A new French threat, a new Volunteer movement

Ultimate victory in the French Wars, particularly the worldwide dominance established by the Royal Navy, was to bring Britain nearly a century of security. However, concerns of the reassertion of French power began to be voiced in Britain by the late 1840s. Military and political voices began to rehearse the old worries about the small size of the regular army, and the fact that its extensive imperial commitments left little for home defence. The threat from France was enhanced by new developments in naval technology, and the reforming, modernising agenda of Louis Napoleon, president of France, who, following his coup d'état of December 1851, became Emperor Napoleon III. With a new Napoleon, a popular dictatorship, and a new spirit of innovation in French industry and the military, the supposed weakness of Britain's defences became a major talking point among the military, politicians, the press, and patriotic members of the public.

It was citizens, animated by their patriotism, the long rivalry with France, and the belief in the role of the citizen-soldier, who forced the government's hand in the face of this new Bonapartist threat. The British public seemed to be 'peculiarly susceptible to the phenomena of the invasion panic',[3] and that susceptibility was exploited by the press. Newspapers such as the *Morning Star, Daily News, Examiner*, and, above all, *The Times*, enthusiastically stoked fears that Britain was open to a rapid crossing of the Channel by French forces possessing temporary superiority in those narrow seas, and thereby able to land an army that would quickly overwhelm the defending British forces. Further, as would be the case later in the century, invasion fiction also played on fears of rampaging foreign soldiers destroying Britain and its place in the world. The fact that in 1850, for example, there were only some 37,000 regular soldiers stationed in Britain, whereas the French could call on 400,000 regulars and two million *Garde Nationale*,[4] seemed to lend credence to these fears. Added to this was the knowledge that, unlike many of Europe's main cities, London at that time was unprotected by fixed fortifications. This was the background to the invasion panics of 1846–47 and 1851–52. In both periods, there were calls for the creation of new volunteer forces that would defend the British homeland; calls that neither governments nor the military were keen to hear. However, the final invasion panic of the period was enhanced by new factors that did, finally, lead to the emergence of the great volunteer movement that would last for some fifty years.

In January 1857, Napoleon III appointed Dupuy de Lôme as the director of construction for the French navy. De Lôme was a renowned naval innovator, and, following the success of France's armoured floating batteries in reducing the Russian fort of Kinburn at the mouth of the rivers Bug and Dnieper during the Crimean War, began a programme to create the first ironclad fleet. The initial French ironclad in the programme, *La Gloire*, was an armoured frigate, laid down at Toulon in March 1858. Its very design made it clear that this ship was not a blue water warship, for 'its gunports were barely six feet above the waterline. This feature, and bunkers capable of carrying just 700 tons of coal, reflected the fact that the ship was designed not for traditional frigate duties but for line-of-battle service in European waters'.[5] This was taken, not unreasonably, to represent a threat to Britain in its home waters. Further, an earlier attempt on Napoleon III's life by the Italian liberal nationalist Felice Orsini on 14 January 1858, in which eight people were killed and 142 were injured, led to popular outrage in France when it became clear that Orsini's bombs were made in Britain, where the plot was also hatched by Italians. The French military, in particular, was incensed by the attack on Napoleon III and Britain having harboured the terrorist and would-be assassin. The heightening of tension, and the threat posed by new naval technology, fed what became known as the 'Third Panic' in Britain, and finally brought success to the demands of the press and supporters of the volunteer cause.

The popular demands for the raising of volunteer corps for home defence were met on 12 May 1859, when the government authorised Lords Lieutenant to raise such units. Both government and the military were still largely unenthusiastic. Despite the government's reservations, 'the Volunteers had the over-riding advantage of satisfying public opinion at absolutely no cost to the Government'.[6] The corps were supported financially by public donation and subscription, with Volunteers providing their own uniforms and equipment. The details of service, training, and the actual role of the Volunteers were, at first, unclear, but the enthusiasm for the force was undoubted. Even before the official founding of the Volunteers, some 60,000 men had come forward. Three weeks after the official announcement, there were 134,000 Volunteers;[7] and the movement proved to be no flash-in-the-pan. By 1863, for example, the Volunteers numbered 200,000 men,[8] and the typically grey-clad Volunteers became a social and military fixture of the Victorian age – the 'wonder of the age'.[9] It quickly established itself as: 'the most significant of the auxiliary forces of the Victorian era in terms of its effect upon social, political and military affairs. Certainly, by the beginning of the twentieth century a far larger section of society had become exposed to military values than would have been possible before 1859'.[10]

This chapter examines the history of that wonder of the age. In nearly half a century of existence, the nature, composition, role, and place of the Rifle Volunteers in society and defence changed and developed. Finally, this most characteristic element of Victorian society experienced its first and last taste of military action, not on home soil but in South Africa, just as the Victorian age drew to a close.

The Rifle Volunteer Movement, 1859–1908

A popular movement

The Rifle Volunteer Movement retained its popularity throughout the half century of its existence. From its inception in 1859 until its replacement in 1908, there were some short-lived falls in the total number of Volunteers enrolled, but the overall trend across the life of the Volunteer Movement was of an increase in numbers enrolled. The temporary falls in enrolment, between 1863 and 1864, and 1868 and 1873, appear to have been responses to reforms and stricter regulations being applied.[11] Between the latter trough of enrolment, when numbers fell to 170,000, until the outbreak of the second Boer War in 1899, when total Volunteer enrolment was 230,000, and would jump to over 280,000 within a year, the trend was upwards. This, of course, was in the context of the continuous rise in the British population, from 23 million in 1861, to 33 million in 1891, a rate of growth which never fell below 10 per cent per decade during the lifetime of the Volunteer Movement.[12]

The Volunteer movement was popular right across Britain,[13] and flourished in cities, towns and the countryside. The class composition of the Volunteers changed over time, with the proportion of professional and middle class men falling, while artisans and labourers made up increasingly greater numbers, as will be seen. The Volunteers quickly established themselves as part of local community life, their activities providing a source of entertainment, and not just to cynics who treated the amateur soldiers with scoffing disdain. Volunteer reviews and displays of military prowess drew large crowds. In July 1861, for instance, up to 50,000 visitors flocked to the small county town of Warwick to watch the midland counties Volunteer review. The year before, between 150,000 and 200,000 spectators gathered at Knowsley, Lancashire, to watch a Volunteer review.[14] That review brought together all of the new Rifle Volunteers of Lancashire, along with no fewer than four battalions of artillery, 'one composed entirely of shipyard workers employed by the Cunard Company; and another commanded by a Colonel Brown, said to contribute £3,000 a year to its maintenance'.[15] It was not just large, set piece tournaments, however, which gave the movement a place in the social life of the country:

> Activities of financial necessity such as fund-raising balls, concerts, bazaars and theatrical performances also added to the entertainment available through the volunteers as did the activities purely internal to units such as dinners, prize givings and the variety of clubs that sprang up attached to corps or companies. Indeed, volunteers athletic and football clubs were especially important in popularising sports previously confined to the wealthier classes.[16]

In the great cities of Britain, the movement flourished, with Liverpool, London, Glasgow, and Edinburgh all being centres of early Volunteer activity, enthusiasm for which was maintained throughout the life of the movement. In Glasgow, for example, 300 men formed themselves into a Volunteer unit a week before the official sanctioning of the Volunteers, in May 1859. That 300 grew to 3,000 Glasgow Volunteers within a month, and 10,000 by the end of that summer, and 'a leading Glasgow citizen, Mr. Archibald K. Murray, whose letter to a Glasgow newspaper had brought about the meeting, claimed that the response of Glasgow to the War Office circular was twice that of London.'[17] Surprisingly, perhaps, Mr Murray made no comparison with the Volunteer movement in Edinburgh, where 22,000 men paraded before Queen Victoria in Holyrood Park in the autumn of 1860. Throughout the existence of the Volunteer Movement, Scots were around twice as likely to be in a Volunteer unit as their English or Welsh counterparts. In 1881, for example, there were 48,936 Scottish Volunteers, which represented one in thirty-six of the male population, compared to the 159,372 English and Welsh Volunteers, representing one in seventy-nine of that population, with the proportions in 1901 being one in thirty-six, compared to one in sixty-eight.[18] The enthusiasm of Scottish volunteers more than matched that of their compatriots south of the border. One account of the early days of the movement in Edinburgh, written over forty years later, gives us some insight into the keenness of the early volunteers:

> The volunteer of to-day can have little idea of the enthusiasm of that time. When a citizen joins the volunteer ranks to-day he enters a developed organisation in which his duties are prescribed, all that is necessary is provided, and he fulfils his part if he goes through a limited amount of training. In 1859 everything was novel, unorganised, and ill-provided. But what a life was in it! The volunteer of that day had no thought of minimum in his drills. Many went regularly to two and even three drills a-day. I have myself drilled at seven in the morning with the Writers of the Signet, in the forenoon in the Parliament House, and in the afternoon out of doors with the Advocates, and in the Queen's Park in the evening with an artisan company. ... My roll-book when I commanded a company showed many volunteers attending ninety drills in one season, and very few below fifty. And how and where did we drill? In Exchange Square and Meadow Walks, by the light of the rat's-tail gas-burners of those days, when weather permitted; in small steaming rooms below the Council Chambers when driven by rain or snow. Night after night, through the long winter and into spring, we laboured. Rich companies had drill instructors in their pay, but we who had artisan companies had to do all our own drilling, getting our musketry certificates by judging distance in two inches of snow in the Meadows, and firing our course when one was glad to warm one's fingers between shots on the heated barrels of our muzzle-loaders.[19]

This affectionate memory of the early days of the Edinburgh Volunteer Movement contains within it the breadth of the social mix of the movement, from the legal elite to the 'artisans' of the Scottish capital, the central importance of musketry, and the enthusiasm generated by a spontaneous amateur military organisation.

As the Volunteer Movement became firmly established, so successive governments moved to integrate it more closely with the needs of the defence of Britain, and the demands of the regular army. Nonetheless, the popularity of the Volunteer Movement was maintained, even as its independence was gradually, though never completely, eroded. By 1871, for example, when Edward Cardwell,

Secretary of State for War, was engaged in his great reform programme, the Volunteers were a crucial, and numerous, element in the defence of Britain. In that year, Britain had nearly half a million men to call upon, with the Volunteers representing the largest number:

Regular Army:	135,000 (at home and abroad)
First Army Reserves:	9,000
Second Army Reserves:	30,000 (mostly pensioners)
Militia:	139,000
Yeomanry:	14,000
Volunteers:	170,000
Total:	497,000 [20]

The continued enthusiasm and support for the Volunteers was also amply demonstrated in the closing decade of its history when Volunteers were called upon for service in the Second Boer War. Not only did thousands of men volunteer for South African service, but recruitment to the Volunteers jumped. Further, private subscription to support the Volunteers on active service in South Africa quickly raised over £100,000, while two shipping companies, Union Castle and Wilson's of Hull, transported the first 1,000 Volunteers to South Africa free of charge.[21] The war in South Africa proved to be not only the Volunteers main experience of active service, but also the swansong for the movement that had been able to maintain popular support since the first, heady days of 1859.

Patriotism, rifles, and leisure – explaining the popularity of the Volunteer Movement

In explaining the long-term popularity of the Volunteer Movement, factors such as patriotism, developments in firearm technology, along with changing work patterns and the quest for new leisure opportunities combine. In effect, the long-term buoyancy of the movement reflected changes in Victorian life, technology and society. Hugh Cunningham, in his social and political history of the Volunteer Movement, discounted patriotism as a major explanatory reason for the popularity of the Volunteers.[22] He allowed that patriotism might have explained middle-class adherence to the movement, particularly in the initial period of the movement's establishment, and also at times of increased tension in Europe, such as during the Franco-Prussian War. Beyond this, however,

Cunningham gave little weight to patriotism, particularly among the ranks of working-class volunteers, who became increasingly more numerous as the Volunteer Movement developed. However, Cunningham drew his definition of patriotism too narrowly. Rightly, he linked the politics of Liberalism and Conservatism with attitudes to Britain intervening in European affairs. In the 1850s and 1860s, it was the Liberal Party that was most keen on intervening in foreign affairs, with a general enthusiasm for Liberal crusade against the *ancien regimes* of Europe. As a result, patriotism was often framed by members of the Liberal middle classes as being supportive of the Liberal nationalism that was typified by the amateur soldiery famously gathered around Garibaldi. In opposition to this approach was that of the Conservatives, who argued that British policy should be guided by what Disraeli said, in 1877, was 'the Imperial policy of England [rather than] a policy of crusade', the latter being that of the Liberals.[23] However, the patriotism of the early years of the Volunteer Movement, which enabled the ideologically charged Liberal to serve alongside the Briton concerned, above all else, with homeland defence, had been transformed by the 1870s. During that decade, patriotism became much more a stance built upon the interests of Britain alone, and a standpoint more in tune with that of the Conservative Party than that of the Liberals. Above all the party politicking, however, it is hard to review any period of the Volunteers' history and not recognise a fundamental, patriotic (in a non-party political fashion) impulse sustaining the movement. It was the popular creation of the British peoples, determined to push what they regarded as sluggish government in the face of foreign threat, and it maintained itself as the embodiment of both local and national pride and the latest expression of the long tradition of Britons prepared to defend their country in the face of foreign attack. In this, patriotism was a strong thread that ran through the movement.

The birth of the Volunteer Movement coincided with the founding of the National Rifle Association (NRA) in November 1859. Modelled on the 'Swiss *tir federal* to promote the [Volunteer] movement and encourage rifle shooting as a pastime',[24] the NRA, and the sport of rifle shooting, quickly became a key factor in the continuing success of the Volunteer Movement. Indeed, from its first annual meeting, held at Wimbledon on 2 July 1860, a meet that was later moved, in 1889, to the still famous Bisley, the NRA became the central pillar of competitive shooting in Britain, long outlasting the Volunteer Movement which the NRA did so much to support.

The rifled musket had already established a position for itself in military history. In the Anglophone world, the exploits of American militia in their war with Loyalists and British had established the weapon's value. Subsequent adoption of the weapon by British light infantry in the American Revolution, the Peninsular Campaign, and the War of 1812, established the importance of the weapon. Moreover, technological development, in terms of craft-based mass production and the development of the breech-loading rifle, brought a new importance to the individual soldier, or Volunteer. The core aspects of Volunteer training revolved around drill and 'musketry', and through a series of reforms, these skills remained at the heart of Volunteer efficiency. Marksmanship was at the very heart of a Volunteer's pride in his effectiveness. But the importance of rifle shooting extended beyond mere military skill, as it became a popular Victorian sport that attracted prizes, underpinned inter-unit rivalry, and drew in the wider community:

> In shooting the volunteers took a leading part in the country, their marksmen even showing the way to the regular army, and through them a taste for rifle-shooting was developed throughout the country. Prize-lists were subscribed for in all corps; local bodies, land-owners, merchants, and the heads of great works and firms offered prizes or trophies for shooting, and provincial rifle associations, on the model of the National Rifle Association, sprang up all over the country. A healthy rivalry between corps was also established by the institution of matches, and the records of the volunteers of those days teem with descriptions of the interest which these excited, not only in the corps, but in the locality from which they were recruited.[25]

The Volunteer riflemen were, from the outset, envisaged as largely playing a light infantry role, and skill at arms was essential to that function. But the importance of the rifle, as an accurate, targeted weapon as opposed to the line infantry's volley firing, also matched the ideal of the Volunteer as a citizen-soldier, whose individuality would play an important part in battle. For some, the technological advance of the rifle suggested an earlier version of the common soldier, with *The Times* stating in 1860 that 'just as the longbow seemed a weapon peculiarly suited to the English, so was the rifle peculiarly adapted to Britain's "national spirit of independence and self-reliance" '.[26]

Many of the original founding members of Volunteer units may well have seen their new organisation as representing exclusive clubs for the professional classes, something that was, in part, guaranteed by the fact that Volunteer units were, at the outset, totally self-financing. However, there was recognition by leading founders of the movement that excluding artisans, members of the 'labour aristocracy', skilled, time-served men, would in the long-term be detrimental to the force, as the professional classes would form too small a pool of potential recruits. Indeed, as the movement matured, so the professional and middle classes provided a small proportion of the Volunteers, and 'evidence from 1862 onwards illustrates a continuing process of change with volunteers becoming younger and more working-class'.[27] By 1877, according to the *Volunteer Service Gazette*, the middle classes had simply 'melted away', and by 1904, 70 per cent of Volunteers were working class.[28] A range of factors underpinned this change, including government capitation funding for the Volunteers, and stricter training and efficiency standards, but also including changes in leisure patterns. By the 1870s, half-day holidays were in place in many towns and cities, the Bank Holiday Act was passed in 1875, and the Factories and Workshops Acts of 1878 and 1901, all enabled workers to devote more time to leisure. It was 'primarily as a recreational pursuit that the volunteer movement appealed to the artisan and thereby survived, particularly as the disciplined pursuit of leisure endowed volunteering with a strongly moral purpose'.[29] Drill evenings, field days and annual camps loomed large, but Volunteer units also created their own social clubs 'with chess, skittles, dominoes, cards and a pea rifle range. Athletic, gymnastic, cricket and drama clubs flourished under Volunteer aegis'.[30] Nonetheless, the non-military social aspects of a Volunteer's life were always secondary. The military purpose and values of the movement were at its heart, and 'to join the Volunteers indicated a willingness to wear military uniform, to learn elementary duties, and to both receive and obey orders'.[31] Thus, the Volunteer Movement cemented military virtues into the social life of Victorian Britain, providing important scaffolding to support the social order and cohesion that came to characterise the view that many late nineteenth-century Victorians had of their own country.

Preparing to defend: roles, training and innovation

At the beginning of the Volunteer Movement, the spontaneous emergence, in a short space of time, of units up and down the country led to a proliferation of ideas relating to uniforms, organisation, and the role of the Volunteers.

Further, as the government only accepted, via Lords Lieutenant, applications for new units on the basis that they would not be a burden to the public purse, the financial independence that implied gave the Volunteers greater leeway in military matters. That, of course, changed as the movement grew and matured, which was something that was reflected in the level of government funding. In 1860, government expenditure on the Volunteer Movement was £3,000, but by 1897 that figure had risen to £627,000.[32] Unsurprisingly, in return for increases in government funding (which underpinned the increasingly working-class membership of the force), there were greater demands for better organisa-tion, stricter control and higher efficiency standards.

Prior to the establishment of the first volunteer units, rifle clubs and amateur military enthusiasts were agitating at local level for a new defence force. One of the most notable early enthusiasts for a Volunteer Movement was Hans Busk, who had campaigned for such a force from his postgraduate days at Trinity College, Cambridge. In 1858, he published *The Rifleman's Manual,* one of many publications aimed at boosting interest in defence. He was an early member of the 'Victoria Rifles', and was extremely active in promoting the concept of rifle-armed volunteers, and between 1858 and 1861 he travelled the country address-ing some 147 meetings.[33] In 1859 he published his best-selling *Rifle Volunteers; How to Organise and Drill Them.* Busk's manual rapidly became a standard for units, especially those not wealthy enough to employ drill sergeants. In addition to instructions on rifle training, Busk also addressed the issue of the role of Volunteers in the field, and how they would complement both the Regulars and Militia. The Rifle Volunteer role was, in the opinion of Busk and most other enthusiasts, that of a light infantryman:

> One important duty [of the Volunteers] would be, to hang upon the skirts of the enemy, compelling him to be constantly on the watch, and continually harassing him with the apprehension of an attack. If Light Infantry discharged their duties efficiently, no detachment or reinforcement could be dispatched, no movement of consequence effected on the side of the enemy – scarcely, indeed, could a return be transmitted, or even a messenger sent off, without information being conveyed in a variety of ways to the head quarters of the army from which these light troops were detached … Rifle Volunteers would upon almost all occasions have the advantage of choosing the

time and the point for their attack, which could only be resisted at a disadvantage, not only at the part where the enemy was weakest, but where the ground was most difficult to hold. If ably led, they would frequently be enabled to penetrate through his flanks, to the very rear of the enemy, stealing their way through his outposts, and, after inflicting severe injury, making good their retreat.[34]

Needless to say, this vision of the amateur Volunteers as some form of early special forces on a large scale was not one shared by many regulars. The actual value of amateur soldiers was much discussed by contemporaries at the time of the first major battle of the American Civil War, First Bull Run/First Manassas, in July 1861. On both sides, volunteer units had played a significant role, so for the partisans of the British Volunteers, the success of Confederate arms proved the value of volunteers, whereas the professionals argued that the chaos and rout of the Union forces at the battle was a result of the presence of volunteer units. In his manual, Busk gave other examples of successful light infantry operations, including American militia against the British, and German Student Volunteers against Napoleon. He went on to argue that with well-practised, basic rifle drill, and with high levels of local knowledge conferring tactical advantage on volunteer forces, they could be 'formidable' guerrillas.

Despite the willingness of the early Volunteers to look to their own training and organisation, the need for some form of government funding for many units, added to the concerns of the army about how the force could, if at all, be effectively integrated into any defence of the country, opened the way for greater official control over the Volunteer Movement. On the Volunteers' part there was always the tension between wanting to keep as much autonomy as possible, while at the same time receiving official recognition as an important element in Britain's defence. Even at the outset, it was recognised that not all units would be financially capable of fully arming their men, and as early as July 1859 the government agreed to make available enough rifles to equip a quarter of the force. That proved to be a temporary arrangement, as by the end of the year the government had conceded the military logic of supplying all the force's rifles.

In 1862, a Royal Commission on the Volunteer force made a series of recommendations which put the force on an official footing, established it as being state-sponsored, and set down the rights and duties of Volunteers. The Commission's recommendations were almost all adopted in the subsequent Volunteer Act,

1863. That Act provided capitation grants for each efficient Volunteer, increased the pay of fulltime adjutants, and set standards for uniforms. The reforms brought improved efficiency, and greater military status; at least in the eyes of the Volunteers. The end of the Volunteers' first decade brought further changes, arising out of the appointment of the reforming Edward Cardwell as Secretary of State for War in December 1868, and the impact of the Franco-Prussian War on thinking about the organisation and use of the Volunteers.

Cardwell's reforms, codified in the Regulation of the Forces Act of 1871, and additional organisational changes enforced from 1872, were initially opposed by many Volunteers. The motivation of the Secretary of State for War was to continue the process of making the Volunteers more militarily effective, more able to be incorporated into the defence of Britain, while extending government control over the Volunteers. Cardwell's 'new regulations required from [the Volunteers] a higher level of training, laid down standards of proficiency for officers and non-commissioned officers and tied the amount of government financial assistance to each corps' success in meeting the new requirements'.[35] Additionally, control of the Volunteers passed from the Lord Lieutenant of each county to the Crown; Volunteers became subject to military law when brigaded with the Regulars or Militia; and the Volunteers' own adjutants (mostly retired officers) were replaced by regular army officers on five-year secondments. Further reforms came in 1878 aimed at increasing the ability of the Volunteers to work with the regulars and the Militia, as well as introducing compulsory uniform distinctions to mark out Volunteers. The final major reforms of the nineteenth century came in 1881, when the Volunteers were reorganised on a territorial basis, by counties, and fully integrated with the structure of defence. For example, following the 1881 reforms, the 1 and 2 Edinburgh, 1 and 2 Midlothian, 1 Berwick, 1 Haddington and 1 Linlithgow Volunteers were grouped into the The Royal Scots (Lothian Regiment), which also incorporated the regular battalions of the 1 and 2 Battalions 1 Foot, and the Edinburgh Light Infantry Militia.[36] In this reorganisation we can see the first signs of what would become the territorial force following the 1908 reforms that ended the history of the Volunteers.

One of the spurs to reform in the 1870s was the Franco-Prussian War, which saw the defeat of Napoleon III and the establishment of the German Empire. The large-scale battles, marked by heavy casualties and the use, and tactical misuse, of the latest military technology, all combined to focus minds on

Britain's preparations for defence, with the newly emergent continental power of Germany taking over from France as the most likely opposition. The reforms sought to take full advantage of the numbers of troops that the Volunteers represented, and one of the first results of the new thinking was large-scale manoeuvres combining the regulars, Militia, and Volunteers. There had been small-scale Volunteer manoeuvres alongside the regulars as early as 1862, but the first large-scale, joint manoeuvres were held near Aldershot in 1871, with succeeding manoeuvres, on a more ambitious scale, on Salisbury Plain from 1872 onwards. Reform also brought reorganisation of Volunteer units into larger formations, first at battalion level, then from 1888 onwards to brigade level organisation of Volunteer units.

Although the greater part of the Volunteer Movement took the form of units of light infantry, the Volunteers also encompassed engineer, fortification and coastal and field artillery units. The Volunteers themselves, in many cases, were keen to extend their remit beyond that of light infantry, and throughout its history the Volunteer Movement was associated with a readiness to adopt the latest technological developments. Despite the fact that the Volunteers became increasingly dependent on government funding and subject to War Office regulation, they always had the leeway to raise funds privately for equipment and innovation. Volunteer units experimented early with the military use of the bicycle, the machine gun, and the armoured train, and adopted equipment, such as the 12.5-pounder Vickers-Maxim field guns Volunteers took on active service in South Africa that were not army issue. This willingness to experiment with the latest technology, and to take advantage of the civilian skills that many Volunteers possessed, was held to be one of the great benefits of the Volunteer Movement. The argument was that in engineering, metalworking, telegraphic communication, the railways, and a host of skilled trades, it was civilians who were in the van of technological development, and could therefore bring the latest innovations of Victorian industrialism to the battlefield. To a limited extent, officialdom accepted this argument, and the first, small Volunteer units to experience active service beyond Britain's shores did so because of the technological skills they possessed.

The first unit to see overseas service was a company-sized unit of men from the 24 Middlesex (Post Office) Rifle Volunteer Corps, which served in Egypt in 1882 as an army post office corps. Success in that role led the battalion to form two telegraph field companies, a platoon of which was sent to Suakin in March

1885, where a small number of men from the 1 Newcastle and Durham and the 1 Lancashire engineer volunteer corps also served on railway duties.[37] The abortive Suakin campaign was part of the initial efforts to avenge the death of General Gordon at Khartoum by the troops of the Mahdi. The failed attempt to relieve Khartoum had convinced the British and Egyptians that a more reliable method than Nile-borne steamers was necessary to support any attempt to reconquer the Sudan. A 300-mile-long railway was planned from the port of Suakin, and it was to provide additional expertise that the Lancashire engineer Volunteers were sent to Sudan. The campaign was, however, abandoned, and little of the railway was built. It would be another twelve years before Gordon was avenged.

Although early Volunteer units embodied specialised industrial skills, that fact was seen to be incidental to the purpose and role of the units concerned, which was that of the light infantryman. Nonetheless, the 1862 Royal Commission reported that in addition to 134,096 riflemen, there were 24,363 artillery Volunteers, 2,904 Volunteer engineers, and very small numbers of mounted men – 656 mounted riflemen, and 662 light horse.[38] The Regular Army was far from enthusiastic about non-light infantry Volunteer units, the argument being that the training limitations faced by Volunteers meant that they could not possibly reach the necessary standards required of horse artillery. The result of this thinking was that Edward Cardwell forbade the use of the capitation grant for the maintenance of horses, harnesses, or field guns. Similarly, rivalry between the older Yeomanry units meant that in 1875, for example, the horse artillery troops of the Yeomanry in Buckinghamshire and Essex, 'the dismounted rifle troop in Northumberland, and the rifle troop raised in Wiltshire in 1859 to ride in specially constructed carriages' were all disbanded.[39] Notwithstanding this type of opposition from rival military forces whose vested interests made them unwilling to accept any developments that they saw as role-creep on the part of the Volunteers, non-light infantry Volunteers still flourished, in part because of perceived weaknesses in Britain's defence schemes that neither Regulars, Militia, or Yeomanry were able to meet.

The defence of London was a perennial issue throughout the nineteenth century, and the source of much concern in both popular and official circles. The dominant, official view was that the strength of the Royal Navy guaranteed the safety of the capital, and made the extensive fortifications that characterised many continental towns and cities unnecessary. However, powerful voices, including the Duke of Wellington's, questioned this view, and the subsequent development of fast, steam-powered warships also provoked the popular fear that an enemy could mount a quick invasion of Britain's southern coastline, opening up London to rapid assault and capture. However, maintaining large, static garrisons and the manning of fixed fortifications by regular troops, raised questions of costs and morale among regulars. The answer to this problem came with the Volunteers. Over two years from 1888–90, the War Office reorganised its planning for the defence of Britain. This entailed organising the Volunteers into combined units of a higher level than battalions. The overall plan for the defence of the country had three elements to it: 'a mobile regular force for active operations, a force for the defence of the capital, round which a series of defensive positions had been selected, and a force for coast and local defence'.[40] The Volunteers' place in this grand plan was that they were:

> increasingly projected as a viable and cheap 'second line', 97 out of 209 volunteer battalions, including 21,000 men in defence of London, were utilised in the mobilisation scheme of 1886 while that of 1888 took a major step forward in proposing to organise volunteer brigades of six battalions each in large camps at Aldershot, Caterham, Chatham, Tilbury, Warley and Epping occupying a line between the immediate defences of London and the two regular army corps operating to the south. The defence of London itself was also entrusted to volunteers in fixed fortifications. Volunteer engineers had already been used to supplement the manpower available for submarine mining defences of mercantile ports from 1884 onwards and additional submarine mining companies and position batteries were now raised to meet deficiencies in the mobilisation scheme.[41]

The Volunteer movement had, without doubt, come of age by being fully integrated in the defence of the nation's capital.

The Volunteers' enthusiasm for innovation was one of their minor, but noted, characteristics. Always enthusiastic in anything to do with the development of rifle technology, Volunteer units also pioneered the use of the machine gun. By 1893, nineteen Volunteer units had equipped themselves with machine guns, while the arrival of the 'safety bicycle' in the late 1880s, as a much-needed alternative to the 'penny farthing' bicycle, opened up new possibilities. The new bicycle, the basic design of which has remained unchanged, was seized upon by Volunteers as a way of enabling rapid movement in the field, as an ideal tool for reconnaissance, providing a mount for messengers, and as a way of carrying more equipment than a man could. At the beginning of the 1888–90 reforms, every Volunteer unit was given the authority to raise a cyclist section, comprising of one officer, two NCOs, and thirteen to twenty-one men, including a bugler. Eventually, bicycle-mounted messengers took their machines on active service in South Africa, where the Volunteers' commanding officer, Major General W.H. Mackinnon, recorded them as 'doing splendid work … taking mails, telegrams &c., to and from Johannesburg and other places. They have frequently taken letters thirty-five miles across the veldt under conditions which were none too safe. They are always eager to go anywhere, and neither risk nor distance is too much for them'.[42]

The Volunteer movement also had the distinction of being the initiators of the armoured train in Britain. Although there had been earlier use of armoured trains by the British, these were extempore armoured units in Egypt and Sudan. In India, British and Anglo-Indian volunteers had developed armoured train usage, building bespoke armoured trains in the mid and late 1880s. In Britain, the Volunteers of the 1 Sussex Artillery Volunteers, under Captain F.G. Stone, developed and operated the 'Brighton Casemate Wagon' throughout the last decade of the century. The armoured train consisted of a 40pdr Armstrong breech loader mounted in an armoured wagon; the gun was complete with its wheeled field mounting and was fixed to an armoured revolving platform. 'A pair of inclined chocks up which the wheels of the gun ran absorbed part of the recoil, the rest being damped by a centrally-mounted recoil cylinder as fitted on the fortress mountings used with this gun. A system of screw jacks stabilised the wagon during firing'.[43] Drawn by an unarmoured engine, the gun wagon was followed by two fully armoured coaches, the first to accommodate the gun crew, and the second to hold the necessary harnesses and equipment that would enable the gun to be deployed, if necessary, away from the train. The crew coach was loopholed so that the gunners could use their artillery carbines. The armoured train was fully operational by 1894, and took part in public demonstrations, as well as accompanying Volunteers on manoeuvres. During the invasion scare of July 1898, prompted by the Fashoda Incident, the train was mobilised. Although the intention of the train's designer, Mr Billinton, had been for the Brighton armoured train to be the first of a series of improved armoured trains acting as mobile coast-defence batteries, the 1 Sussex Artillery Volunteers' train was both the first and last Volunteer armoured train.

For almost all the Volunteers, their only experience of field life came with annual camps, field days, and manoeuvres. For the typical Volunteer, these events were the highlight of the Volunteer life. Annual camp represented to the Volunteer a taste of the military life, and a real change from the daily grind of employment. Military training, drill, 'musketry' practice, sports, and evening concerts and music all made annual camps popular. A reporter for the *Leicester Daily Mercury* described the life of Leicester Volunteers in summer camp in 1879:

> The daily life of a military camp is interesting to those who have to experience it once a year, and then only for one week. Reveille is sounded at half-past five in the morning, when the men have to turn out and wash the 'bishop' from their eyes. The walls of the tents are then neatly rolled up if the weather is fine, the bedding rolled into a small compass, and the tents made tidy, the non-commissioned officers in charge being called to account if everything is not clean and respectable. At half-past six o'clock they have to be on parade, and woe be to any fellow who is then found gaping, or drowsy. At 7.30 the canteen is opened, and at eight o'clock breakfast is served, and at half-past ten there is another parade, which gives an appetite for dinner which is partaken of at one o'clock. An hour or an hour and a half is allowed for digestion, and at three o'clock there is another parade, and tea at five. The day guard and piquet mount at 9 a.m., but piquets fall in with their respective corps on all parades. At half-past eight o'clock in the evening the night guard march out, and half an hour later tattoo is sounded. At half-past nine the subalterns of the day collects the reports on the parade ground, the canteen having closed at 9.15 and at ten o'clock, on a prolonged G being blown on the bugle, lights are put out ... Strict silence is enforced in camp between lights out and reveille, not the least noise being allowed. This order was well observed in our Leicestershire camp each night.[44]

This contemporary account appears more concerned with the gastronomic rather than the military experiences of a Volunteer camp on home soil, but a generation later, thousands of Volunteers would see active service in South Africa, enduring harsh conditions, and shortages of rations, in addition to death and disease. It was to be the Volunteer Movement's swan song.

War at last: Volunteers on active service in South Africa, 1899–1900

For much of Queen Victoria's reign, the Volunteers had been a fixture of British society, and one that she had high regard for. It was, therefore, fitting that the Volunteers saw their first and only actions during the war that ended both her reign and the nineteenth century. War between the British Empire and the Boer republics had been on the cards since the 1870s at least. The expansion of the Empire into South Africa, even as it removed the threat to the Boers presented by the Zulus, opened the way to Britain's high-handed treatment of the Afrikaners. But the Afrikaners – tough, indomitable, independent and possessed of an absolute belief in their status as a people Covenanted with God – were not likely to put up with interference. Following the defeat of the Zulus in 1879, the British found that they now faced an Afrikaner population in the Transvaal that was free to resist Britain. The short, and for the British disastrous, First Boer War of 1880–81, led to the feeling among Afrikaners that their citizen-soldiers were more than a match for poorly-led, incompetent British troops. The resulting peace treaty gave the Transvaal a high level of independence; indeed, the Afrikaners saw it as giving them full independence. Against this backdrop of a somewhat tense peace, a new development drastically changed matters for both Afrikaners and the Empire, when, in the late 1880s, huge gold reserves were discovered near Johannesburg. What had been a poor, agricultural country now became a magnet for non-Afrikaners, the *Uitlanders*, who joined the ensuing gold rush. The Transvaal also became far more attractive to the diamond king, and Prime Minister of Cape Colony, Cecil Rhodes, who organised the spectacularly badly planned Jameson raid in December 1895. Jameson and his men were captured and the raid defeated, but the event made war increasingly likely. In preparation, 'from 1896-9 the Transvaal openly re-armed, importing 80,000 modern rifles and 80 million rounds of ammunition, re-equipping their army with the most modern French and German guns and recruiting professional foreign officers for their artillery'.[45] The final ingredient to the potent mix that led to the Second Boer War was the mutual antagonism between President Kruger of the Transvaal and Sir Alfred Milner, Britain's High Commissioner in South Africa from May 1897. Negotiations over the rights of non-Afrikaner whites in the Transvaal between the two men continued until the summer of 1899, but proved futile, and war preparations began to be made. On 11 October, Britain and its Empire found itself at war with the Transvaal and the Orange Free State.

The Boer War was a war in two parts. Not for the first or the last time, Britain proved unprepared for the defence of its Empire. The Boers mobilised rapidly, putting 60–70,000 'burghers' into the field in Commandos of between 300–3,000 men and boys. To these were added the small number of Afrikaner and foreign professionals in the artillery and police. These men quickly invested small British garrisons at Ladysmith, Kimberley and Mafeking. In all, the British only had around 27,000 men, including newly raised volunteers and police, in Natal and Cape Colony, and were in no position to do anything but grimly hang on in the besieged towns. Reinforcement had to come from Britain and India, and that took time. Eventually, and to great popular relief and celebration in Britain, the sieges were lifted, after the British Army made its customary early war mistakes, being defeated at Stromberg, Magersfontein and Colenso during the 'Black Week' of December 1899. The early months of 1900 marked a new phase in the war, as the Boers suffered a number of defeats in the field and lost Pretoria in June. However, this did not prove to be the end of the fighting, as many supposed. Instead, the war turned into a war of movement and pursuit across thousands of miles of difficult terrain, as the British tried to hunt down Boer columns, which proved highly mobile, and quick to deliver bloody noses to their pursuing British antagonists. This was guerrilla war on a grand scale, and it was during this period that Britain earned undying enmity from the Afrikaners, as a result of scorched earth tactics and the deaths of thousands of Afrikaner women and children in poorly run concentration camps. The war dragged on until the spring of 1902, marked by three 'de Wet hunts', as the British called their pursuits of the great Boer guerrilla leader, Commandant General Christiaan de Wet. It was this second phase of the war that the Volunteers took part in. The big battles were past, but the long, hard slog, by horse and foot, interspersed by sharp fighting, took its toll. It was this phase that was immortalised by Rudyard Kipling in his famous poem of infantry endurance, 'Boots' – 'Seven-six-eleven-five-nine-an'-twenty mile to-day/Four-eleven-seventeen-thirty-two the day before/(Boots-boots-boots-boots, movin' up and down again!)'.

The need for manpower to fight the war was particularly acute, and the Volunteers represented an obvious source of trained men. Although there was no obligation at all on Volunteers to serve outside Britain, there was widespread keenness to help the Empire at a time when, in late 1899, it began to look as if it could sustain a major blow, and one that would be welcomed by Britain's enemies and rivals. The spirit of the Volunteer movement was noticeable in the offers that poured into the War Office. The most significant of these came from the Lord Mayor of the City of London, who had 'offered to raise a regiment of [Volunteer] infantry, with mounted infantry attached; to clothe, equip, and transport them by sea to Cape Town, where they were to be taken over by the War Office'.[46] This unit became the famous 'City Imperial Volunteers' (CIV), with whose ranks, sixty-four Volunteer officers and 1,675 other ranks served.[47] The fortunes of these Volunteers were recorded at the time by the commanding officer of the CIV, Major General W.H. Mackinnon, whose journal was published early in 1901, just months after the CIV returned home. This journal provides a detailed, almost daily account of the fortunes of the Volunteers on active service. But this is not the only contemporary record, as the famous author of *The Riddle of the Sands*, later an Irish Republican, and one of the victims of the Irish Free State's firing squads, Erskine Childers, left his account of service in South Africa as an artillery Volunteer with the CIV's artillery battery.[48] Together, these two contemporary accounts act as a worthy memorial to the Volunteers at war.

Once the War Office had accepted the offer of the CIV, mobilisation was rapid, as the situation in South Africa in December 1899 was, for the British, a far from happy one. In the first week of January 1900, 1,265 Volunteers were sworn in at the Guildhall by the Lord Mayor of the City of London and five aldermen and sheriffs. At the same time, the Honourable Artillery Company (HAC), that famous and somewhat esoteric unit, was given permission to send a battery of their new, private-purchase, 12.5-pounder Vickers-Maxim field guns, which Childers described as 'having practically no recoil, and with a much improved breech-mechanism. They turned out very good, but of course, being experimental, required practice handling, which could not have been obtained in the few weeks in the London barracks'.[49] The first detachments of Volunteers marched out on 12 January, with great ceremony and to huge popular acclaim:

> All ranks received the Freedom of the City of London, the presentation of which to the officers was made with much ceremony and picturesqueness, in the presence of the Duke of Cambridge. The men also drew their rifles from the Tower. At 8 p.m. the detachment attended a farewell service in St. Paul's, subsequently marching through dense masses of people to the Temple, where they were entertained at supper by the Inner Temple. The enthusiasm of the

populace was very marked, and the formation of the ranks could not be kept. After supper the detachment returned to Bunhill Row, were they slept.

The detachment marched out of Bunhill Row at 7am, but, owing to the enormous crowds lining the streets, it took three hours and twenty minutes, instead of seventy minutes, to get to Nine Elms.[50]

The Volunteers' departure was an amalgam of late Victorian Imperial enthusiasm, involving the City of London, the Church, the heart of London's legal world, and huge, enthusiastic crowds turning out in freezing early-morning weather to cheer the Volunteers off on their defence of Empire. Later drafts were sent on their way in similar style, and, in all, 1,260 men in the CIV served in South Africa. They were drawn from forty-seven different Volunteer units, were deemed fit for overseas service, were categorised as 'efficient' and had an average age of twenty-four. In terms of occupations, the largest number, some 308, were 'clerks', with solicitors, students, printers, engineers, schoolmaster, civil servants, warehousemen, builders, carpenters, tailors, and labourers all figuring among a wide range of trades and occupations.[51]

Service in South Africa during the 1900 campaign involved, for the CIV, campaigning in a harsh environment, with the ever-present threat of deadly disease, and vast distances to be covered in the pursuit of an elusive foe that remained capable of inflicting sudden reverses. Childers's diary gives a good account of campaign life, with its shortages of food, extremes of heat and cold, and the long pursuit, broken by sudden artillery actions. The halcyon days of peacetime summer camps were behind the Volunteers on active service, but, at first, the gunners of the CIV found themselves in reserve, and taken up with the monotonous daily tasks of caring for horses, while familiarising themselves with their new guns. This was not what the men had hoped for, and the knowledge that the CIV infantry were seeing action did little for the HAC's morale. However, in May the move came, and they were taken by train to Bloemfontein, where numerous field hospitals struggled with high levels of mortality arising from dysentery and 'enteric' fever. Finally, towards the end of June, the artillery were sent in pursuit of the enemy. Interestingly, the Volunteer artillerymen moved off in conjunction with an array of different regular, reserve and volunteer units – men from the 'Buffs Militia, Yorkshire Light Infantry, Australian Mounted Infantry (Imperial Bushmen Contingent), and some Middlesex Yeomanry'.[52] There was a brief taste of action on 26 June, with the Volunteers firing on entrenched Boers, and suffering two light casualties, then the chase continued. This set the pattern for much that followed, and the campaigning was as much about endurance as fighting:

> The change of life since we left Bloemfontein has been complete; no tents, no washing, no undressing, only biscuit and tinned meat for food; and not too much of that, very little sleep, etc., but we have enjoyed it, for it is the real thing at last. The lack of water was the really trying thing, and the cold at night. We had fresh meat for supper this night from a sheep commandeered on the march, and weren't we ravenous! Another very cold night …[53]

The 'commandeered' sheep was, in all probability, taken from a Boer farm. The British regarded the Boers who resisted as rebels, and farms were burnt and livestock taken. Childers made some commentary about this 'doubtful policy', and, with hindsight, the experience can be seen as contributing to his change of heart about British policy that led him to gun-running for the Irish Republicans.

Clashes with the enemy became more frequent, typically characterised by Boer artillery and rifle fire from prepared hilltop positions, answered by counter-battery fire, and infantry assaults that found the main Boer force gone, living to fight another day. Childers described such an artillery duel:

> This is the warmest work we have had yet. Our [ammunition] wagon is with the guns, unhooked, and we and the team are with the limbers in rear. There is no shelter, for the ground is level. Boer guns on a kopje [small hill] have got our range, and at one time seemed much interested in our team, for four shells fell in a circle round us, from thirty to forty yards off. It was very unpleasant to sit waiting for the bull's-eye[54]

Among the Boer artillery that caused the British problems were heavy pieces like the Cresout 'Long Tom', and the one-pound 'Pom-Pom', a quick firing weapon that proved to be a particularly effective anti-personnel gun – 'far off you hear pom-pom-pom-pom-pom, five times, and directly afterwards, like an echo, pom-pom-pom-pom-pom in your neighbourhood, five little shells bursting over an area of about eighty yards'.[55] The effect of the 'little shells' was devastating, with Mackinnon describing the wounds received by a Volunteer infantryman, Private Eatley, who had 'five wounds, one in the head, one in the chest, out of which the doctor has extracted a fragment of pom-pom two inches long, two fingers of his left hand smashed (they will have to be amputated), his right hand crushed, the arm will have to come off'.[56] Private Eatley later died from these wounds. By the end of October 1900, sixty-one Volunteers in the CIV had been killed, or died of illness, sixty-one wounded, 155 invalided out of the service, and forty-eight were sick.[57]

If the campaigning by the men of the HAC was tough, the infantry of the CIV had a longer period of active service in the field, and marched hundreds of miles, fighting numerous actions. In the first fifty-four days of the CIV's infantry campaign, the Volunteers marched 545 miles over forty-one marching days, at an average of thirteen and a third miles a day in harsh conditions, with poor rations, and afflicted by illness and disease.[58] Four months of this campaigning took its toll, with the CIV's commanding officer noting in his diary:

> Bitterly cold night and morning. We leave behind here [in the township of Springs] no less than 126 men, who are unfit to go on, fifty-three of them being slight cases of exhaustion and sore feet, and seventy-three being cases of collapse, utter collapse. The poor fellows are completely done, and many had struggled on longer than they should have done ... Sorry though I am to leave so many behind, there is nothing in it discreditable to the battalion.[59]

The fighting was tough too, and the CIV were involved, for example, in heavy fighting at Doorn Kop in May, which was the first major action that the Volunteers took part in. Other actions included Diamond Hill, against some 4,000 Boer, on 11–12 June, 1900. A few days before that action, the role of the CIV had received recognition in Lord Roberts' army orders:

> The newly-raised battalion of the City of London Imperial Volunteers marched 500 miles in fifty-one days, only once having two consecutive days' halt. It took part in twenty-six engagements with the enemy.
>
> During the recent operations, the sudden variations in temperature between the warm sun in the daytime and the bitter cold at night have been peculiarly trying to the troops, and owing to the necessity for rapid movement, the soldiers have frequently had to bivouac after long and trying marches without firewood and with scanty rations. The cheerful spirit in which difficulties have been overcome and hardships disregarded are deserving of the highest praise, and

Grenadier of a Volunteer regiment, c.1805. This oil painting, by Arthur William Devis, shows a Volunteer in officer quality uniform, yet wearing the equipment of a private, a conundrum that is unexplained. (NAM, 1980-07-25-1)

'A Military Squabble about Dress'. A characteristic Gillray cartoon, lampooning the uniform obsessions of Volunteers, with the martial heroes arguing for the style of Mark Anthony or Adonis.

St George's Volunteers charging down Bond Street. James Gillray capturing the view of many that the Volunteers were merely figures of fun – 'St George's Volunteers charging down Bond Street, after clearing the Ring at Hyde Park, and Storming the Dunghill at Marlybone'. Yet, at Fishguard, it was the various amateur units who moved rapidly to seal the invaders' fate.

'Push on, brave York Volunteers!';
painting, by John David Kelly, of
the mortally wounded General
Isaac Brock urging on his men at
the Battle of Queenston Heights, 13
October 1812. This British victory
saw British regulars, along with the
York and Lincoln militias and
Mohawk warriors, defeat an
invading force of US regulars and
militia, some of which refused to
leave US soil despite seeing the
heavy losses among their
attacking comrades.

The Battle of Châteauguay, 1813.
This battle was one of the great
victories of the amateur soldier in
the War of 1812, effectively stopping
one of the US's most formidable
invasions of British North America
in its tracks.

Lieutenant Colonel Charles de
Salaberry leads his volunteers and
militiamen at Châteauguay. The
volunteers who defeated a US force
ten times their number were ably
led by experienced, professional
officers, under the command of
de Salaberry.

Lieutenant Colonel de Salaberry, victor of Châteauguay.

The Victorian amateur soldier, Staffordshire Rifle Volunteers, c.1860. The highlight of the Rifle Volunteer's year was the annual camp, here at Lapley, South Staffordshire (Alamy).

Officers of the 1st Aberdeenshire Rifles, 1881. Very smartly turned out Scottish Volunteers (Alamy).

Uniforms of the 1st Sutherland Volunteer Rifle Corps, 1860–1908. One of Major General J.M. Grierson's illustrations from his *Records of the Scottish Volunteer Force, 1859-1908* (1909).

Bicycle-mounted Volunteers in South Africa, 1899. The Volunteers were quick to adopt, and pay for, the latest technology, including the 'safety bicycle' which they used to good effect in the South African War.

Officers of the 1st US Volunteer Cavalry, 'Rough Riders', at Long Island before embarkation for the invasion of Cuba, 1898. The officers of the famous elite unit of US Volunteers, the 'Rough Riders'. Their second-in-command, Teddy Roosevelt, is sitting in the second row, second left. (Library of Congress, LOC)

The 1st US Volunteer Cavalry, the Rough Riders, in their first action on Cuba at Las Guasimas. The artist has caught well the difficult country the Rough Riders found themselves fighting in, against seasoned Spanish troops who were well concealed and in prepared positions. (Alamy)

One of Captain Parker's Gatling guns on Cuba. Captain Parker was a consummate professional soldier whose Gatling gun command was key to the US victory. His memoir of the Spanish-American War contained some biting commentary about the relative value of professional and amateur soldiers. (LOC)

71st New York Volunteers in quarantine in the USA after the Cuban campaign. Yellow fever, dysentery and enteric fever ravaged the ranks of Volunteers and Regulars alike, and the medical facilities of the US Army were overwhelmed. Surviving soldiers were quarantined on their return home. (LOC)

The Spanish Falangist leader, José Antonio Primo de Rivera, inspects his blue-shirted militia before the outbreak of the Spanish Civil War. The para-militarisation of politics in the Spanish Second Republic was both a symptom and cause of the collapse of democracy. The leading right-wing militia was, prior to the war, that of the Falangists.

Republican militia besieging the Alcázar. Anarchist and socialist militias dominated the Republic's attempt to defeat the determined defence of the Alcázar in 1936, but the failure of leadership, as well as the heroic nature of the defence, brought defeat.

Heroic portrayal of Falangist militia in July 1936.

Weapons inspection for Castroist MNR militiamen. The MNR was vital for the defence and consolidation of Castro's Communist regime on Cuba. Here, MNR look every bit like the popular image of the militiaman, with outdated personal weapons and little in the way of uniformity about their dress.

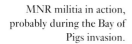

MNR militia in action, probably during the Bay of Pigs invasion.

Castroist troops advance behind T34/85 tanks during the Bay of Pigs fighting. Soviet weaponry was essential to the defence of Castro's regime; here the famous World War Two Soviet tank leads an assault on the invaders. However, it was British and US-made fighter aircraft that struck the most decisive blows.

MNR militia in action.

MNR militiamen with Czech-made Soviet anti-aircraft artillery. The two militiamen, centre-left, are wearing the regulation chambray shirts of the MNR.

in thanking all ranks for their successful efforts to attain the object in view, Lord Roberts is proud to think that the soldiers under his command have worthily upheld the traditions of Her Majesty's army in fighting, marching, and in the admirable discipline which had been maintained throughout a period of no ordinary trial and difficulty.[60]

This high praise from 'Bobs', the popular Commander-in-Chief South Africa, was a fitting tribute to the CIV, and what was to be the swansong of the Volunteer movement.

The end

The Volunteers returned home from South Arica to a reception that was, happily, as enthusiastic as that which had seen them off to war:

The rest seems a dream; a dream of miles of upturned faces, of dancing colours, or roaring voices, of a sudden dim hush in the great Cathedral, of more miles of faces under gaslight, of a voice in a packed hall saying, 'London is proud of her ------,' of disconnected confidences with policemen, work-people, street-arabs, and finally of the entry once more through the old grey gateway of the Armoury House. I expect the feelings of all of us were much the same; some honest pride in having helped to earn such a welcome; a sort of stunned bewilderment at its touching and passionate intensity; a deep wave of affection for our countrymen; and a thought in the background all the time of a dusty khaki figure still plodding the distant veldt – our friend and comrade, Atkins.[61]

It was a fitting end to the enthusiastic service of the Volunteers in South Africa, and, almost, to the history of the Volunteer Movement. The shock of the Boer War, and in particular the reverses suffered at the hands of the Afrikaners, fed into extended reflection by many, both official and amateur, on the need for reform of the British Army and the system of reserve forces that supported it. Seven years after the CIV returned to Britain, the Haldane reforms saw the end of the Volunteer Movement, as its function was absorbed into the new Territorial Force, which had but a few years to wait until it was thrown into the First World War.

Chapter 5

The Spanish-American War, Cuba 1898

The USA, the Americas, and Spain

From the founding of the United States an important element in its foreign policy was to establish and maintain US pre-eminence on the American continent. The defeat of Britain in the American Revolution opened the way to the beginnings of trans-continental US expansion, and in the War of 1812 an attempt to incorporate British North America into the young American republic. Although the US's strategic aims regarding British North America were foiled by its failure in that war, it did not in any way end the desire for US dominance throughout the continent. By the 1840s the concept of the United States' 'manifest destiny' to occupy and dominate as much of the North American land mass as possible was a commonplace. This sense of a God-ordained future later came to encompass South America, a destiny that first required the expulsion of European powers from the region. By the late 1880s, the Indian Wars within the territory of the US were drawing to a close, and US interests were expanding in the Caribbean, where Spain, France and Britain held numerous territories.

US strategic interests in the region were focused on the long-term plan of cutting a sea canal through the Panamanian isthmus. The initial French attempt to do this had come to grief due largely to the appalling death rate of workers, and construction had been abandoned in 1889. But the idea was key for advocates of US naval power. A canal would link both seaboards of the US, allowing naval ships to be quickly transferred between the Atlantic and the Pacific rather than enduring the long and dangerous route via Cape Horn. Among the enthusiasts for a crossing through the isthmus was Theodore 'Teddy' Roosevelt, who was appointed to the post of Assistant Secretary of the Navy in the spring of 1897 by the new President, McKinley. Roosevelt would become nationally famous thanks to his part in the Spanish-American war, leading a volunteer unit subsequently lionised in the US press. Teddy Roosevelt was a supporter of the naval theories of Captain Alfred Thayer Mahan, a lecturer at the US Naval War College and an advocate of naval power. An Anglophile, he took British naval supremacy as a model, arguing that a combination of Britain's geography, commitment to the sea and outward-looking governments had brought trading success and global power, protected by a strong navy, all of which could be emulated by the USA. Mahan made the idea of naval power a fundamental concern, and 'it is no exaggeration to say that Mahan's writings had a worldwide impact that changed the shape of armaments for a generation, and thinking about strategy for much longer than that'.[1] In his *The Naval War of 1812*, Mahan argued that the US needed a great fleet, and that in order 'to support the great fleet he envisioned, Mahan called for bases in the Caribbean and the Far East and for a canal across Central America'.[2] Those, like Roosevelt, who believed that the US's manifest destiny lay beyond its continental boundaries, appreciated that a future US-controlled canal through the Panamanian isthmus would need to be protected from European powers in the Caribbean. Foremost among those powers was Spain, with its strategically important colonies of Cuba and Puerto Rico. Both islands had been Spanish colonies since the fifteenth century, and although Spain's long, slow decline meant that it was no longer anything approaching a first-class power, it nevertheless had a sea-going fleet, and successfully fought insurrection in Cuba between 1868 and 1878, a revolt which reignited in 1895.

The US's strategic interests in Spain's colonies in the Caribbean were enhanced by its commercial interests in the sugar and tobacco plantations of Cuba. The Spanish government's failure to keep its promises to rebellious Cuban patriots following the Ten Years War of 1868–78 had brought a renewal of fighting in which both sides used economic warfare in their efforts to defeat their opponents. The destruction of plantations and mills by both rebels and government troops impacted heavily on US investors, who helped stoke public outrage in the USA. The question of public opinion was central to any possibility of US war against Spain, and, indeed, to the Mahanist dreams of advocates of a bigger US Navy, foremost among these advocates being Roosevelt, who set himself the task at the Navy Department of, 'Building up our Navy to its proper standing'.[3] Yet popular opinion in the US was far from concerned with the idea of foreign intervention, with the 1896 Presidential election being fought on the entirely domestic issue of currency reform, couched in terms of 'Silver versus Gold; the People against the Interests; Agriculture against Industry; the common man against the banker and speculator'.[4] But the war party in the new McKinley government had an ally in Spain's repression in Cuba, which mirrored in ferocity and brutality that of the Cuban insurgents. Spain's tactics were widely reported in the popular US press. Foremost among the masters of the 'yellow press', dealing in scandal, violence, sex and outrage, were the newspapers of William Randolph Hearst, who owned a string of newspapers including the *New York Journal*. Hearst ensured that Spanish atrocities, real and imagined, were given full coverage, especially in the *Journal*, which was in a circulation war with its New York rival, Joseph Pulitzer's *New York World*. The effect was to enflame anti-Spanish feeling among the American reading public, enabling Cuban exiles to raise funds to run guns and men into Cuba.

The pressures on McKinley to 'do something' about Spain in Cuba mounted, but McKinley's strategy was to approach the question through diplomatic means. McKinley was faced by competing pressures at home, with differing business interests pushing in different directions. Just as in the War of 1812, some interests thought war with Spain would end the threat to US investments, while others sought to avoid any disruption of international trade, which war on the US's eastern seaboard could involve. McKinley's position was that what was needed was order and stability on Cuba, either from a Spanish victory over the rebels, or as a result of Spain abandoning the island. In the summer of 1897, it began to look as if a new liberal government in Spain would solve the issue by giving Cuba home rule within the framework of the Spanish Empire. This led to an easing of US-Spanish tensions, and there was little sense in the US War Department that any conflict with Spain was likely in the immediate future.

The optimism that characterised Washington in December 1897 regarding the Cuba issue was ended in the first weeks of the New Year. The Cuban rebels rejected Spain's home rule proposal, and continued to demand full independence. To make matters worse for the Spanish government, Spanish Army officers on the island also rejected the idea, and rioted against the plan in Havana. The US press ramped up the pressure on McKinley's administration, then, as tensions reached new heights, the US battleship, *Maine*, which was in Havana harbour to protect US interests, was sunk in a massive explosion on the night of 25 January, with the loss of 254 men. The loss of the *Maine* is now generally accepted as being a result of 'an accidental ignition of its forward magazines, [but] at the time the US public and government were certain of Spanish treachery, ignoring the obvious fact that it would not have been in Spain's interest to provoke a conflict'.[5] McKinley was now convinced that Spain could not remain in control of Cuba, and demanded Cuban independence under US supervision. On 7 March, Congress voted $50 million for 'National Defense and for each and every purpose connected therewith to be expended at the discretion of the President'.[6] McKinley intended the 'Fifty Million Bill' to be used to address shortcomings in US military readiness, particularly that of the US Army. The reality was that in 1898 the US 'did not have an army in the operational sense of that word'.[7]

The United States – ill-prepared for war

Naval strategy

The United States' military strength in 1898 lay in the US Navy, and the problem of pursuing the war against the Spanish Empire in the Caribbean and the Pacific was envisaged by US planners as being primarily a naval question. It was changes in that planning that led to the US Army entering the war ill-supplied, and with logistical support that was so weak as to lead to heavy losses to disease and poor medical care. Although the US Navy quickly destroyed the Spanish squadron in the Philippines, at the Battle of Manila Bay, enabling a US Army landing and occupation of Manila, the same strategy failed in the Caribbean. Instead, the Spanish were able to thwart a navy-led US victory against Cuba by putting a Spanish squadron to sea within a week of war being declared. That squadron, under Rear Admiral Pascual Cervera left the Cape Verde Islands in the Atlantic and headed west. The Spanish squadron consisted of four armoured cruisers, and three destroyers. The Spanish Navy was not the force it had been as recently as the 1860s, and although the squadron included the new armoured cruiser, *Cristóbal Colón*, it was without its main armament, the navy believing that its secondary armament of fourteen six-inch guns was sufficient. Cervera managed to elude two US Navy squadrons in the Atlantic, and this success introduced a new element into the problem of Cuba for US planners, a problem that was compounded by the political strength of the US National Guard and the Volunteer movement that exploded onto the scene in a US suddenly keen for war.

Initial US planning had been for a navy victory over the Spanish squadron, leading to the surrender of what would then have been unsupported Spanish forces in the Caribbean. The small US Regular Army would have had what was primarily an occupation role on both Cuba and Puerto Rico. But with a Spanish squadron on the loose in the western Atlantic, the US faced the threat of Spanish attacks on the US mainland, which demanded greatly strengthened US coastal defences. That, in turn, needed more manpower than the Army had at its disposal. It also opened up the need to mount a concerted, combined arms assault on Cuba.

The US Army, Regulars and Volunteers

The United States Army in 1898 was little more than a militarised police force. It had an authorised strength of 25,000 officers and men, which amounted to twenty-five infantry, ten cavalry and five artillery regiments, all of which were understrength. Two companies from every infantry and cavalry regiment were paper companies only, and:

> The Army's manned companies and battalions, scattered across the continent in over seventy small posts, functioned mainly in police actions against rebellious Indians or striking laborers. It had no permanent troop formations larger than regiments – seldom were entire regiments assembled at a single post – and neither detailed war plans nor a staff for making them existed.[8]

There were signs of hope in that some senior officers had begun to think about the likely future of an expansionist US, and, under General William T. Sherman (officer commanding, 1869–83) officer schools had been established, along with the increasingly influential Military Service Institution of the United States. However, there were few officers who had experience of commanding large units above battalion level, and although the army had technical experts in the key and emergent sciences such as engineering, military medicine and signals, the necessary staff skills to bring all branches of service together effectively were lacking.

Reforms and re-equipment were taking place in the 1880s, but slowly. For example, attention had begun to be paid to the country's coastal defences following the Endicott report, which highlighted the weaknesses of fortifications and their equipment. However, by 1897 only thirty of the 500 heavy guns called for by the Endicott report, and seventy of the 1,000 mortars, had been mounted in coastal forts. Part of the problem was that US industry was not geared to providing the necessary armaments needed for a modern army. This would have repercussions in the field in 1898 when the new standard artillery piece, the 3.2-inch 'bag gun', proved inferior to Spanish artillery, while the new 30 calibre, five-shot Krag-Jörgensen, using smokeless powder, was not available in large enough numbers because there was not enough industrial capacity to produce sufficient smokeless cartridges.

Just as planning for the US's previous wars, from the Revolution to the Mexican-American War, and indeed, the Civil War, had an expectation that Volunteer forces would underpin action by the regular army, so, too, did that expectation exist in 1898, particularly among the ranks of the Volunteer state militias. All the states and most of the territories possessed Volunteer militias whose function was to support law and order within their respective states, and be ready to defend against invasion. The majority of the state militias were, by 1898, called 'National Guard', but other titles, such as 'Volunteer Guard', were also in use. In theory, there were around 114,000 officers and men in these units, 'including 4,800 cavalry, 5,900 field and fortress artillery, 100,000 infantry, and a few thousand supply and service troops'.[9] As in the previous wars, the position of the militias in 1898 was far from straightforward, and their state of readiness varied widely. Once again, the issue of just how far the Volunteers could be committed outside of their own states, or whether they could be ordered beyond the US by the President, came to the fore. There was also a legal issue regarding the actual status of the force. Most National Guard argued that they were simply the continuation of the militias raised in 1792, but there was a legal case that they were, in fact, a different beast that the states should not possess. Added to these concerns was the pressing military problem presented by very poor equipment, with most being armed with the single-shot, black powder Springfield rifle, little in the way of field-worthy uniforms or other vital material, and, of course, the perennial issue of just how well trained the men were. The reality was that many National Guard units were armed social organisations, a sort of aggressive camping club. None of these issues, however, dampened the enthusiasm of those National Guard Volunteers who saw in the war with Spain a chance for glory, and in the eyes of many officers an opportunity to boost political careers at state and federal level.

War Department planning focused not only on the need for an expeditionary force to support the navy, but also the necessity of bolstering coastal defence. Improving coastal defences had been speeded up early in 1898, with a rapid increase in the number of cannon and mortars mounted, and the stockpiling of ammunition. Defences were further enhanced in mid-April by the mining of all major harbours. Despite these efforts by the US Ordnance Department and the Army's engineers, the recommendations of the earlier Endicott report were still far from being completed, and it was necessary to detach a strong naval squadron to help defend the eastern seaboard. Manning the coastal defences was not seen to present a problem, as this would be largely in the hands of the Volunteers of the National Guard. As the Army and Navy Journal of 12 March 1898 noted, 'With a regular Army of sufficient strength to form the fighting line, and with the organized militia for local service, we should have a force sufficient for our needs against Spain'.[10] That 'sufficient strength' was, in the weeks and months prior to the outbreak of war, deemed to be around 104,000 officers and men, which figure could be attained by expanding the regular army with fresh recruits who would be absorbed into existing infantry regiments enlarged with more companies and the addition of a third battalion. This plan was submitted to the House of Representatives as the 'Hull bill' on 17 March. Under that plan there was no role for the National Guard in offensive operations, its role would be to defend the coasts, and provide support for the Regulars. Needless to say, such a view of the distribution of military tasks sat well with the regular officers, who had little regard for the abilities of the state militias. The sponsors of the Hull bill, and those who drafted the plan in the War Department, had, however, failed to take account of the political power of the National Guard, and the yellow press-enhanced enthusiasm of large sections of the public for war with Spain. That combination of popular forces, plus the enforced change in War Department strategy caused by Spanish naval activity in the western Atlantic, meant that the Spanish-American War would, after all, offer scope for the Volunteer spirit that had animated all US military history hitherto.

The Spanish position

Spain's military position on Cuba and Puerto Rico was a combination of strengths and weaknesses. Foremost among the weaknesses was the fact that the two possessions were isolated from Spain by the Atlantic, and the more powerful US Navy. However, the initial success of Cervera' s squadron in evading the US Navy stretched the Americans' naval assets, demanding ships to cover the US coast, others to escort troopships, as well as carrying out the hunt for the Spanish at sea. On Cuba, the Spanish Army was, on paper, strong, with 150,000 Spanish Regulars in addition to 80,000 Cuban loyalist Volunteers (known, confusingly, as 'Guerrillas'). However, of this large force only around 55,000 men were capable of effective field operations. Disease, particularly yellow fever, was rampant, and was a deadly limitation on any operations on the island. Between 1895 and 1898 over 13,000 Spanish soldiers had died of yellow fever in Cuba, and that death rate also loomed large in the minds of US planners. The role of mosquitos in driving infection was not appreciated, and the general standard of Spanish, and indeed US, military medical care was poor. The combination of the two meant that, for example, around 6,000 of the 18,000 men in the Spanish

garrison of Manzanillo were hospitalised at any one time. Added to the problems of disease and poor medical facilities, Spanish soldiers also laboured under
an inadequate training regime. A British observer at the time noted:

> It makes one sad to see the quality of the expeditions packed off in
> heartless shoals to Cuba, boys, to look at, at fifteen and sixteen, who
> have never held a rifle till this moment, and now are almost ignorant
> which end it fires, good lads – too good to go to such uneven butch-
> ery – with cheerful, patriotic, willing faces, but the very antithesis of
> a soldier.[11]

These 'good lads' faced some 25–45,000 rebels, the numbers in the field
varying according to events. Although the rebels would receive little in the way
of praise from the Americans when they arrived, they had managed to maintain
an insurrection for a decade, and been able to return to the field in 1895. They
were well equipped with modern rifles, thanks to arms smuggling from the US,
and typically they carried heavy machetes used on the sugar plantations. The
rebels were strongest in the eastern part of the island, and engaged in a brutal
guerrilla war which was met, as is the custom in such wars, with equal brutality
by the Spanish authorities.

The Spanish response to the insurrection foreshadowed in some respects the
later British strategy in the Second Boer War. The Spanish built blockhouses
and barbed wire barriers across the island, aiming to restrict the ability of the
rebels to move freely. This tied down large numbers of Spanish in small packets
of men garrisoning the blockhouses and patrolling the wire. The strategy was
not as successful in the close country of Cuba as the British found it to be in the
latter part of the South African War, but there the British had sufficient mobile
forces to scour the country while restricting enemy movement. The Spanish
also adopted a policy of clearing the rural populations of some of the Cuban
provinces, concentrating the displaced Cubans in camps. The thinking was that
the rebels would lose any support they had, or could coerce, while food supplies
could be destroyed. But, as in British South Africa, the Cuban camps were
mismanaged, and quickly became death traps, with thousands dying through
lack of shelter, food and medical care. The 'reconcentration' policy did little
to undermine the insurrection, but plenty to undermine Spanish authority.
The situation in Cuba had reached an impasse, with neither the government
nor the rebels capable of winning the war.

'Remember the *Maine*!' The Volunteers flock to the Stars and Stripes

The news that the USS *Maine* had been sunk in Havana harbour sparked an outpouring of patriotic outrage in the USA, which manifested itself in heightened support for the Cuban rebels and saw hundreds of thousands of men volunteering for the expected war against Spain. Men flocked to National Guard regiments, offered the President entirely new regiments of Volunteers, and set up their own recruiting offices. It was an extraordinary manifestation of the American ideal of the citizen in arms, the Volunteer coming away from his place of work and home to fight for the United States. It was also an expression of the belief that soldiering was something that could be done just as well by the civilian turned Volunteer as by the professional soldier. Some contemporaries realised that what they were witnessing represented the latest iteration of a long tradition. Charles Johnson Post, whose account of his service on Cuba with the 71 New York (Volunteer) Infantry, *The Little War of Private Post* was published in 1960, left this lively account of Volunteer recruiting:

> Enlisting then was not like enlisting today. When you enlisted then, you first shopped for a regiment. Anyone with money or credit to rent a vacant store could recruit for his regiment, and he would be colonel. There was vast enthusiasm. In fact, one had only to go into any of the three or four saloons at each street intersection and start a conversation with almost any casual stranger and, first thing you knew, the bartender would invite you to have one on the house and recommend a regiment for you to join or to transfer to. Mr. William Randolph Hearst had just bought the New York *Journal* and was mixing war, patriotism, and romance with Eva Cisneros – a Spanish captive in Havana, reported by Hearst to be of superlative and languishing beauty. This reporting was fragrant with circulation results, while we commoner folk began to boil and seethe with ardor to kill a Spaniard. So it was that vacant stores on every avenue suddenly blossomed into recruiting stations, with pictures of the *Maine* before and after the sinking, and with pullers-in at their doors straight from the Social Register or the nearest ward leader. Each store was intent upon recruiting a regiment. Officers were needed. And before each store was a line of expectant officers. This was a system that dated

back to the Civil War – probably back to the barons of the Magna Charta. You wanted to be an officer – and who did not? You brought in enough fellows to make a platoon, and you became a lieutenant. Enough for a company, and you became a captain. And who made you an officer? Why, the man who paid the rent for the store and who was going to be the colonel of the regiment.[12]

Here were three of the popular ingredients of the war: the power of the press, the unchained patriotism of the American in arms and the challenge to the idea of a professionals-only army of the Republic, and politics. It was that combination of politics and popular enthusiasm for a Volunteer army that added to the War Department's problems, and faced the US Army with the possibility of being overwhelmed by the demands of the Volunteer. When the Hull bill reached Congress, it faced strong opposition from the supporters of the National Guard and Volunteers. These Congressmen, especially from the interior states of the Union recognised that under the Hull bill, their state militias and Volunteers would have no role in the forthcoming war, as the Army would be able to directly recruit up to the necessary strength. There was no way that the various pro-National Guard interests were going to permit the sidelining of the Volunteer soldier, and the strengthening of the regular army, and, 'together with Southern Democrats who still resented military reconstruction, Populists who feared an enlarged Regular Army as an instrument of internal repression, and a few dissident Army officers with technical objections to the Hull bill, the National Guardsmen formed a powerful alliance against the War Department and the Regulars',[13] and defeated the Hull bill on 7 April, just over two weeks before the declaration of war.

The way was now open for the Volunteers to be incorporated into military planning, and a revised bill went before Congress. The War Department still aimed for an expeditionary force of 100,000, but the new plan, drawn up by General Miles, was for that force to consist of all the regulars in an expanded Army of 60,000, plus 40–50,000 Volunteers. On 13 April, the plan was finalised, with 60,000 Regulars, 40,000 Volunteers for field service, and another 20,000 Volunteers for the coastal defence of the US. The Volunteers were to come almost exclusively from the state militias, the National Guard and Volunteer regiments. It was a political victory for the Volunteer movement, and those wary of a greatly expanded Regular Army.

The Volunteers

In keeping with the foundation myths of the USA, and subsequent conflict against British North America, Mexico and the Confederate States, contemporaries saw the Volunteers as representing the people in arms, the best of American manhood, expressing the patriotism that had created the republic. Much of Roosevelt's memoir of the war was devoted to identifying the men that he saw as typifying the perfection of American manhood. Lauding the virtues of the frontiersmen that provided many of the 1,000 Volunteers of the Rough Riders, Roosevelt also praised the ideal of the American scholar-warrior-sportsman:

> One of the most useful members of the regiment was Dr Robb Church, formerly a Princeton football player. He was appointed as Assistant Surgeon, but acted throughout almost all the Cuban campaign as the Regimental Surgeon. It was Dr. Church who first gave me an idea of Bucky O'Neill's versatility, for I happened to overhear them discussing Aryan word-roots together, and then sliding off into a review of the novels of Balzac, and a discussion as to how far Balzac could be said to be the founder of the modern realistic school of fiction. Church had led almost as varied a life as Bucky himself, his career including incidents as far apart as exploring and elk-hunting in the Olympic Mountains, cooking in a lumber-camp, and serving as doctor on an emigrant ship.[14]

O'Neill was promoted to the rank of captain, and refusing to take cover under heavy Spanish fire at San Juan, was shot through the head, 'so that even before he fell his wild and gallant soul had gone out into the darkness'.[15]

Across America, Volunteers entrained for the training camps at Tampa, Mobile and New Orleans, on the Gulf of Mexico. Their fellow citizens turned out en masse to send them off:

> In April, everywhere over this good, fair land, flags were flying … Trains carrying soldiers were hurrying to the Southland; and little children on fences greeted the soldiers with flapping scarfs and handkerchiefs and flags; at the stations, crowds gathered to hurrah for the soldiers, and to throw hats into the air, and to unfurl flags … the fluttering of the flags drowns the voice of the tears that may be in the air.[16]

It was the Volunteers, in particular, that were seen to represent the nation in arms. Interestingly, the rush to war on the part of these men was used by both the US government and American commentators as evidence of the unity of the nation. Racial divisions, and the still–potent post-Civil War divisions were, it was claimed, being overcome by a shared American enterprise to bring freedom to Cuba. Teddy Roosevelt made much of this in his rapidly published memoir of the war and the role that he and his Volunteers in the First US Volunteer Cavalry played in the US victory. His Volunteers came mostly from the 'Four Territories' – New Mexico, Arizona, Oklahoma, and Indian Territory – and included native Americans. Roosevelt made much of the wide range of American 'types', from Ivy League sportsmen to cowboys and 'lawless spirits' that joined his 'Rough Riders', and among these there were, 'a number of Indians – Cherokees, Chickasaws, Choctaws, and Creeks. Only a few were of pure blood. The others shaded off until they were absolutely indistinguishable from their white comrades; with whom, it may be mentioned, they all lived on terms of complete equality'.[17] Some 3,000 Black Americans were also part of the expeditionary force, but in the Regular Army in segregated 'colored' regiments: 9 and 10 Cavalry, and the 24 and 25 Infantry. Roosevelt's Rough Riders, as a cavalry regiment (albeit without their mounts on Cuba) were brigaded with the Black Regulars, and both took part in the famous assault on San Juan Hill. Paying tribute to them, he said, 'Between you [the Black Regulars] and the other cavalry regiments there is a tie which we trust will never be broken'.[18]

The Volunteer enthusiasm for the war was also used by many as a way of attempting to bury the lingering but strong resentment that existed in the South against the US government and army. The federal government in Washington was keenly aware of the potential for a violent reaction that shipping tens of thousands of soldiers in blue through Southern states to Florida might have. Volunteer Post recorded how the 71st New York Volunteers, entrained for Florida, were routed away from the old Confederate capital of Richmond:

> It seemed that there were two ways to get to Florida by rail. One of them would take us through Richmond, Virginia; the other would go around it.
>
> Which route? We were a Northern regiment. We were 'Boys in Blue'! It was only 1898 remember, and the question was profound. Would we be fired upon or would we not?[19]

The troop train went through Virginia, but avoided Richmond. Post then went on to describe, at length, the warm welcome he and his fellow New York Volunteers received in the South, and noted that, in fact, Richmond had been preparing a great welcome for these US Volunteers, which, he said, included, 'a delegation from the Confederate Veterans!'[20] It was the consideration of the need for support in the states of the old Confederacy that also fed into the decision to appoint the former Confederate cavalry officer, 'Fighting Joe' Wheeler, to his old rank of Brigadier General, under Major General William Shafter, a Union veteran of the Civil War. It was not just the high-profile figure of Wheeler who was now uniformed in blue, as President McKinley was highly sensitive to the need to gain the support of Southern Democrats:

> McKinley was careful to give Democrats, and especially Southern Democrats, a large proportion of the ranking military appointments. He did this for two reasons: First, he wanted to increase Southern support for his Administration and its politics; second, as the first war President since Appomattox, he wanted to demonstrate that sectional animosity was a thing of the past, that Blue and Gray now stood united against the national enemy.[21]

For politicians and patriots alike, it was to be a war of national unity in which the Volunteers, drawn from across American society, would represent the best of America manhood.

Training and equipping the Volunteers

Between the sinking of the *Maine* and the first landings of US troops on Cuba, there was only four months during which men who rushed to volunteer were sifted, sorted and incorporated into those Volunteer and National Guard regiments that would be deployed, either at home or overseas. The larger part of those Volunteers had little, or no, previous military experience, and, even existing members of National Guard regiments had indifferent and irregular training. The War Department and the Army had to concentrate the Volunteers in the training areas in Florida, and equip and train them for the forthcoming war. In the event, only three Volunteer regiments were incorporated into Fifth Corps, which was tasked with the invasion of Cuba; these were the 71 New York, the 2 Massachusetts, and the First US Volunteer Cavalry (the Rough Riders). The 71 New York, which was an established New York National Guard regiment that was mustered into United States' service on 23 April, 'with a core of veteran guardsmen … expanded to its war strength of about one thousand officers and men by enlisting civilian recruits,'[22] including Private Post. His account of the problems in supplying and training the Volunteers provides the detail of the situation that a contemporary of Post's, and later Brigadier-General described:

> One by one, regiments began to arrive in one concentration camp or another, pulled themselves together, spent a day or two making things shipshape, then settled down to training as training was understood in those days. Organization of a kind was gradually effected but under many handicaps. With few general officers or staff officers, everything had to be extemporized. Unprepared in every sense for war, we went about our job with a cheerfulness, activity and zeal born of our own vast ignorance. Most of our efforts would have caused a modern commander to go gray and would have bred hysterics in our present highly-schooled staff.[23]

Very little was in place for the Volunteers, and largely consisted of missing or obsolete equipment. The US Army was in the process of introducing a new khaki cotton uniform, based on British imperial experience, but among the Volunteers only the Rough Riders were issued with it. For the rest, the old blue uniform, in wool, was issued, a uniform totally unsuited to the tropical conditions of either the Caribbean or the Pacific. Similarly, the Volunteers were issued with the single shot Springfield rifle, using a black powder cartridge that both obscured vision for the firer, while clearly marking his position for the enemy. In addition, packs, tents and other field equipment was missing, rations were poor, while training was limited.

Private Post was issued with an outsized blue uniform, including 'cerulean-blue pants with a broad, deep blue stripe down the sides,'[24] and was fortunate enough to find a tent, and be issued with a blanket and rubber poncho. His training began and largely consisted of learning the various bugle calls that were the commands 'that had not varied from the time of the Civil War',[25] and were for close order movement and fighting. Not only was this questionable in the era of magazine-fed rifles and machine guns, but, in the close country of Cuba, would prove less than useful:

> The sergeants and corporals were as sergeants and corporals always are. They knew their book. Those were the days of close order, and we drilled in it much as in the days of Waterloo or Gettysburg, when troops formed for battle at long-range cannon shot, and in full view of the other, unless one side was entrenched. The only substantial innovation was the 'advance by rushes' when each squad alternatively advanced while the other covered them with volleys.[26]

Not only was this in the tradition of the famous error of training to fight the last war, but it also took little cognisance of the fact that the latter stages of the American Civil War had seen the emergence of trench warfare and the 'empty battlefield'. But this was the case of the US Army, and particularly the Volunteers, doing their extemporised best in a very short period. For Graham Cosmas, the leading historian of the war, it was an achievement that the War Department organised, officered, and equipped within three months a force of 275,000 men while at the same time, 'it launched and pressed to victory overseas campaigns on opposite sides of the world'.[27]

Volunteers to war in Cuba
Shipping out
War was officially declared by Spain on the US on 23 April, and was reciprocated by the US on 25 April. On 1 May, the Spanish Asiatic Fleet was completely destroyed in Manila Bay by the US Pacific Fleet under Commodore Dewey in a one-sided battle that left the US with few casualties and little damage to its fleet. Attention now turned to the Atlantic and the Caribbean. The threat of Cervera's squadron constrained US action, for until the Spanish could be challenged and defeated in the Western Atlantic only the US Navy had an active role. But on 19 May, Cervera anchored at Santiago, Cuba, having evaded the US Navy, which, under Commodore Winfield Schley, arrived there nine days later to blockade the Spanish Navy. Schley's squadron was joined on 1 June by Rear Admiral Sampson's larger force, which bottled up the Spanish using almost every American warship except those sent to the Philippines. The Spanish Navy

was trapped, but at the same time the difficult approach to Santiago harbour, and the protection of the harbour defences, meant that it was unlikely that the US Navy could repeat the success of Manila Harbour in Cuba. Now the way was open for the US expeditionary force to ship to Cuba.

Transporting the expeditionary force to Cuba was another headache for US planners. There was no standing fleet transport available. Instead, the Army's Quartermaster General's office had to scour the US mercantile marine to find steamers capable of being converted to troopships. In 1898, the American merchant navy was limited, but under international law it was not possible for the US to hire foreign-flagged ships, and attempts to transfer such ships to the US flag foundered when the East Coast shipping interests, fearful of post-war competition, blocked the move in Congress. The result was that the expeditionary force had to depend on the 'small, slow vessels that plied the Gulf and the Caribbean in peacetime, most of which were little suited to carrying men and animals in large numbers'.[28] The practical effects on the men, mules and horses were over-crowding, sickness, and extraordinary difficulties in landing in Cuba. Second Lieutenant (later Captain) John H. Parker, whose Gatling gun detachment was to make a powerful contribution to the US victory on Cuba, recorded, in a letter home:

> We have now been on board the transport a week, and are getting into a frame of mind suitable for desperate work. If you can imagine 1,000 men crowded into space needed for 500, and then kept there without room to stand or move or sit for seven days, under a tropical sun, in foul holds utterly without ventilation (just imagine it!), endured without a single murmur or complaint, not stoically, but patiently and intelligently, while every officer on board is kicking as hard and as often as possible for the relief of his men, then you will have some idea of the situation. The men are very patient, but they know someone has blundered. Talk about the heroism of the Light Brigade! It is nothing to the heroism that goes cheerfully and uncomplainingly into the Black Hole of Calcutta (there is nothing else that will compare with these transports), all because it is duty. When will the people appreciate the heroism of the Regular Army?[29]

Parker's appeal concerning the heroism of the Regular Army was also a deliberate dig at popular enthusiasm for the Volunteers, about whom Parker, the Regular, was at times scathing. But the Volunteers, too, endured the same conditions aboard the inadequate and slow transports, until the main expeditionary force landed at Daiquiri on 22 June.

Landing on Cuba

The initial US Navy plan was for a combined arms assault on Santiago, with US troops mounting an amphibious assault against the town and harbour, while the US fleet broke into the harbour to sink the Spanish ships at anchor. Admiral Sampson put this plan to General Shafter shortly after he had landed on Cuban soil, some eighteen miles west of Santiago, where the US leaders met, for the first time, the Cuban rebel commander, General Calixto García. Fortunately for the US Army, Shafter had a much better appreciation of how incapable his men were of carrying out an opposed landing. Further, Shafter had, on the way to Cuba, been reading about a disastrous British frontal assault, of the type Sampson was in favour of, in April 1748. The strength of Santiago, facing seaward, was not diminished, and Shafter was supported by the Cuban rebel leadership when he proposed a landing at Daiquiri, fifteen miles east of Santiago, with the intention of fighting his way to the heights overlooking the harbour, thereby forcing the Spanish squadron out into the Caribbean and the waiting guns of Sampson's ships.

US troops came ashore at Daiquiri and at nearby Siboney, following an ineffectual naval bombardment, ineffectual because the few Spanish positions were hidden from the sea. Fortunately for the US troops, there was little opposition, and the Spanish withdrew. The biggest obstacle was the fact that the US ships were not equipped to facilitate an amphibious landing, and, as the masters of the extempore troopships were mercantile marine officers and therefore not under military discipline, they refused to take their ships close into shore. The result was a confused and lengthy disembarking that saw some men, and many horses and mules, drown. Private Post described the problems:

> The horses and mules were jumped overboard and swam ashore. And not a colonel or a wagon master had the power to tell a ship captain how close in to shore he should come. The transports were under charter merely, and it was the ship captain who could tell the colonel what he, the skipper, would or would not do with his ship. The horses and mules were jumped overboard from a half to a quarter mile off shore – depending upon the skipper's digestion or his judgement – and then swam. Horses by the hundred were drowned.[30]

These were not cavalry horses, as the cavalry regiments were to fight on foot. Instead, the losses were sustained by the artillery and supply elements of the expeditionary force, both of which had an impact in the weeks to come; for

example, 'when Captain Best's battery was on San Juan and had to be withdrawn, they did not dare risk horses ... two infantry companies were sent to
screen the withdrawal [and] over twenty infantrymen were casualties in three
minutes'.[31] The loss of wagon horses and mules was even more problematic, for
as the army fought its way inland towards Santiago, its supply line grew weaker.
Little in the way of regular or sufficient rations could be brought up, tents were
left at the beachheads, and the wounded and sick could not easily be brought
down to the shore and the ships. Landing the men also presented problems, as
they went ashore by ships' boats, and, heavily laden, some men fell between the
boats and the small landing stage, becoming the first casualties.

Las Guásimas

As soon as the first Americans landed, they began to advance through the close,
dense country, with the Volunteers of the Rough Riders to the fore, chasing
retreating Spanish units. On 24 June, the Rough Riders clashed with a Spanish
rear guard at Las Guásimas, some three miles from the coast. It was here that the
characteristics of the Volunteers became apparent, being a mixture of military
ignorance and Volunteer enthusiasm. The Rough Riders failed to carry out any
reconnaissance, or put out a point, but instead moved as fast as they could, in the
heat and thick undergrowth, in the direction of the Spanish. Post, who was helping
to move ammunition boxes when the Rough Riders set out, heard a Regular officer
say, 'Goddam it – they haven't even got a point out!',[32] with Post commenting that
the Volunteer cavalry moved out 'in column of fours, solid, and only lacking a
band at its head to give it a thoroughly festive and inconsequential air'.[33]

The skirmish at Las Guásimas was a short, confused, but hotly contested
affair. The Rough Riders and other Regular cavalry discovered that attacking an
entrenched enemy, and two small blockhouses in close, hilly country was a far
from easy task. According to Roosevelt, General Young, riding a mule, examined
the Spanish positions prior to the attack. A Hotchkiss one-pounder light field
gun was brought up, and opened the American attack. That fire almost immediately drew counter-battery fire from a few light guns and well-hidden Spanish
skirmishers and snipers. For the first time, the Americans realised how difficult
it was to locate the enemy in 'the denseness of the jungle and [with] the fact that
they used absolutely smokeless powder, [which] made it exceedingly difficult to
place exactly where they were'.[34] The US Cavalry then advanced up the narrow
road, and on both sides of it, in the thick jungle. The going was difficult, and
the heat intense, so when the Rough Riders went into action, they first 'had to

climb a very steep hill. Many of the men, foot-sore and weary from their march of the preceding day, found the pace up this hill too hard, and either dropped their bundles or fell out of line, with the result that we went into action with less than five hundred men.'[35] The dense jungle made it difficult to maintain contact with other units, and with men in the same unit. Control over the advancing Volunteers was difficult, but the men kept advancing, while the Spanish fired both volleys and sniper fire. In the confused fighting the Americans kept on, clearing first the right of their line before breaking through to the ranch buildings on the summit of Las Guásimas. The engagement had cost sixteen Americans killed and fifty-two wounded, while total Spanish losses were around 250 men.[36] In the heat, and with the presence of vultures, the dead had to be buried quickly:

> Next morning we buried seven dead Rough Riders in a grave on the summit of the trail, Chaplain Brown reading the solemn burial service of the Episcopalians, while the men stood around with bared heads and joined in singing, 'Rock of Ages'. Vast numbers of vultures were wheeling round and round in great circles through the blue sky overhead. There could be no more honorable burial than that of these men in a common grave – Indian and cowboy, miner, packer, and college athlete – the man of unknown ancestry from the lonely Western plains, and the man who carried on his watch the crests of the Stuyvesants and the Fishes, one in the way they had met death, just as during life they had been one in their daring and loyalty.[37]

The fight at Las Guásimas had not only blooded the Volunteers, but had also earned them recognition from the Regular Army for their steadiness under fire. Notwithstanding both Roosevelt's, and the press reporters' skill at lauding the Rough Riders, those Volunteers had a strong sense of being an elite among all the Volunteer units. Even Parker, whose account of the campaign carried a number of critical asides concerning the Volunteers, acknowledged that the Rough Riders were, 'the most unique aggregation of fighting men ever gathered together in any army … every man determined to get into the fight'.[38] The US victory at Las Guásimas had opened the way to the outer ring of Spanish defensives around Santiago.

El Caney

General Shafter was acutely aware that time was not on his side, as the yellow fever season was approaching, and it was essential that the campaign be success-fully concluded before then. If not, then it was likely that disease would become a formidable enough ally of the Spanish to compel a US withdrawal. Shafter spent the week after the Las Guásimas success concentrating his troops there, and refining his battle plans. At first it looked as if the Spanish had withdrawn onto Santiago, and 'Fighting Joe' Wheeler reported that:

> We can see Santiago very plainly from this point [Las Guásimas], about seven or eight miles distant. The country appears level for six miles this side of the city except on the heights on the south which extend to within three miles of Santiago, and from which the city can be shelled. The hills now appear deserted. The country is fairly open, a good tract for campaigning over.[39]

In fact, the hills were far from deserted, and the Spanish were busy extending their trenches and barbed wire, and fortifying the village of El Caney, about four miles north-west of Las Guásimas. This formed part of the extended outer defences of Santiago, with a line of blockhouses, including a stone fort at El Caney. In all, there were some 4,000 yards of trenches and rifle pits, with defence in depth, protected by barbed wire and breastworks. The Spaniards had been constructing this line since the end of April, and in the week after the Las Guásimas clash were able to add the final elements. Between the Americans and Santiago there were three strongpoints, one being El Caney, and the other two being the fortified hills of Kettle Hill, backed by San Juan Hill. General Linares had 13,000 men to defend Santiago, a mixture of Spanish Regulars and Cuban Volunteers. Reinforcements, in the shape of 3,600 men from the Manzanillo garrison, forty-five miles from Santiago, were on the way, but there was a limit to how many men Linares could pull into the defence of Santiago as food supplies in the city were low.

General Shafter was told by the Cubans who were harassing the reinforcements on the march to Santiago that there were 8,000 Spanish troops in the Manzanillo column, accompanied by a large herd of cattle and other supplies. This news forced Shafter to bring forward his plan to attack the outer defences of the city. Shafter's plan was to mount a staged attack, with Brigadier-General Henry Lawton's 2 Infantry Division, which included the Massachusetts Volunteers, opening the offensive by attacking and quickly clearing El Caney, something that was expected to take two hours. The capture of El Caney would remove any outflanking threat to the main thrust which was to be made as a frontal assault against Kettle Hill, then San Juan Hill, to be made by Wheeler's dismounted cavalry, including the Rough Riders, along with Brigadier General Jacob Kent's 1 Infantry Division, which included the 71 New York Volunteers. Lawton's force was expected to take part too, moving rapidly from their expected victory in El Caney to attack the San Juan heights from the north. Support for these attacks was to be supplied by the artillery's 3.2 inch field guns, and, for Wheeler and Kent's men, the Gatling gun battery under Parker. The expectation in the US headquarters was that it was to be a straightforward offensive, 'when Shafter made his plan, and until the advance on July 1, the information reaching the Fifth Corps commander indicated that San Juan Hill was weakly held if at all and that the El Caney garrison was unlikely to put up determined resistance'.[40]

El Caney was held by 520 Spaniards under the command of one of the notable heroes of the war, General Joaquín Vara del Rey, who were to face some 6,653 Americans. The experienced Spaniards were well dug in, and had fortified the small stone church, which formed a key defensive position, along with a stone fort, El Viso, and three blockhouses, all protected by wire, and supported by some guns. The US attack was started at 6.35am on 1 July, when Captain Allyn Capron's four-gun battery of 3.2-inch guns began firing on El Viso on the edge of El Caney. Although the guns were the latest in the US Army's inventory, they were already obsolete by world standards. Not only were they using black powder, which produced plumes of white smoke which clearly identified their position, but they also had no recoil mechanism so had to be constantly re-laid on their targets. A US artillery officer later wrote, 'such was our backwardness in military science that the whole Army was ignorant of the tremendous advance in Field Artillery that in 1898 was an accomplished fact'[41] The Spanish response was to reply with heavy fire, both at the US guns, and at skirmishing Cuban rebels who had moved close to the town in support of the US attack. Far from the assault on El Caney being a two-hour affair, it quickly became clear that heavy fighting was ahead. The British military attaché with US forces, Captain Lee, believed that weakness of the US artillery, with just one battery in action, was the root cause of the difficulties faced by the attacking force:

> [It] was a heavy price to pay for the possession of an outlying post, defended by an inferior force ... but it only bore out the well-known military axiom that the attack on a fortified village cannot succeed,

without great loss of life, unless the assailants are strong in artillery … That the attack succeeded was entirely due to the magnificent courage and endurance of the infantry officers and men.[42]

The Massachusetts Volunteers suffered particularly badly, as their black powder Springfields gave their positions away, with one Volunteer shouting out to Black soldiers of the 25 Infantry Regiment, 'the buggers are hidden behind rocks, in weeds and in underbrush, and we just simply can't locate them; they are shooting our men all to pieces'.[43] The Volunteers' casualties were so heavy that, around midday, they had to be withdrawn. By that time, it was quite clear that the men of Lawton's division were not going to be taking part in any attack on the San Juan Hill to the south, even though as late as 1pm Shafter was urging Lawton to leave a screening force in place, and move the bulk of his force to support the main assault to the south. In fact, it took until late afternoon before the Spanish, short on ammunition, and having suffered heavy casualties, surrendered. General Vara del Rey and his two sons died in defence of the town, along with 235 of his men, while the Americans took 120 prisoners, with some eighty managing to slip through the American and Cuban rebel lines back to Santiago. El Caney was captured, but what had been intended as a clearing operation had cost the Americans 441 men, including eighty-one killed.

Kettle Hill and the heights of San Juan

The advance towards the Kettle and San Juan Hills began around 8am. The attacking divisions had first to move through the thick jungle approach to the foot of the hills. That approach was made down the only trail available, and it was while this movement was underway that the first problems arose. The dismounted cavalry, including the Rough Riders, led the way and by 11am were in position at the foot of the heights. At the same time, other Regiments were still moving up, including the 71 New York Volunteers. What happened next revealed both the inexperience of the Regular Army Signal Corps, and the lack of training of the Volunteers. The Spanish knew that there were only three trails available to the Americans moving up to their attack positions, and they rained fire down into the jungle, but much of this indirect fire was indiscriminate as the defenders were unsure as to which of the three trails the attack was coming down. However, the chief US engineer, Colonel Derby, sent forward the US Signals detachment's balloon to try and gain a better idea of Spanish positions.

The balloon detachment's officer in charge objected, but was over-ruled, and the balloon went forward, and was deployed, tethered, above the trail that the Regulars and Volunteers were moving up. The balloon became a huge target marker, showing the Spanish exactly where to drop their fire. The 71 New York Volunteers were on the trail that cut across a creek that would become known as 'Bloody Ford':

> Through the tunnel of our jungle trail we could see the water of the creek. Beyond, we could hear the louder reports of our own men who had already crossed the ford and were sheltered by a little bank back from the farther shore. But these were only glimpses; where we were was a crowded mob of men pressing steadily forward. My foot slipped, and I looked down. The trail underfoot was slippery with mud. It was a mud made by the blood of the dead and wounded, for there had been no showers that day. The trail on either side was lined with the feet of fallen men and the sprawled arms of those who could not quite make it.
>
> This was Bloody Ford.
>
> Because Lieutenant Colonel Derby's balloon had told the Spaniards we were in that cowpath, they turned all they had upon it and its approach. Over four hundred men were killed or wounded in that trail and at that ford, in an area that was, perhaps, a city block in length – some eight hundred feet – in a path not as wide as a city sidewalk.[44]

In the face of this fire, the Volunteers of the 71 New York lost all cohesion and went to ground, with eighty of their men casualties. This partially blocked the advance to following units, which included Captain Parker and his battery of four Gatling guns, who were under orders to accompany the 71 into action. But Parker could not get a clear indication from either the 71's colonel, or its adjutant, about whether their men were going to re-form and continue. So, 'still the Gatling Gun Detachment lay beside the road with the 71, waiting, swearing, broiling, stewing in their own perspiration, mad with thirst and crazed with the fever of battle'.[45] The 71 were blocking the advance, and 'General Kent and his staff, unable to restore order, herded the New Yorkers off the trail into the brush to allow Regular regiments to go past'.[46] The Volunteers would recover, but meantime Parker's Gatlings moved on with the other Regulars.

By about 1pm, the Americans had created a somewhat haphazard firing line facing Kettle Hill and the longer ridge of the San Juan Heights. The Spanish artillery, two small pieces, had run out of shrapnel, and their positions were now under fire from the US Infantry, and, most effectively from Parker's Gatlings, which opened a heavy fire against the San Juan blockhouse:

> Corp. Steigerwald turned and asked, 'What is the range, sir?'
>
> To which was instantly replied, 'Block-house, 600 yards; the ridge to the right, 800 yards,' and Steigerwald's piece was grinding 500 shots a minute within a quarter of a second, playing upon the San Juan block-house.[47]

The Spanish replied, killing two of the Gatling gunners and wounding three, but they kept up a continuous and heavy fire. At the same time, the American line surged forward, cheering, under the cover of the Gatlings. Spaniards began to climb out of their trenches in retreat, but the Gatlings caught many of them, and they 'were seen to melt away like a lump of salt in a glass of water'.[48] The Rough Riders, 9 and 10 Cavalry and some men of other regiments attacked Kettle Hill:

> The three regiments went forward more or less intermingled, advancing steadily and keeping up a heavy fire. Up Kettle Hill Sergeant George Berry, of the Tenth, bore not only his own regimental colors but those of the Third, the color-sergeant of the Third having been shot down; he kept shouting, 'Dress on the colors, boys, dress on the colors!' as he followed Captain Ayres, who was running in advance of his men, shouting and waving his hat.[49]

Clearing the summit of Kettle Hill, the Americans were exposed to heavy rifle and artillery fire from San Juan Heights, but Roosevelt and his men were then able to see the start of 'the charge on the San Juan block-house to our left, where the infantry of Kent, led by Hawkins, were climbing the hill'.[50] The cavalrymen on the summit of Kettle Hill began firing to cover the infantry attack up San Juan Hill, adding to the attackers' fire and that of Parker's Gatlings which laid down a continuous wave of bullets, forcing the Spanish defenders to stay below the parapets of their trenches and rifle pits.

The infantry attack up the slopes of San Juan Hill was led by Lieutenant Jules Ord, a Regular officer of Hawkins' staff. Hawkins had hesitated to order the men into a frontal assault up the steep hill against the Spanish blockhouse and trenches. But Ord received his permission to lead a charge:

> Lieutenant Ord jumped forward from the brush in a running crouch with his saber in one hand and his pistol in the other.
>
> 'Come on – come on, you fellows!' he yelled.
>
> 'Come on – we can't stop here!'
>
> In the next instant the scraggly undergrowth burst in a ragged fringe of blue-shirted men, crouching and running, with Ord in the lead. There went up what the academic histories call a cheer, but it was nothing more than a hoarse scream of relief from scores of men and the yell that soldiers give those whom they wish to honor. It was Hawkins' brigade, its two regiments, the Sixth and Sixteenth running in a pack, unleashed from the jungle, and hell-bent for the red-tiled roof [of the blockhouse] that crowned San Juan Hill. It was a running spearhead. There was no nice order, no neatly formed companies crossing that plain or mounting the slope.[51]

Richard Harding Davis, one of the many journalists that had accompanied the expeditionary force, described the assault in similar terms, 'they had no glittering bayonets, they were not massed in regular array. There were a few men in advance, bunched together, and creeping up a steep, sunny hill, the tops of which roared and flashed with flame'.[52] What had appeared to General Hawkins as a suicidal assault up towards a heavily defended position proved not to be the case, and the attacking infantry suffered very few casualties in their climb. This was for two reasons: firstly, the suppressive power of the three Gatling guns that were in action, with one Spanish officer reporting, 'it was terrible when your [Gatling] guns opened – always. They went b-r-r-r, like a lawn mower cutting the grass over our trenches. We could not stick a finger up when you fired without getting it cut off'.[53] The second factor, not discovered until the attackers reached the summit of San Juan Hill, was that the Spanish had entrenched on the geographic, not the military, crest of the hill. As soon as the attackers began their climb, they had been out of reach of Spanish fire from their trenches. To have been able to fire at the attackers, the Spanish would have had to leave their trenches, exposing themselves to the full force of the Gatlings.

As the US infantry neared the summit, covering fire ceased and the surviving Spanish began to leave their trenches and retreat quickly. Some remained to contest the issue with the Americans, and one of these shot and killed Lieutenant Ord. The Spaniard was himself quickly killed, and, as in El Caney, battle-enraged Americans shot down some Spaniards who attempted to surrender. The Americans held San Juan Hill, but it was a tenuous position. More men, including the 71 New York Volunteers and the Gatling battery, were brought up and contested the hill top, exchanging fire with Spaniards in nearby positions. The Spaniards put in two counterattacks, but these were driven off, with casualties among the Americans. There appears to have been little in the way of command and control in evidence, with men from various regiments, Regulars and Volunteers intermingled, acting on their own initiative. Post, who was on the hill soon after it was taken, noted that the Rough Riders and other cavalry had attacked and taken other Spanish positions near San Juan Hill, and that 'down below, in the plain we had crossed, more men were straggling across and climbing the Hill. There was little order, but there were plenty of men'.[54] By nightfall, the Americans were established on the hill, and nearby ridges. They were now a mile and a quarter from Santiago. It had cost US Fifth Corps over 1,300 casualties.[55] Both the 71 New York Volunteers and the Massachusetts Volunteers had sustained casualties of around 12 per cent.

The Siege of Santiago and US victory

Despite the hard-won victories of 1 July, the US command were far from sanguine about their position. It greatly over-estimated the number of Spanish defenders it had faced on the 1 July, and the number that continued to face them after having broken the Spanish outer defensive line. As fighting continued, Roosevelt believed that, 'we are in measurable distance of a terrible military disaster',[56] while General Shafter held a commanders' conference on the night of 2 July. He asked his officers to decide whether their front line should be withdrawn from the San Juan ridge to defensive positions nearer the coast, or whether they should hold the ground they had. The decision was to remain where they were. The next day, Shafter telegrammed Washington, outlining his position as he saw, and feared, it. Washington responded almost immediately, urging Shafter to hold his line, as the 'effect upon the country would be much better than falling back'.[57] The Regulars and Volunteers now settled down to besiege Santiago.

The situation for the Spanish was, unbeknown to General Shafter, serious. Their losses on 1 July had been heavy, with the units defending San Juan Hill losing between 30 and 50 per cent of their men, while General Linares was seriously injured. Had the Americans pushed on from the San Juan ridge on the evening of 1 July, they would have been faced by 'barely 300 men, 100 of them convalescents from the military hospital [holding] the Spanish trenches on Santiago's outskirts'.[58] As for being able to withstand a prolonged siege, that was highly unlikely, with only 190 rounds of ammunition per man, and very low food stocks, while the city's main reservoir and water supply was in the hands of the Americans at El Caney. The Spanish authorities in Havana then made the decision to try and at least save the Spanish naval squadron, and Admiral Cervera was ordered to lead his ships out in a dash for freedom. Outnumbered and outgunned, the Spanish squadron sailed out on 3 July into the arms of the waiting US fleet. In a running encounter lasting four hours, the Spanish lost all four of their cruisers, and two destroyers, along with 474 men. The US Navy lost one man killed and ten wounded. The loss of the Spanish squadron now meant that Santiago held no real military significance, and Shafter was convinced that it would soon be surrendered. Negotiations began between the US and Spanish commanders, interspersed with US naval and artillery bombardments. The Spanish commander, General José Toral, who had replaced the wounded Linares, stretched out the negotiations, hoping that disease, especially the dreaded yellow fever, would soon take hold in the American lines, and force a withdrawal. In fact, yellow fever had begun to make its presence felt, and the continuing severe supply problems meant that the besieging US troops were low on food, water and anything approaching decent medical support. But US reinforcements were being brought into Cuba, and the navy was able to bombard the city with heavy shells without fear of response. Finally, on Sunday, 17 July, the Spanish surrendered:

> General Shafter, together with the generals and their staffs, rode to a large field in front of Santiago, accompanied by a troop of cavalry; there they met General Toral, who was also accompanied by a company of one hundred men ... General Shafter rode up to General Toral and presented him with the sword and spurs of the Spanish General Vara del Rey, who was killed at El Caney. The Spanish troops then presented arms, and the Spanish flag, which for three hundred and eighty-two years had floated over the city, was pulled down and furled forever.[59]

The war with Spain was not over, however, as Puerto Rico still remained, but after a short, and well-coordinated campaign, it, too, fell to US forces before an Armistice was agreed between the USA and Spain on 13 August.

For the US Volunteers and Regulars who had defeated Spain in Cuba, the difficulties were far from over. The challenges that the War Department and the US Army faced in terms of supplying and supporting what, for the US, was an exceptionally large force, continued. Disease swept through the ranks, and neither logistical, nor the medical services, were able to cope with the situation. It was a poor reward for the men who had flocked to the Stars and Stripes.

An important little war

In 1898, the United States did not possess an army suited for what was to be the next stage of American expansionism, beyond its continental borders into the Pacific and the Caribbean. The war with Spain highlighted the limitations of the US Army, but also revealed the role that politics, popular sentiment, and the press had in the making of US policy and the US's way of waging war. As it became clear that war with Spain was likely, the proponents of an enlarged and revitalised regular army were overwhelmed by the political demand for the incorporation of the citizen in arms, in the form of the National Guard and Volunteer movement, into any US Army ready for war. This movement channelled the enthusiasm of ordinary Americans, fuelled by the power of the press barons and the 'yellow press', for military service, and by the local and national figures who saw Volunteer service as a way of bolstering political ambitions. In consequence, the US forces that landed in Cuba included Volunteers, whose performance in the defeat of Spanish forces on the island, was, in the popular imagination, a vindication of the long-held American belief in the value of the citizen in arms. The role of the Rough Riders, in particular, was lauded throughout the USA, and helped propel Theodore Roosevelt to the Presidency in 1901 following the assassination of President McKinley. The undoubted courage of the Rough Riders was, nevertheless, magnified by the press, and Volunteer Post, of the 71st New York Infantry, caustically commented:

> The Rough Riders were the supreme of the élite; no regiment has ever received the newspaper space that was devoted to them. They were good men – make no mistake about that, even if some did admit it easily – and they could man the trenches or a cotillion with

intrepidity. In addition to having Teddy as its second in command, this regiment had its own press agent in Richard Harding Davis, to whom the human beings not listed in the Social Register were merely varied forms of pollution.[60]

The military value of the Volunteers was disputed by some Regulars, of whom Captain Parker of Fifth Corps' Gatling detachment might be taken as typical. He took a nuanced view of the Volunteers, criticising in particular poor camp discipline, but reserved his ire for the press and a gullible public:

> The Volunteers presented many different types: some good, some otherwise. There should be no sympathy with that servile truckling to popular sentiment which speaks of our brave Volunteers indiscriminately, as if they were all good and all equally well instructed. There were Volunteers who were the equals of the Regulars in fighting and leadership. And there were some who should have been at home pulling on a nursing-bottle or attending kindergarten. To praise them indiscriminately creates a false impression on the public, and works a rank injustice toward those who were really good and efficient in the service. It does even worse than that: it fosters the popular idea that all there is to do to make soldiers is to take so many labourers, clerks, hod-carriers, or farmers, and put on them uniforms, arm then with rifles, and call them "gallant Volunteers"! Out upon such an insane delusion![61]

This was the authentic voice of the professional, a Regular soldier who saw war as a scientific endeavour, but struggling to make his voice heard in a country where the ideal of the citizen in arms, the Volunteer, had a powerful resonance, both politically and militarily.

Chapter 6

Spain, 1936–39: Ideological War and Murder; Militias in the Spanish Civil War

The descent into civil war

In January 1936, Spain faced a general election against a backdrop of multiple and ever-deepening political divisions, which the election would do nothing to heal. To the casual outsider, Spain's general election seemed to be a reflection of wider European political trends. At the beginning of the election campaign, most left-wing political parties signed an electoral pact to form a 'Popular Front'. The Popular Front idea was the brainchild of the communist international, the Comintern, and was a tactical response to the rise to power of Hitler and the national socialists in Germany. In that case, the powerful German Communist Party, obeying Comintern instructions, had refused an alliance with the Social Democrats, dooming both to defeat at the hands of the Nazis. Ranged against Spain's Popular Front alliance was a range of right-wing parties, conservatives, monarchists, and a small fascist party, the Falange. All this could be taken as characteristic of the struggles that were taking place across Europe, but there were important differences in the Spanish case.

In many respects, Spain was atypical in comparison with other major European countries like France, the United Kingdom, or Germany. Whereas these countries had experienced rapid economic and industrial change in the nineteenth century, and had been the major players in the First World War, Spain had experienced comparatively little industrial change and had avoided the First World War. It might have avoided that conflict, but it had an equally damaging recent history: 'for while there had been no civil wars in most of Europe since the seventeenth century, Spain ... had fallen back into conflict within her national frontiers three times in the nineteenth century'.[1] Spain was both oddly isolated from Western Europe, and, at the same time, receptive to wider European ideas and movements, with new political ideas being enthusiastically added to an already crowded ideological landscape in Spain.

In the coming civil war, the ideologies of anarchism, communism, socialism, and fascism were all to play their role, but intertwined with other, particularly Spanish concerns, such as land-holding, Catholicism, monarchism, and the early loss of a global imperial role. In this context, it is perhaps unsurprising that parliamentary democracy was doomed in a country where compromise and consensus were not seen as virtues. In Hugh Thomas's words, 'each of the leading political ideas of Europe since the sixteenth century has been received with enthusiasm by one group of Spaniards and opposed ferociously by another, without any desire for compromise being shown by either side'.[2] The combination of fanatically pursued ideologies, deep-seated economic and social problems, the politicisation of the military and security forces, anti-clerical and Church obsessions, and regional divisions, gave the Spanish conflict both a strongly national character with overtones of wider, European struggles. This context also meant that by the time of the narrow electoral victory of the Popular Front on 16 February 1936, (it won 47 per cent of the vote and 263 seats in parliament, compared to the right's 46 per cent and 156 seats) significant elements had already begun the process of the para-militarisation of politics.

The para-militarisation of Spanish politics
Politics and armed struggle
Many political parties in Spain had, before the civil war broke out, already adopted para-militarism to one degree or another. Parties of the left and right fielded armed supporters, and gunmen (*pistoleros*) skilled in assassinations and the killing of opponents, as a matter of course. This was not only a reaction to the violence that was endemic in Spanish politics, but also because some parties and groups had ideological stances that incorporated, and indeed exalted, the role of armed struggle. The existence of party militias, and gunmen, helped undermine Spanish democracy, and as the botched military rising turned into all-out war, provided an already existing framework for the rapid expansion of militias that made a significant contribution to the development of the war, particularly in 1936, when conventional forces were in short supply. The role of armed struggle, political violence, party militias and gunmen prior to the start of the civil war is examined here through the examples of anarchism and fascism in Spanish politics.

Anarchism in Spain

Anarchism was one of the European political ideas that took root in Spain to a degree that exceeded anywhere else in its depth and longevity. The anarchists had emerged in the mid-nineteenth century, particularly in France, Italy and Russia. The movement's foremost figure in the late nineteenth century was Mikhail Bakunin, a peripatetic Russian exile, rival to Marx, and the leader of an armed uprising in Lyon in 1870, which was a foretaste of the Paris Commune. Bakunin's writings and example provided a model for the military organisation of the Paris Communards, with a militia being established on anarchist principles, including the election of officers. By the end of the nineteenth century, anarchism was a by-word for terrorism, with many anarchists in Europe and America following Bakunin's policy and tactic of 'propaganda by deed'. In effect, this meant assassinations, bomb attacks and other violent attempts on individuals, institutions and representatives of the middle and ruling classes. For example, in 1878, Giovanni Passannante attempted to stab to death King Umberto I of Italy; Umberto survived, only to succumb to another anarchist attack in 1900, an anarchist success that led directly to the assassination of US President McKinley a year later. In 1893, the anarchist, Auguste Vaillant, threw a bomb into the French Chamber of Deputies (Parliament). This latter attack led to a chain of events culminating, in 1894, with an Italian anarchist, Sante Geronimo Caserio, stabbing Sadi Carnot, the President of France, to death. Kings, princes, politicians, business magnates, and police were all victims of anarchist propaganda by deed. But despite the decades of anarchist terror, the anarchists never managed to establish themselves as a successful mass movement, except in Spain.

In Catalonia and Aragon, Bakunin inspired the creation of an anarchist movement that combined politics with armed struggle. Although anarchists could be found in many parts of Spain by the 1880s, it was in Catalonia, and, in particular, in industrial Barcelona, that the movement struck root. From the first, it combined revolutionary trade unionism with violence. In the 1890s, anarchist propaganda by deed in Catalonia included bomb attacks in the Liceo Theatre in Barcelona, and an attack on a Corpus Christi procession. The attacker escaped, but hundreds of anarchists were rounded up, and detained under torture, during which some died. That, in turn, led to the assassination of the Spanish Prime Minister, Antonio Cánovas. The to and fro pattern of state and anarchist violence was established, and reached a new peak during the 'Tragic Week' in Barcelona in July, 1909, when anarchists, socialists and republicans fought government para-military police and troops. Not only did the Tragic Week add to the long history of political violence, but it also added a new chapter to anarchism in Spain, and led directly to the creation of what would become the most significant anarchist movement.

In the aftermath of the Tragic Week, a new union was formed, the *Confederación Nacional de Trabajo* (CNT – the National Confederation of Labour), which was, from the outset, dominated by anarchists. Although it was a national movement, it was always most strong in Barcelona and Catalonia. Unlike 'reformist' trades unions, characteristic of those in Great Britain, the CNT was a revolutionary union, which was syndicalist. Syndicalism proposed to organise all workers in one, general union which would, at some point, be in a strong enough position to use the tactic of a general strike to paralyse society, government and the state. As a result, the state and government would collapse, and the syndicalist union would take power. Although the CNT were a minority among workers in Barcelona, the union's adherents and supporters exhibited such fervour that their particular brand of revolutionary politics produced admiration, fear and hatred among friends and enemies: 'their verve and violence commanded attention. Their tactics included sabotage, riots and anti-parliamentarianism, above all, the revolutionary general strike'.[3] From the outset, the CNT used violence as a tactic, not only to defend the union, and the anarchist movement, from state-sponsored violence, but also as an integral part of its political struggle. By 1918, there were some 700,000 members of the CNT, and over 200 anarchist newspapers and magazines.[4] But hopes of a syndicalist revolution were crushed during the rule of General Primo de Rivera, Prime Minister under King Alfonso XIII, between 1923 and 1930. CNT leaders were arrested, exiled, and jailed, and the anarchist movement was forced underground. It was during this period that the movement became even more committed to revolutionary armed struggle and a 'pure' form of anarchism that would resist all reformism.

In 1927, underground anarchist leaders formed a secret society, the *Federación Anarquista Ibérica* (FAI – the Spanish Anarchist Federation), committed to leading the wider anarchist movement on a path to violent, insurrectionary action. Two men in particular came to symbolise and personify the FAI's belief in revolutionary violence and warfare. These were Buenaventura Durruti, who would become the most famous militia leader during the Spanish Civil War, and Francisco Ascaso, who would be killed in action during the first days of the civil war. These two anarchists were 'formidable men of violence [... and] for some, Durruti was a "thug", "killer", or "hooligan"; for others he was the "indomitable hero" '.[5] Men like Durruti and Ascaso set the standard for the revolutionaries of the FAI, who sought to keep the much larger anarchist-dominated CNT on a narrow revolutionary path, resisting both the state and those erstwhile allies who were deemed less than totally committed to revolution.

The anarchists' belief in the necessity of armed struggle survived the end of the Primo de Rivera dictatorship and the proclamation, on 14 April 1931, of the Second Republic. Further, the commitment to terrorism and the necessity of insurrection led to the October 1934 to a general strike which turned into an uprising. Quickly crushed in Madrid by the centre-right government, the revolutionaries of the Asturias proved to be a tougher nut to crack. Socialists, communists and anarchists took part in the Asturian uprising, with anarchists, in particular, able to take advantage of their experience of organising for combat by creating workers' militias. Militia units blocked the advance of government forces, and, for a fortnight, revolutionary conditions held sway in what was later called the 'October Revolution in the Asturias'. But, in an ominous foretaste of what was to come in less than two years' time, the rising was crushed with great severity by men of the Spanish Foreign Legion, under the overall command of General Francisco Franco. Executions, torture and imprisonment followed for over 30,000 people involved in the uprising,[6] but the government was, in many ways, no more secure than before the uprising. The left was able to capitalise on the severity of the repression, and, for the anarchists, the experience of the Asturian uprising merely confirmed them in their analysis of the political situation in Spain, and of the role of armed revolutionary organisations.

The Falange

Unlike communism, fascism was not an international creed that, eventually, was adapted to suit national conditions. Instead, fascism was a trans-national experience that found particular national expression, and development. Fascists throughout Europe had to provide a determinedly national expression of the ideology, not least because fascists exalted the nation-state above all else. Fascism as a political ideology was a latecomer in Spain, but in the form of the Falange, it would make a contribution to the collapse of parliamentary democracy out of all proportion to its size, provide an armed opposition to the gunmen of the left, and, in the first months of the war recruit tens of thousands to its militia ranks.

A young graduate of the Complutense University of Madrid, Ramiro Ledesma Ramos, was the first Spaniard to attempt to develop a fascist programme early in 1931. Ramiro Ledesma drew upon a wide range of Spanish and European thought to develop what he called 'national syndicalism'. He was influenced both by the fascism of Mussolini, and the national socialism of Hitler, but also by Spanish anarchism, with its stress on the syndicalist model of revolution and societal organisation. He pursued the development of his new approach to Spanish politics in his magazine, *La Conquista del Estado* (The Conquest of the State), which argued for the create of a revolutionary, anti-parliamentarian vanguard of militants dedicated to creating a new Spain which would reject both the reactionary conservatism of the right-wing parties, and the internationalism and class warfare of the left. Ramiro Ledesma' appeals were couched in military-style language, with national-syndicalist groups being envisaged as 'military-type teams without hypocrisy before the rifle's barrel'.[7] Ramos quickly attracted another young enthusiast for fascist revolution, a graduate of the University of Salamanca, Onésimo Redondo Ortega. He had spent some time in Germany in the late 1920s, was influenced, like Ramos, by an eclectic group of Spanish and European thinkers, and was hostile to communism and capitalism. In August 1931, he founded a small fascist grouplet, *Juntas Castellanas de Actuación Hispánica* (the Castilian Hispanic Action Groups), which he took with him when he and Ramos created the *Juntas de Offensiva Nacional-Sindicalista* (JONS, or Unions of the National-Syndicalist Offensive) in October of that year. Its name made it quite clear that what mattered for these 'national syndicalists' was revolution, not parliamentary politics.

The new party was little more than a bit player in the drama of Spanish politics, drawing its support from undergraduates in Madrid, and some peasants and workers in Valladolid. It focused on establishing small workers' syndicates, and building its support through these groups, and a number of newspapers and periodicals. As with other political ideologies, a rival appeared in October 1933, in the form of the *Falange Española* (the Spanish Phalanx), founded by José Antonio Primo de Rivera, the son of the former dictator. From the outset, José Antonio mixed the rhetoric of para-military politics with the idea of solidarity, and participation in elections. However, despite the fact that José Antonio was a much more well-known figure than his rivals in JONS, the Falange made little impression on the voters in the November 1933 elections. Failure at that election led to the unification of the Falange and JONS in February 1934, to create the *Falange Española de las JONS*. The new, unified movement, adopted a national-syndicalist approach, combined with a commitment to militant action. In some respects, the FE de las JONS was a mirror-image of the Spanish anarchist movement. The new fascist movement adopted, and adapted, symbols from Spain's past, but also from Spanish anarcho-syndicalism. So, as with the anarchists, the Falange's flag was black and red, though with the 'yoke and arrows' symbol of King Ferdinand and Queen Isabella superimposed, monarchs who symbolised Spanish unity and its Imperial glory. In addition, the movement adopted the blue work shirt as its uniform, symbolising its celebration of productive labour.

The politics of the Falange was combined with a willingness to use paramilitary violence. Membership of the Falange, for many of its militants, represented a way of life. As militants committed to a future that would be made by new, fascist, men, they believed in a life that was seen as 'trenchant, ardent and militant'.[8] Against the wider backdrop of political violence, José Antonio's speech at the inaugural meeting of the Falange, on 29 October 1933, welcomed the likelihood of armed conflict with political opponents, while rejecting parliamentary politics:

> We are not going to argue with habitués over the disordered remains of a dirty banquet. Our place is outside, though we may occasionally have to pass a few transient minutes within. Our place is in the fresh air, under the cloudless heavens, weapons in our hands, with the stars above us. Let the others go on with their merry making. We outside, in tense, fervent, and certain vigilance, already feel the dawn breaking in the joy of our hearts.[9]

For the Falangists, their creed was 'not a trend of thought, but a way of being – *una manera de ser*'.[10] It was not surprising, perhaps, that the similarly militant and hyperbolic anarchist hero, Durruti, had two brothers who were members of the Falange.[11] The presence of so many elements in Spanish politics, of left and right, willing, and happy to use violence, allied to the frequency with which political leaders resorted to high-flown justifications of armed struggle, created a situation that normalised the role of political militias and the activity of gunmen.

Socialist, anarchist and Falangists fought a low-level, para-military war. In the Falange's case, José Antonio proved to be unable to control the activities of his armed followers, who fought a rising tide of left-wing violence. The Falange soon gained their inspirational martyr, in the person of a 20-year-old student, Matias Montero, who was gunned down in 1934, becoming the movement's Horst Wessel, the famous, much-celebrated Nazi martyr.[12] The Falange was forced to recruit more gunmen, some of whom were ex-Spanish Foreign Legionnaires who had fought in Spain's war against the *Rif* in Morocco. But the situation became increasingly serious, and in the spring of 1936, the Falangist militiamen and gunmen needed to boost their capabilities with better weaponry. Luis Bolin, who was later to act as Franco's Press and Intelligence Officer, was asked to source sub-machine-guns for the movement. Bolin had extensive contacts in foreign capitals, and his first thought was to approach friendly figures in England. Eventually, Bolin was given a contact:

> Who bore a well-known name [who] told me to be at Claridge's on a certain day and hour, wearing a white carnation on my lapel. Someone would in due course appear and work out the deal, but he and I were never again to recognize each other publicly. I kept my appointment. The business was settled in a matter of minutes. He guns were to be purchased in Germany and shipped to Portugal in champagne cases aboard an ocean-going yacht. From Oporto, they would be smuggled across the Spanish border in the vicinity of Salamanca ... Before the guns could be landed, civil war broke out in Spain.[13]

For the Falangist militia and gunmen, the outbreak of war would bring the transformation of their movement, the deaths of most of their leaders, and the fulfilment of their conception of politics as armed struggle.

Militias on the eve of the civil war

The political militias became a permanent feature of the Second Republic. In the aftermath of the October 1934 rising, and the repression in the Asturias, militias were, supposedly, banned, and their members imprisoned. But, in reality, they simply took on the guise of sporting and athletic clubs, and after the February 1936 election, they returned to open activity, with left-wing militias boosted by the release of members from gaol by the new Popular Front government. The right-wing response to the electoral victory of the Popular

Front, the release of militiamen and their open parading, was to enhance the strength and activity of the Falange. The movement had only around 25,000 members at the time of the February general election, but their militancy and willingness to fight left-wing militias and gunmen, meant that in the aftermath of the election many more young right-wingers joined their ranks, boosting the Falange to nearly 40,000 activists. Meanwhile, the militiamen and gunmen of the anarchists and revolutionary socialists attacked opponents, assassinated individuals, burned churches, and intimidated employers. On the 16 June, just under a month before the Generals' uprising that began the civil war, José María Gil-Robles y Quiñones, the leader of the Catholic party, *Confederación Española de Derechas Autónomas* (CEDA, Spanish Confederation of Autonomous Right-wing Groups), many of whose younger members were abandoning CEDA for the Falange, addressed the Spanish parliament, reading out a list of political violence in the four months since the election:

> It comprised 169 churches totally destroyed, and another 257 partly burned down or looted, 269 persons killed and 1,879 wounded, 161 armed robberies, 113 general strikes, and 228 local strikes, 381 private or political clubs destroyed, looted or attacked, 43 newspaper offices and printing presses gutted or sacked, 146 bombs exploded, and 78 more discovered before they blew up.[14]

Against this backdrop, even parties like CEDA which had, for a while, seemed extreme, paled before the fanaticism of the party militias and youth groups dedicated to armed struggle. The failure of the Popular Front government to stamp its authority on extra-parliamentary violence provided just the excuse that anti-democratic, right-wing military men needed to continue their plotting against the Republic. All that was needed by the summer of 1936 was one more outrage of sufficient moment to enable a military coup.

That outrage took place during the early morning of Monday 13 July, and was part of a chain of events that led to the military plotters initiating their coup attempt. The protagonists included officers of the Assault Guards, the socialist militias and the Falange. The Assault Guard – *Guardia de Asalto* – was a largely urban-based para-military police force created by the Republican government in 1931, following the end of the Primo de Rivera dictatorship. It was a mobile police reserve along the lines of the older, rural-based *Guardia Civil*. That force was seen by many to represent reactionary interests in Spain, while the Assault

Guards, the *Asaltos*, were seen to be strongly pro-Republican. In Madrid and Barcelona, many of the *Asaltos* were recruited from left-wing groups, particularly the socialists. One such was Lieutenant José Castillo, who, in addition to his police duties, helped organise and train socialist militias in the capital. That activism, as well as his part in putting down a right-wing riot, had made Castillo a marked man, and on 12 July he was gunned down by four Falangists. His Assault Guard comrades took his killing as a challenge, and a murder that had to be avenged, and during the night of the 12/13 July, a squad of Asaltos drove around Madrid in a futile attempt to arrest or kill Falangists. Finally, in the early hours of the 13 July, they made their way to the home of José Calvo Sotelo, the monarchist leader of *Renovación Española*, and spokesman of the right-wing parties in the Spanish parliament. The Asaltos drove Calvo Sotelo away, and 'after a quarter of a mile, Luis Cuenca, a young Galician socialist sitting beside the politician, shot him in the back of his neck'.[15] The enormity of the act – a leading parliamentarian murdered by the police – was the spark that set off the planned military uprising, which began on the night 16–17 July.

Into the civil war
A failed coup d'état
The conspiring generals, led by a junta comprising of Mola, Quiepo de Llano, Cabanellas and Franco, planned for a coup d'état which would involve, first, a rising of the army elite, the Army of Africa, consisting of the Spanish Foreign Legion (the *Tercio*) and colonial troops from Spanish North Africa, the *Regulares*, some 30,000 men in total. This would be followed quickly by the rising of all other troops stationed throughout Spain. However, the plan miscarried, with poor communications, conflicting loyalties, and the rapid response of left-wing militias all frustrating the rebels' coup. Instead of a new military government taking power, Spain found itself in a civil war. From the very first days of that war, militias, on both sides, played crucial roles, both in defeating the coup plan, and in shoring up the government and the rebels.

Defeating the rising – the left-wing militias in Madrid and Barcelona, 19–20 July, 1936.
In the initial hours and days of the rising, confusion took hold on both the government's and the rebel's side. Far from seizing all the main garrison towns and cities, the rebels found that their most potent forces were stuck in Spanish

Morocco, where the rising had succeeded, while in key, mainland areas, officers either declared for the government, prevaricated too long, or adopted a 'wait and see' position. For many, delay proved fatal. But the government was slow to react, too, and it was soon besieged by left-wing parties demanding the release of weapons to their militias. It was the militias which were primarily responsible for halting the rising, particularly in Madrid, and in industrial Barcelona, and in towns where the left-wing militias were unable to acquire enough weapons, it was members of the militias who were the first to be executed by the rebels. But in Madrid and Barcelona, socialist, communist and anarchist militias seized the initiative and, with the support of loyal troops, the majority of *Asaltos*, and some loyalist Civil Guards, crushed the rising. Following the initial fighting, accompanied, as would become the norm throughout the war, by the murder of captured opponents, militia columns then took their new revolution out into other areas of Spain, in attempts to beat back rebel troops and their supporting militias who had seized parts of south-west Spain, and much of the heart of the country, west and north of Madrid.

In Madrid, as elsewhere, the government refused the demands of the left-wing parties to distribute arms to their followers. The militias had their own armouries, but not of a size to fight an all-out urban battle against the military, especially given the large numbers that were flocking to the militia ranks, some 40,000 within a few weeks.[16] From the outset, and in contrast with Barcelona, the most important militia in the capital was that of the Communists – the *Milicias Antifascistas Obreras y Campesinas* (MAOC, Workers and Peasants Anti-fascist Militia). The MAOC formed five battalions of around 1,000 militia apiece, partly equipped with some of the 5,000 rifles the government had distributed. Their first actions on the night of 19-20 July were to burn around fifty churches. This was quickly followed by militiamen seizing government ministries, and ensuring that left-wing loyalists were in control. Then the militias turned their attention to the main army barracks in the city, the Montaña barracks, held by 2,000 soldiers and around 500 Falangists and monarchists. The army in Madrid had botched the rising, with poor communications and confusion delaying their attempt to seize the city and government until it was too late to do anything other than retreat to their barracks and await developments in the rest of Spain.

The militias brought up artillery to shell the Montaña barracks, and loyalist aircraft bombed the defenders too, while the militias exchanged fire with the besieged defenders and bombarded the barracks with loud-speaker appeals for the rank and file soldiers to turn on their officers. During the morning of the 20 July, General Fanjul, the leading military rebel in Madrid, and Colonel Serra, the Montaña barracks garrison commander, were both wounded. The wounding of the two officers, and the continued bombing and shelling, led to confusion among the garrison. When a white flag appeared at one of the windows, militia ran forward to take the surrender, only to be fired upon from another part of the barracks. Eventually, the militia broke into the barracks, and began a massacre. Photographs taken at the time show the parade ground strewn with the bodies of the defenders, their throats cut by the left-wing militias and the mob. Several hundred defenders were murdered, and the wounded were thrown into the Model Prison. The militia victory at the Montaña barracks was followed by the defeat of other pockets of the military uprising. With Madrid secured, 'hastily-armed militia forces, along with elements of the demoralized civil guard and assault guards as well as what remained of the army, were dispatched in taxis, lorries, or requisitioned private moto-cars, southwards towards Toledo and north-east towards Guadalajara'.[17] As will be seen, the militias' fortunes at Toledo would be somewhat different from that in Madrid in the first days of the war.

In Barcelona, the most important militia forces were those of the powerful anarchist movement, along with the anti-Stalinist *Partido Obrero de Unificación Marxista* (POUM. Workers' Party of Marxist Unification). The POUM, led by the courageous and charismatic Andrés Nin, was the main Marxist party in Spain in 1936, and was opposed by the Communist Party of Spain (PCE) which was represented in Catalonia by the *Partit Socialista Unificat de Catalunya* (PSUC, or Unified Socialist Party of Catalonia), part of the Soviet international, the Comintern. The anarchist and POUM militias took control of Barcelona by the evening of 20 July. The rebels had only been able to muster around 5,000 men, with an equal number of loyal civil guards and *Asaltos* to oppose them. It was the anarchist militias who decided the outcome, with 30,000 men and women, who were quickly issued with rifles when the anarchists seized the San Andrés barracks, Barcelona's main armoury. The anarchists of the CNT/FAI were, as a result of their military success, able to pursue their revolution, and become a key element in the new 'Anti-Fascist Militias Committee', composed of representatives from the socialist trade unions, the CNT, the FAI, PSUC, the POUM, and Catalan nationalists. At first, thanks to the strength of the anarchist militia, it was the CNT/FAI which dominated, but, as the war continued, the balance of power would shift against them.

The rapid response of the various left-wing militias to the military uprising was the primary reason why the ill-conceived coup failed. Although a significant minority of the army, along with a majority of the air force and navy, and the *Asaltos* and some civil guard, rallied to the government, without the militias' intervention it is likely that the rising would have prevailed. The militias combined political motivation, not to say fanaticism, with prior street-fighting experience, significant wider support and a willingness to act which outweighed the confusion of the government, to stymie the rebel generals in the first two days of what would become nearly three years of war. The left-wing militias would continue to be at the very heart of the defence of the Republic for the rest of 1936, and into the first months of 1937. Each of the left wing-militias had their own character, arising out of their political outlook, but there were also similarities, especially in the non-Stalinist backed militias. The organisation, effectiveness and performance of the left-wing militias was, and has been, subject to much political debate give their fate from 1937 onwards, when the Republican side descended into inter-factional fighting. But it is clear that the militias were a vital element in the defence of the Republic in 1936.

The Anarchist, Socialist and POUM militias – personnel, organisation, effectiveness

At the time of the military rising, several thousand left-wing athletes from all around the world were gathered in Barcelona for what was to be the People's Olympiad. In the event, the rising put paid to what was intended to be an alternative Olympics to that which was held in Berlin. Around 200 of the left-wing athletes (usually sponsored by political parties and trades unions) joined the various militias, while other foreign left-wing activists also travelled to Spain to see what was happening on the ground. In the early days, people made their way to Spain on their own initiative, though later it was the Comintern's International Brigades that brought most foreigners to fight for the Republic and communism. One of the very early foreign participants in Barcelona was Richard Kisch, who went to Spain as a stringer (or 'leg man' as he called it), for John Langdon-Davies, chief of bureau for the British newspaper, the *News Chronicle*. In Barcelona, he joined the POUM, and took part in the ill-fated, poorly organised anarchist invasion of the Balearic Islands, where he was wounded and returned to England. After recovering from his wounds, Kisch began to recruit for the British International Brigade, then returned to Spain in a support role for the International Brigades. Kisch was on the spot in the very early days of militia operations, and gave accounts of the men and women in the militia, militia organisation and effectiveness.

Kisch arrived in Barcelona, along with three other Britons, less than a week after the defeat of the rising in the city. He noted that although there had been a 'spontaneous' emergence of militias, the cutting edge of the Republican forces in the city had been provided 'by the Assault Guards and 1,000 Civil Guard under Colonel Escobar'.[18] The importance of both loyal Civil Guards and, more particularly, Assault Guards, to the Republic, as trained, disciplined, para-military forces is a recurring theme of the early days of the fighting. But Kisch underestimated the value of the politically-committed, pre-existing militia men, which provided the core of fighters around which thousands of new militiamen and women coalesced. On joining the POUM militia, Kisch and his friend, Tony Wills, reported to a newly 'liberated' army barracks, renamed the Karl Marx barracks. The barracks had been stripped and looted by the mob, and left in a filthy condition, with all the latrines and wash houses inoperable – 'the place stank of piss and shit'.[19] The lack of basic hygiene in Spain was something that struck all British and American volunteers for the Republic forcefully. Kisch described the characteristic atmosphere of the newly victorious militias:

> Few *milicianos* had much experience of weapons. Many of the kids had none. There were few instructors and no time for training, at first. Discipline was voluntary, a matter for discussion, particularly in the Anarchist brigades. New recruits brandished weapons like banners and continually shouted brazen defiance of the Generals and fascism. They all seemed a bit gun-crazy but at that time, perhaps, it helped.[20]

Both Kisch and Wills turned out to have more military training, particularly weapons training, than most of the militia, as they had both been in their public schools' Officer Training Corps (OTC). George Orwell, who also joined the POUM militia, found that his OTC service with the Eton 'Corps', and his para-military training with the Imperial Burmese police, also made him one of the better trained militiamen. His Spanish and Catalan comrades also assumed that, as an Englishman, he would, as a matter of course, know how to handle machine-guns.

In the early days of the war, women joined the various militias, and served alongside men. Kisch explained that the women, 'fought, ate and slept with other milicianos on a basis of absolute equality. But, in fact, it was not long before the Republican authorities gradually withdrew women from the fighting zones'.[21] It was while she was with a militia unit from Huesca that the English communist and artist, Felicia Brown, was killed in the abortive militia attempt to take the town. She was probably the first international volunteer to be killed, and the only Englishwoman.[22] Other foreign women also fought with the militias, including Brown's friend, Patricia Fernhurst, and, in the POUM's Women's Battalion, the Australian, Mary Low.[23] More unusually, Ethel MacDonald, the secretary of the 'Anti-Parliamentary Communist Movement', became a radio propagandist at the CNT headquarters, and later took part in the internecine fighting between Republican forces in Barcelona in May, 1937. MacDonald was fortunate to escape with her life, and returned to Glasgow, saying: 'I went to Spain full of hope and dreams. It promised to be Utopia realised. I return full of sadness, dulled by the tragedy I have seen',[24] which reflects Kisch's much later comment that 'foreigners flocked to Barcelona and Madrid to get a glimpse of history in the making through whatever tinted spectacles they used'.[25] Although for many disillusionment soon set in, there were plenty of glimpses of history in the making to be seen, and the left-wing militias, often 'uniformed' in blue boiler suits and overalls – the ubiquitous *mono* – with coloured side-caps, in red and black for the anarchists, and red for the socialists and communists, their enthusiasm for various brands of the revolution, provided sufficient spectacle for many foreigners. The leaders of the various militias also played their part, with, for example, Andrés Nin, the POUM leader, fulfilling a foreigner's ideal image of a revolutionary:

> He greeted us warmly as international comrades. He was dressed in corduroy breeks with an open-neck plaid shirt. He had a Sam Browne belt slung over his shoulder and carried two heavy automatics, one on each hip. He also had two cartridge bandoleers slung crossways over his shoulders. There was a machine gun leaning against the back of a chair behind his desk.[26]

This flamboyance was part of the militia appeal, but the unorthodoxy of the militias was also apparent, especially in the CNT/FAI and POUM militias, with regard to the issue of discipline.

One of the most marked aspects of anarchist and socialist militia organisation was the belief discipline should be voluntary. This came as something as a shock to George Orwell: 'I had brought with me ordinary British Army ideas and was appalled by the lack of discipline'.[27] Orwell's experience with firearms and military organisation led him to be quickly voted in as a corporal, and he was then in a position where he had to try and get orders obeyed, 'a) by appealing to party loyalty and b) by force of personality, and for the first week or two I made myself thoroughly unpopular'.[28] For the anarchist and socialist militias, the issue was about trying to reconcile their strong ideological commitment to revolutionary principles with the practical need to have orders carried out. These two factors were not easily reconciled: 'it was generally agreed that in the Militia, discipline was a voluntary matter; decision and orders were the subject, as far as possible, to consultation and conference. Officers were regarded as delegates subject to control and recall'.[29] This was not the best approach when a militia unit was in action, although it worked better when, like the POUM militia unit that Orwell served with, they held static, frontline positions for a long time, but even then matters were only improved in Orwell's words, by 'endless arguments and explanations as to *why* such and such a thing was necessary'.[30] After his long period on the relatively static Aragon front, when the militia units were left unrelieved for up to five months, Orwell came to believe that the key to militia discipline lay in the political commitment of each individual. He put this argument in his inimical style, and in English and middle-class terms of reference:

> A man who has fully identified with some political party is reliable in *all* circumstances. One would get into trouble in left-wing circles for saying so, but the feeling of many Socialists towards their party [in Spain] is very similar to that of the thicker-headed type of public school man towards his old school.[31]

Eventually, the 'revolutionary discipline' became a major issue on the Republican side, and led to the demise of the militias which had dominated in the first six or seven months of the war. It was not just the ordinary demands of warfare that brought about the end of such voluntary discipline, but the also the political manoeuvring of the Communists as they grew ever-stronger in the Republic. The Communists used the issue of military and political discipline as a *casus belli* to provide cover for their policy of crushing their left-wing opponents and rivals.

The militias on both the Republican and Nationalists sides were organised in very similar fashions, especially in the early days and weeks after the start of the war. The Nationalists' militias were fairly quickly re-organised along army lines, but the left-wing militias kept their organisation for longer. As soon as the military rising in Barcelona was defeated, the militias established a Central Committee of Militias to act as a general headquarters with responsibility for recruiting, transport and supplies. The first meeting of the Central Committee of Militias agreed to organise a 12,000 strong Militia Column, led by the anarchist, Durruti, and advised by the loyalist army officer, Major Farras.[32] A militia column was the largest organisational unit, but there was no standard figure for the numbers of effectives in a column. However, sub-groups did have some degree of standardisation. In the Durruti Column, the smallest unit was a 'Group' of ten men, with one of the ten being elected as the Group's delegate. Ten groups made up a Century, with ten Group delegates and a Century delegate. Five Centuries made up an Assembly, with an additional Assembly delegate. All the various elected delegates formed the 'War Committee of the Assembly'. The POUM militia was organised in a similar way to the anarchists of the Durruti Column – 'the basic unit of men was the Section with around 30 militia, then the Century with a 100 militia, the Battalion with around 500 militia and the Column, which was usually over a thousand militia.[33]

When the initial fighting was over, it was clear that most of Spain's industrial assets were in the hands of the Republic. Catalonia was the most industrially developed area, and, in particular, Barcelona. The dominance of the anarchists in Barcelona enabled them to take advantage of the industrial strength of the region. The Anarchist Metallurgy Union of the CNT were able to provide the militia columns with makeshift armoured cars and lorries, using commercial chassis. Since the 1920s, there had been continued interest in building *protegido camion* (protected trucks) for internal security duties, and the militias continued this approach. The resulting armour was usually heavy, lacking in mobility, protected using non-amour steel or iron plate, and effectively confined to roads.[34] Daubed with revolutionary slogans, party symbols, and nick-names such as 'King Kong', these behemoths proved to be of little practical use.

More effective were armoured trains, which were almost exclusively fielded by the republic. Towards the end of 1936, a Railway Brigade was created, centred on Madrid, which brought together the Railway Militias, the Railway Shock Battalion, the armoured trains and the railway workshops.[35] The Republic used armoured trains on all fronts, taking advantage of its industrial capacity in the Basque country, Catalonia and Madrid. Many of these trains were heavily armoured and armed, and formed formidable units; for example, 'Armoured Train A' 'was designed by Engineer Lieutenant Colonel D. Ramón Valcárel, and comprised four wagons and a steam engine, all armoured, and armed with two 70mm guns, nine machine guns and eighty-nine rifles, considerable firepower for the period'.[36]

The militias were undoubtedly central to the defeat of the uprising in July 1936, and they also turned what was the defence of the republic into a revolution, especially in the areas where the anarchist, POUM, and socialist militias were dominant. However, their subsequent effectiveness was less clear. The initial successes of the left-wing militias in putting down ill-prepared attempts to support the military rising convinced many in the militias that they were more than a match for the army. The militias 'even in the smallest town, began to think of themselves as soldiers as well as street fighters, along-side the police, assault guards and civil guard or regular army'.[37] Right across republican Spain, the militias took control, and where they were faced by the likelihood of Nationalist attack, began preparations to defend their towns. In Madrid and Barcelona, the rapidly organised columns moved out of these two great centres of revolution to secure the republic in Aragon, and, to the north-west and south-west of Madrid, to Guadalajara and Toledo. These columns were largely made up of the party militias, but with an element of regular army loyalists, assault guards, and a few civil guards. They set off in high excitement, and it was that enthusiasm which the republican government hoped would carry the columns through the forthcoming fighting.

The Nationalists also needed militia support, but the rebels' trump card in the early week and months of the war was the 'Army of Africa' – the men of the Foreign Legion, and native Moroccan troops, the *Regulares*, officered by the most experienced, battle-hardened officers. The loss of most of the Spanish Navy to the Republic was an initial blow to the rebels, but the rapid agreement of Mussolini to send SM81 transport/bomber aircraft to Spanish Morocco in order to airlift the Army of Africa to Spain overcame this difficulty. The Nationalists then organised a column of around 8,000 men, under the field command of Yagüe, with Colonels Asensio, Delgado Serrano, Barrón, and Tella, along with Major Castejón, to advance from Seville deep into Republican territory. The training, experience, discipline, and ferocity of these soldiers was to show itself in the rapidity of their advance, and the limited capacity of the Republican militias to resist:

> Each of these officers commanded a *bandera* of the Legion and a *tabor* [225 men] of *Regulares*, with one or two batteries [of field guns]. The whole force [of 8,000] travelled in detachments of a hundred strong, in lorries commandeered in Seville by Quiepo de Llano, driven fast up the centre of the road … . On arrival at a town, the lorries would halt, artillery and aircraft would bombard it for half an hour. The legionaries and Moroccans would then advance. If there was resistance, a regular assault would be made. The militiamen might fight bravely while their ammunition lasted, and thereafter panic, with no discipline to prevent a rout: no one told them to spread out to defend a village. Afterwards, bodies of those killed in the revolutionary atrocities would be found, and, in reprisal, the leaders of the left-wing parties who had remained would be hunted out and shot … . Few prisoners would be made. The brutality of the Legion and the Moroccans was unexpected.[38]

In this brutally effective fashion, the Nationalist column advanced over 200 miles in under a week until it reached Mérida, on the Guadiana River, on 11 August 1936. Part of the column, some 3,000 men under Yagüe, advanced west to Badajoz on the Portuguese frontier, where one of the worst wartime massacres by the Nationalists took place. The remaining force was split, with one part heading north-west to meet up with other Nationalists, and a small force under Colonel Tella being tasked with taking Mérida. The militia defending Mérida had been reinforced from Madrid by 2,000 *Asaltos* and civil guards. These additional forces made the crucial difference, adding discipline and formal training to the enthusiasm of the militias. For the first time, the advancing Nationalists faced an enemy that took the offensive, with militia, Asaltos and civil guards emerging from the town to attack the advancing troops of the Nationalist column. Despite being outnumbered, Tella's men held the attack, allowing the other Nationalist columns to complete their missions.

The militias, which had proved themselves so effective in crushing the rising by isolated and ill-coordinated garrisons, found themselves at a serious disadvantage when it came to fighting the highly disciplined, trained and battle-experienced professionals of the Army of Africa. Revolutionary enthusiasm and courage were not enough, and poor tactics, poor leadership, plus a lack of traditional military discipline, all combined to undermine the militias' efforts. In addition, the militias proved incapable of mounting and sustaining successful offensives. On the Aragon front, the militia was unable to take Huesca in February 1937, and, similarly, the ambitious amphibious attempt to take Majorca, in which Richard Kisch was wounded, also collapsed. Nonetheless, the stubborn resistance of the militias faced by Yagüe's men bought time for the Madrid government to re-organise their forces, and obtain military supplies from the Soviets (in exchange for Spain's gold reserves), and, to a lesser degree from France.

Supporting the rising

For the rebel Army officers, once their coup attempt had failed, they realised that they were in a war situation. Like the Republic, the rebel Nationalists had to rely, especially in the early months of the war, on militias. For the Nationalists, the two main sources of militia were the Carlists, and the Falange. Harold Cardozo, the special correspondent of the *Daily Mail*, reported from the Nationalist lines in the civil war, publishing his pro-Franco account of the early part of the war in 1937. He was with the Nationalist Column that advanced from Seville, and made this observation about the militias which accompanied the Army of Africa:

> A word must be said as regards the speed with which volunteers flocked to the Nationalist side. At the outset undoubtedly it was the marvellously efficient help brought by the Carlist organisation in Navarre which counted most. Ultimately the Falangist militia, which provided some excellent fighting units, became the larger, but the strength during the first critical days lay with that splendid body of troops, the Navarre Brigades of Requetes, and they continued to show their mettle throughout the war.[39]

If the Republican government's immediate problem was the lack of high quality, trained and disciplined troops, the Nationalists' problem was the need for more men, which was where the right-wing militias came into play. By the end of 1936, the Nationalist army had around 200,000 men, over half of whom were militiamen from the Falange or the Carlists.[40] The latter represented strongly traditionalist, Catholic, monarchist supporters for the Carlist succession in

Spain. The movement had fought three bloody wars in the nineteenth century, and was an important political force in Navarre, in particular. Within a few months of the outbreak of the civil war, the Carlists were able to put 60,000 of their militia, the *Requetés*, into the field:

> At least half of them [the requetés] came from Navarre, which led to the Carlist claim that "Navarre had saved Spain". This arrogance, combined with open contempt for the Castilian Church, which they thought corrupt and pharisaical, did not make them popular with their allies. The famed discipline of the requetés derived, not from strong respect for hierarchy, but from the self-discipline of the hill farmer … . Their medieval crusading faith made them fearless. Colonel Rada described his requetés as men 'with faith in victory, with faith in God; one hand holding a grenade, the other a rosary.'[41]

The Carlists had maintained their tradition of para-military training, and proved an effective addition to the regular Army from the outset. The *requetés* were renowned for their high morale and their particular military style: 'dashing with their scarlet *boinas*, or berets, rather like the tam-o'-shanter but without the tassel, worn hanging down over the right ear, their khaki shirts, wide open on the chest, their buff equipment, and their white socks rolled round the ankle over their *esparagatas*, or cord-soled shoes'.[42]

Unlike the Carlists, the Falange started the war widely scattered, with many of their activists isolated in Republican areas, or, indeed, already languishing in government prisons, like the movement's leader, José Antonio. The first few days of fighting, executions, and murder took a heavy toll on the original, pre-war, membership of the Falange – the *camisas viejas* (the 'old shirts'). The leadership element of the movement suffered particularly badly, not only was José Antonio a prisoner, as were Ruiz de Alda and Fernández Cuesta, along with 2,000 rank-and-file Falangists, but Onésimo Redondo was killed on 24 July, while the chief of the Falange's militia, Luis Aguilar, was killed in Madrid. The result was that during the first weeks of the war, the Falange lacked any form of national leadership, and 'it would be difficult to exaggerate the lack of direction and organisation in the various Falange [militia] units … . Everything was done on a local basis. *Centurias* were recruited and equipped by the provincial and regional leaderships'.[43] But, in military terms, a least, the Falange had one advantage in that it was the militia of choice for Spaniards who did not share the ultra-conservative, monarchist beliefs of the Carlists. As a result, the surviving *camisas viejas* found themselves inundated with volunteers for the Falange's militia, with, for example, 2,000 volunteers coming forward for the militia in Zaragoza in one 24-hour period.[44] By the end of 1936, the Falange would boast nearly one million members.[45] The ideological purity of the original Falangists was, overnight, diluted by the new members, whose main thought was to join the fight against the Republic and the 'Reds'. Neither did the *camisas viejas* have the time, nor the capacity to ensure the principles of national syndicalism were fully absorbed by their new comrades.

By August 1936, the Falange had established two centres of power – Valladolid and Seville – but its militia was fighting on all fronts. In some areas, the Falange was the main military force for the Nationalists. The Falange had taken part in the rising in all areas of Spain, although the movement had no formal agreement, nor recognition, from the military plotters. As far as the army was concerned, the Falange's militia was simply one of the groups of civilian auxiliaries supporting the army's efforts. But, in fact, 'units of the Falange militia or the Carlist Requetés often occupied large sections of the still poorly defined front, while Army leaders searched desperately for new manpower'.[45] As with the left-wing militias, the Falangist militias not only fought at the front, but carried out the usual Spanish Civil War practice of executions, murder and generalised brutality, all under the euphemism of *limpieza*, the 'cleaning up'.[46] Nonetheless, in the first weeks of the war, the Falangist militia, like the Carlists, and their enemies on the Republican side, played a vital role in taking, and holding towns, villages, and key geographic features. For example, the initial stages of the Battle of Guadarrama (also known as Battle of Somosierra) on 24 July 1936, was carried out by Falangist and Carlist militiamen, who attempted to seize the heights on the road to Madrid. A first, the militia were successful, but the advance ground to a halt as left-wing militia, *Asaltos*, Civil Guard and loyalist soldiers were sent to the front from the capital. This was the first real battle of the war, and it was fought with 'extraordinary ferocity'.[47] Shortly afterwards, Harold Cardozo met up with Falangist and Carlist militiamen who had been the first in the field at the battle, some of whom had escaped from Madrid before making their stand:

> The leader of the little group of feverish-eyed survivors who sat around me in their tattered blue uniforms – mechanics' overalls – [said] 'Only ten of us had rifles,' he told me, 'and the rest were armed

with automatic pistols or hand grenades which we made ourselves with dynamite we took from a marble quarry. We started from Madrid a hundred strong. Last night we still held the pass but we were only twenty in number. Our chief, Captain Carlos Miralles, the famous Royalist leader, was killed in the last onslaught and with no cartridges left we had to evacuate our position, carrying the body of our leader with us'.[48]

This description of under-equipped militiamen fighting a die-hard battle, could stand for much militia experience, on both sides, in the early months of the war. The militias ensured the failure of the military rising, but they had also helped create the environment for that rising to happen, and ensured that the rising turned into a full-scale war. And, if one action more than any other in the first three months of the war guaranteed that the war would be long as well as vicious, it was one in which the militia played a central role – the siege of the Alcázar.

The siege of the Alcázar, 21 July–27 September 1936[49]

The siege, and relief, of the Alcázar was one of the key events in the months following the rising. The long-drawn out siege became a focal point of international press interest in those months, and provided the Nationalists with a highly symbolic victory. The siege was conducted by a variety of militias from Madrid, and militiamen were also significant in the defence of the great military academy in the city of Toledo. The besieging forces mishandled the operation, providing the anti-militia critics in the Republic with further arguments to demand their replacement by a regular Republican army. But, ironically, that failure, and the undoubted tenacity and courage of the defenders, prevented the Nationalists from taking Madrid in 1936, thereby ensuring that the war would become a war of attrition and regular armies, not militias.

Toledo is an ancient city, situated about forty-five miles to the south-west of Madrid. It is dominated by the city's cathedral and the massive, largely sixteenth-century palace of the Alcázar. The city was famous for its armaments, military and religious heritage, although, by 1936, these, like the city itself, were of far less importance than they had once been. The Alcázar was still one of the Spanish Army's most prestigious military academies, less for the training it provided and more for what it represented – the historical glory of Spanish arms. It was both an important symbol and a formidable complex of buildings:

> Standing upon the highest of Toledo's seven hills, the Alcázar's rectangular granite bulk dwarfs the rest of the town. Tiny windows penetrate the grey walls, which in some places are twelve feet thick. At each of the four corners is a square tower, crowned by a pyramidal steeple pierced by a tall, lance-sharp spire. The four walls form a large courtyard bordered by two levels of arcades.[50]

In the summer of 1936, almost all the Army cadets from the Alcázar were on leave, and the commandant of the academy, Colonel José Moscardó, a 60-year-old regular army officer, devout Catholic, keen footballer, and director of the army's school of physical education, was preparing to accompany the Spanish Olympics team to Berlin, as Spanish commissioner for the games. Moscardó knew nothing of the planned military rising, and when reports of events in Morocco began to reach Spain, he drove to Madrid to try and find out what was happening. Once he realised that the rising had taken place, but that Madrid had not immediately been taken by the rebels, Moscardó contacted Captain Emilio Vela Hidalgo, a cavalry instructor at the Alcázar who was on leave in the capital, telling him to find as many cadets as possible and return to the Alcázar. Moscardó then returned there himself, fearful that the arms factory in Toledo would be seized by left-wing workers.

In the first few, uncertain days, Moscardó took some vital steps that would ensure the success of his command over the following months. He concentrated on getting as many men, and as much ammunition as possible into the Alcázar, with the intention of holding the barracks until the Nationalist columns from Seville or Salamanca could join up with him. Moscardó believed this would happen within a few days, or a week. In addition to those instructors, the handful of cadets, and various supernumerary officers and men in the Alcázar, the local Civil Guard commander, Colonel Romero, called in the widely scattered men of his provincial command. Captain Vela returned from Madrid, but with only six cadets. But if Vela had not been able to find many of the cadets, he had another source of manpower in his gift.

As well as being a cavalry officer with an active interest in the modernisation of the army through mechanisation and armoured warfare, Vela was a member of the Falange. Army officers were not over enthusiastic about the Falange, with its hostility to the monarchy, its insistence on a modernising revolution, and its similarities with non-Spanish political movements. However, Falangists in the military tended to be young, junior officers, like Vela, as one historian of the siege of the

Alcázar put it, 'just as Moscardó reflected the conservatism of Old Spain, so Vela embodied the aspirations of New Spain'.[51] Vela met up with local Falangist leaders and convinced them that they would have to take temporary refuge in the Alcázar as the rebels were in no position to seize and hold Toledo once the Republican government realised that the barracks was in the hands of the Nationalists. There was one initial problem, and that was that Moscardó was none too keen on allowing the Falangists into his command, even though he needed as many fighters as possible to defend it. Vela presented the Falangists to Moscardó as a fait accompli, and after some face-saving on the Colonel's part, the blue shirted militia were absorbed into the garrison, along with the Civil Guards, some monarchists, and middle-class refugees including 555 women and children. The Falangist militia would, under Captain Vela, play an aggressive and notable role during the siege. One group which refused, fatally, to seek refuge in the Alcázar were Toledo's priests. By the time that Captain Vela read out the rebels' proclamation of war against the government in Madrid, at 7.00am on 21 July, there were 1,205 fighters in the barracks. This number included 690 Civil Guard, twenty-five *Asaltos*, and 106 Falangist and monarchists, in addition to various army officers and men. Between them, they had 1,400 rifles, twenty-two old machine guns, sixteen sub-machine guns, four 50mm mortars (with 200 mortar bombs) and two 70mm mountain guns (with fifty shells), plus hundreds of thousands of rounds of rifle ammunition taken from the Toledo armoury in the face of advancing Republicans.

After some confused negotiating by telephone with Moscardó, who successfully managed not to immediately give his game away, the Madrid government sent a Republican column, led by the loyalist, General Manuel Riquelme, to Toledo. The general was tasked with securing the arms factory, and seizing the Alcázar. From the very outset, Riquelme was faced by the difficulty that he, a regular army officer, had in trying to control the larger part of his command, which was composed of wildly enthusiastic, ill-disciplined militias who fundamentally distrusted the army. As the column of around 3,000 fighters, with artillery and armoured cars, reached Toledo, Riquelme sent his regulars to seize the armoury, and ordered the militias to wait until a reconnaissance had been made of the Nationalists' positions. This order was ignored, and militia, led by anarchists, rushed into the city:

> Just past the bull ring the militia walked into the sights of the Civil
> Guard at the hospital. Window glass popped from the cupola as
> [Major] Villalba's machine guns sprayed the road and the Guards

delivered point-blank rifle fire. At first the militia were too startled to run, then they bolted for protection behind walls and houses beside the highway.[52]

The militia were saved by the intervention of one of the armoured cars, and fire from a 75mm field gun, but the diversion enabled the Nationalists to evacuate the armoury, taking the last of 700,000 rounds of ammunition with them into the Alcázar.

The siege of the Alcázar then settled into a pattern, involving endless sniping, particularly by Republican militia, air raids by Republican bombers, shelling, and attacks on the defenders' positions, particularly the *Gobierno Militar*, an administration building standing below the Alcázar, blocking the way to the to the palace itself. This would be the focus of fierce fighting for most of the siege. But prior to the siege settling into this pattern, the left-wing militias began their occupation of Toledo by hunting down 'fascists', and killing priests and clerics. Militia gangs with names like 'Exterminating Battalion' and 'Vengeance Group' were responsible for murdering 107 priests, along with other clerics. Although Toledo's cathedral was saved by being put under guard, many more churches were burnt by the militias. Modelling themselves on the Bolsheviks, a *cheka* of anarchist and socialist militia was set up, under the command of a local lawyer, Candido Cabello. This group was responsible for arrests, torture, and executions, all in the guise of being a security unit. The killings and atrocities, were, as was the usual pattern, reciprocated by the Nationalists once the siege was lifted.

The siege became a bizarre attraction for Madrid-based militias and sightseers. Militia flooded into Toledo to take part, some doing so at weekends as a sort of militarised 'day trip'. The constant turnover of militia taking part in the action made Riquelme's task even more difficult. Under pressure from Madrid to finish the siege as quickly as possible, Riquelme not only had to defeat the Nationalist defenders, but also had to struggle with the assortment of militias under his nominal command. Even the most basic of tasks, such as establishing how many Republicans were in that command (there were probably around 7,000) was problematic. The reality was that Riquelme and the loyalist officers had no authority over the anarchist, socialist, or communist militias:

On paper, General Riquelme commanded the Republican forces in Toledo, but in actual fact he could do nothing without the co-operation of individual militia leaders, who, in turn, could do nothing without the consent of the men they represented. "Orders" arriving from the Ministry of War [in Madrid] were, in the province of Toledo, little more than recommendations, and the result was military incompetence and general confusion.[53]

Riquelme was eventually forced to operate almost entirely through another army officer, Major Luis Barceló, who had already proved his total commitment to the Republican cause in Madrid, where he had overseen the execution of Nationalist officers. By sheer force of personality, and the operation of his own group of *cheka*, Barceló brought the leaders of the differing militias together in a 'Militia Defence Committee of Toledo'. Barceló's power grew to the extent that General Riquelme needed the major's permission even to be in Toledo.

Despite Riquelme's difficulties, his command did receive support from Madrid. His 75mm artillery were reinforced by 105mm guns, then by 155mm pieces. Air attacks were sporadic, but with Republican bombers flying from Getafe air base, ten miles south of Madrid, was close enough to Toledo to enable the bombers to fly several missions a day when in action. The continued resistance of the defenders became an embarrassment for the Republican government, and a major propaganda coup for the Nationalists, whose columns were still fighting their way towards Madrid. The need to finish the siege intensified the efforts of the attackers. Several attempts were made to burn the defenders out of their positions using petrol sprayed onto the walls of the Gobierno. Two old Schneider CA1 tanks were brought in to provide additional assault capacity, but there was little progress.

The defenders of the Alcázar had little information as to the progress of the Nationalist columns which they expected would lift the siege. The Nationalist air force managed to drop small amounts of supplies to them, along with messages of hope, but the defenders faced increasing food and water difficulties. The horses in the barracks were gradually slaughtered, wheat which was found in Toledo was brought back to the Alcázar and crudely ground, while water was heavily rationed. Fatigue, shelling, assaults, bombing, all took their toll on the defenders. Although the majority of the defending fighters were Civil Guards and regular army, the Falangist militia played a part in the defence of the Alcázar that was out of proportion to their numbers.

The head of the Falange in Toledo was 21-year-old Pedro Villaescusa Bonilla, a member of the Falange's student movement. It was Villaescusa that Captain

Vela had convinced that retiring into the Alcázar was the best option once it became clear that the military rising had failed. Villaescusa and his Falangists formed, under the command of Vela, a shock unit that was repeatedly involved in raids on the besiegers' lines. On 4 September, the Republicans managed to dislodge the Nationalists from the Gobierno, when they succeeded in setting fire to the building. The defenders were forced out, but the Republican militias could not occupy this key feature until the fire died down. The danger to the defence was clear, for if the Gobierno was taken, then the way would be open for a direct assault on the Alcázar itself. By the evening of the following day, the fire had burnt itself out, and a sudden sortie by Vela's Falangists and other troops successfully forced out the Republican militia. One of the heroes of the counter-attack was the Falangist militiaman, Maximiliano Fink, who was mentioned in dispatches for his actions. Fink and his comrades continued to see themselves as crack assault troops, perhaps in an attempt to show the military and Civil Guard that they were not just enthusiastic amateurs. Despite an order from Colonel Moscardó that no further raids were to be mounted, the Falangists continued to attempt raids on the Republican lines. In one of these, on 7 September, Fink was killed. Another Falangist attempted to recover Fink's body which lay in clear sight of the Republican militias, but he, too, was killed. The bodies became a focus of the vicious war being waged between the politically committed on both sides:

> Since a Falangist – even a dead one – was a trophy for the [Republican] militia, they made several attempts to recover the corpse. An intrepid Anarchist managed to grab [a] rope and drag Fink a few feet before he, too, was shot dead. For the rest of the day a savage vendetta raged in the Plaza de Capuchinos. Republicans abandoned their barricades in other sectors to join in the fun along the south wall, alternately try-ing to lasso the body and shooting bullets into it. Inside the building the Falangists were livid. Moscardó finally had to dispatch Captain Vela and other officers to the south door to prevent them making a sortie *en masse*.[54]

The body was recovered by the Falangists during the night, and buried by them with the usual Falangist shout of 'Present!' when Fink's name was called. Fink was not the only *fanático* in the Falangist militia, and, in a desperate, suicidal attack toward the end of the siege, his chief, Pedro Villaescusa, was also killed, by a grenade.[55] Captain Vela survived the siege, and then formed a Falangist assault unit, '*El Alcázar*', with which he was killed in action in the fighting at the University campus in Madrid on 23 December 1936.[56]

Increasingly desperate to end the siege, the Madrid government sent miners from the Asturias to mine the towers and walls of the Alcázar. The distance from the Republican front lines to the walls and towers of the Alcázar was, in places, less than a hundred yards. A cat and mouse game ensued once the defenders realised that mining was taking place, but the Nationalists were unable to discover the head of the mines, and during the first three weeks of September, three of the four great towers were brought down, along with major sections of the walls. The Republicans used their artillery to widen the breeches caused by the mines, and assaults were made, but the defenders still held on, fighting in the ruins of the Alcázar.

By 21 September, the defenders were in a desperate situation. Of the four great towers of the Alcázar, only the south-eastern one remained and it was battered and near collapse. The Republican artillery was pounding the ruins with up to 300 shells a day, and Moscardó was forced to move his office into the cellars. The exhausted, starving Nationalists did not know, furthermore, that the Army of Africa was only twenty-four miles away, at the village of Maqueda, the last real Republican defensive position before Franco's main objective, Madrid. Now Franco was faced with a choice. Should he break through and seize the capital, thereby ending, or greatly shortening the war, or should he relieve the garrison of the Alcázar? Franco's staff, and those military men he trusted, like Yagüe and Colonel Kindelán, the head of the Nationalist air force, recommended pushing on to Madrid, and leaving the defenders of the Alcázar to their fate. But Franco was aware that the world's eyes were on the siege, that, for Spaniards symbolism was of great importance, and, finally, that it was 'easy to imagine the obloquy in which he would have been held had he left Moscardó to his death'.[57] Further, it may well have been that Franco saw advantage in drawing out the war, making it a war of attrition, a war that would enable him to grind the Republicans down, eliminating the Nationalists' ideological enemies by war, repression, and extermination. Certainly, Franco's German advisors would repeatedly chafe at the General's slow military campaigns, and recommend in vain that newer, blitzkrieg style tactics should be used. Whatever the combination of reasons, Franco ordered the relief of the Alcázar, and on 23 September two Nationalist columns struck out for Toledo.

The Republican militias brought the final tower down on 27 September, with a ton of dynamite, followed up by an all-out militia assault by 'a mass of desperate, determined men; the weak-hearted had deserted many days before, when the Army of Africa neared the city'.[58] But their assault failed, as the defenders fought back from mounds of rubble that had turned the Alcázar into a confusion of one defensive position after another. It was the last effort by the Republican militias, who were now faced with the Nationalist columns. Little attempt was made to defend Toledo, and on the morning of 27 September, first Moors followed a few minutes later by Legionaries, made contact with the defenders of the Alcázar. Apart from the bloody mopping up process, and the revenge killings, the siege of the Alcázar had been lifted.

The siege of the Alcázar marked the high point of the Republican militias' operations. Their failure to break the defenders of the Alcázar provided those hostile to the idea of revolutionary militias with extra ammunition in their campaign to create a regular army to fight the Republican's corner. However, the great irony was that the very failure of the Republican militias to subdue the Nationalist defenders in the Alcázar, probably saved Madrid in 1936. It was not a forgone conclusion that the advancing Nationalist columns of the Army of Africa and its Falangist and Carlist militia auxiliaries would turn aside from Madrid in order to relieve the heroes of the Alcázar, but as soon as Franco made that choice he gave the Republic a vital breathing space. In the time the Republic gained, it was able to take delivery of new equipment from the Soviet Union, of tanks, artillery, and, crucially, the latest Soviet fighter aircraft that gave the Republic superiority over its capital during the winter of 1936/37. The defence of Madrid in 1936 meant that the capital did not fall to Franco's men until the end of the war, and that was, in part, due to the failure of the left-wing militias to take the Alcázar from the army, Civil Guard, Falangist and monarchist militia defenders of the palace.

The end of the militias

By the end of 1936, the writing was on the wall for the militias in both Nationalist and Republican Spain. In both zones, the highly ideological militias would, by the summer of 1937, be almost fully subsumed into the regular armies of Nationalist and Republican Spain. That process was far more painful on the Republican side, and was characterised by the vicious, violent repression of non-Communist militias. On the Nationalist side, there was less in the way of repression, but the outcome was the same, with the Falangist and Carlist militiamen incorporated into a new political as well as military structures

In the Republican zone, the central issue that divided the various factions was the degree to which the revolution should be maintained. The anarchists, and the POUM were of the view that maintaining the revolution, which they had won by force of arms in the aftermath of the military coup, was of equal importance to the need to win the war against the Nationalists. Indeed, the anarchists and the POUM argued that victory over the Nationalists depended on the extension of the revolution. By contrast, the communists, and the socialist government under Juan Negrín, who became prime minister in May 1937, argued that winning the war had total precedence. This policy stance, of course, acted as a cover for the deeper ideological rivalry and hatred that existed between the left-wing parties and movements. But the communists, and their socialist allies, had one great advantage in that the greatest source of the Republic's weaponry came from Stalin's Soviet Union. In October 1936, Negrín, then finance minister, had ordered the transfer of all of Spain's remaining gold reserves, some $500 million in 1936 prices, to the Soviet Union. This bought the Republic the latest Soviet arms and aircraft, and it gave the Spanish communists a crucial advantage in the Republican power struggle. The communists grew rapidly, aided by Soviet support, the support of the international communist movement, and their own dedication to a ruthless 'revolutionary discipline'. They were able, therefore, to turn on their enemies in the POUM, and in the anarchist movement.

The anarchist movement of the CNT/FAI was, as a result of its size, too big a movement for the communists to destroy by terror or violence. Instead, the communists used the undoubted need for a more disciplined defence of the Republic to effectively disband the anarchist militias. In this, the communists were supported by most of the Republican government, and many moderates in the Republican camp. The argument against the anarchist militias was a strong one, but, as the Catalan anarchist, and historian of anarchism in the civil war, José Peirats, explained, the argument had more than one level to it:

> To face the enemy army required an army. An army is a very serious thing. It has to be disciplined, under command of officers, militarily prepared, obedient to the voice of a strong government, centralized and representative of all the anti-fascist forces. This argument, unquestionably supported by events, was aimed towards one end that could not be waived: the disarming of the people.[59]

But despite a declaration by the CNT on the issue of militias and a regular army that the anarchists 'cannot support the existence of a regular army, uniformed and conscripted',[60] the Republican government went ahead with the creation of such an army. By December 1936, the reorganisation of the various militias and the army was well underway. The government incorporated militia units into 'Mixed Battalions' and 'Mixed Brigades' along with existing and new units from the army. Newly trained officers along with several thousand reserve or retired officers who were recalled to service, made up the officer corps of the Republican Army. Many anarchist militiamen avoided this process, while others found themselves in mixed units that, they believed, received little in the way of equipment.

If the anarchists' dream of a people's militia was effectively dead by the spring of 1937, the fate of the much smaller POUM was far worse. As anti-Stalinist communists, the POUM were primary targets for the strengthened communist movement. Not only did Spanish communists see the POUM as their enemies, but the Spanish Communist Party was also under Moscow's instructions to destroy the POUM, which Moscow regarded (inaccurately) as Trotskyist and fascist. The communists were supported in their endeavours by the Negrín government, and the campaign against the POUM reached a climax in the spring of 1937. The POUM's militia were overwhelmed in Barcelona, and many of its leaders were imprisoned, tortured, and executed. Andrés Nin was arrested and tortured by Soviet 'experts' who reduced him to a maimed, bleeding pulp, before he was executed. Those foreigners who were serving with the POUM went underground, escaped to friendly embassies, or were caught by the communists and the Republican security forces. It was the end for independent, left-wing militias in the Republic.

In Nationalist Spain, Franco became *Generalísimo* of the Nationalist army and *Jefe del Estado* (Chief of State) on 1 October, 1936, as, following the death of General José Sanjurjo in an air crash on 20 July 1936, Franco held the strongest position among the rebel generals. In part, the Franco's political strength came from the fact that he was not associated with any one particular faction on the Nationalist side. He was able to exploit that 'neutrality', his standing in the army, Hitler's support for him, and his dual military and political role, to carry out the political unification of the various militias, and their absorption into the regular army. His opponents were to be found in the leadership of the Carlists and the Falangists. Both movements realised that Franco was intent on taking control of them, and subsuming them into a Franco-ist movement which would be shorn of the key policy demands of the Carlists and the Falange. Such a move would also drive a Franco-ist wedge between the militias of the two movements and their political leadership. But both movements were in a weaker position than they would have liked. The first few weeks of the civil war had seen the Falange's national leadership all but wiped out. The movement's charismatic leader, José Antonio, languished in a Republican jail and was be executed by the Republic on 20 November 1936. Many in the Falange refused to believe he was dead, and his successor Manuel Hedilla, a former shipyard mechanic, one of the original 'old shirt' founders of the Falange, and an enthusiast for José Antonio's brand of national syndicalism, struggled to fill his place. Further, Hedilla failed to fully appreciate the role of the Falangist militia in any attempt to make the Falange the leading political movement in Nationalist Spain.[61] In fact, the Falangist militia was bereft of any really effective leadership following the death of its national leader and his replacement by an ineffectual street-fighter. The Carlists, by contrast, had a good militia chief in the person of José Luis Zamanillo, who supported Hedilla in an attempt to protect both the Carlist requetés and the Falangist militia.

The exigencies of war, the strength of Franco's position, the fact that the Falange's 'old shirts' were either dead or swamped by thousands of new members who cared little for the details of José Antonio's political theories, meant that Hedilla and his associates were unable to preserve their movement as an independent force. Similarly, the Carlists' political leader, Fal Conde, attempted to build new bases of Carlist influence, including a military college for militia officers (something the Falange tried too). But none of these moves were successful. In December, Franco summoned Fal Conde and offered him the choice of exile in Portugal or execution; the Carlist leader chose exile. Hedilla, meanwhile, became more isolated, although benefiting from greater protection from Franco thank to his links with various Italian and German factions. But Franco was determined to enforce his will. The first moves were made on 22 December 1936, when the Nationalist Army General Headquarters issued an order that unified all civilian militias. In fact, at that stage, 'this was largely a paper unification ... the problems at military headquarters were too numerous to allow constant attention to the militia'.[62] But in that order, Franco and the Army had signalled the future for the militias.

The in-fighting in the Falange came to a head on 16 April 1937, and it looked for a few days as if Hedilla and his old guard had won out. But Franco outmaneuvered them by announcing, on 18 April, that all political parties in Nationalist Spain were being unified under the unlikely title of *Falange Española de las Juntas de Ofensiva Nacional Sindicalista (FE de las JONS) y la Comunión Tradicionalista*, subsequently more usually known as FET. Within a week, Hedilla was under arrest, and under a death sentence. This was not carried out, but the political independence of the various groups had come to an end: from then on, Franco-ism was paramount. As for the Falange's militia, the Army had already begun the process of siphoning off the best recruits for itself, leaving the militia with less able, less capable men who increasingly performed second-line duties, took part in repression, and developed a reputation for being less than effective as a fighting force. Nonetheless, the Falange did, at least until the end of 1942, have some influence, providing important elements of the social and economic policies of Franco's Spain. In military terms, the Falange's strength lay in the popularity of Falangism among junior officers in the Spanish military, particularly among the *alféreces provisionales* (temporary junior officers). It was these men who flocked to the colours again, in June 1941, when Franco agreed to the formation of a Spanish 'Blue Division' to fight alongside the Germans on the Eastern Front. That Spanish contribution, of some 45,000 men, represented, among other things, the last hurrah of the militia heritage of Nationalist Spain.[63]

Chapter 7

Cuba 1960–61: Defending the Revolution – From the Escambray Mountains to the Bay of Pigs

Making and consolidating Fidel Castro's Cuban revolution

In January 1934, a Cuban Army coup, backed by the USA, put Sergeant Fulgencio Batista into power in Cuba. Although the country had elections and a number of Presidents over the next six years, power resided in the hands of Batista and the Army. Batista was elected President of Cuba in 1940, introducing a new, liberal, constitution and ruling for four years before 'retiring' to Florida. But Batista returned to Cuban politics, leading a coup in 1952 and reinstituting a draconian, repressive regime, marked by the use of torture and the execution of hundreds of opponents. However, opposition from numerous groups continued to grow, with one of those groups being led by Fidel Castro, a lawyer and the son of one of Cuba's biggest landowners. Castro led a failed attack by 164 rebels on the Cuban Army's Moncada and Carlos Manuel de Céspedes barracks on 26 July 1953. The rebels were captured, with sixty-five of them subsequently being killed, while Fidel and his brother Raúl were fortunate enough to be jailed, before being released into exile two years later. In exile in Mexico, Castro formed the *Movimiento 26 de Julio* (the 26 July Movement) as his new anti-Batista movement. The new movement drew on supporters from a wide range of backgrounds and ideologies, and at this stage of the revolution-to-be, it was 'an alliance more than a party',[1] and a loose alliance at that. That characteristic of Castro's movement was to have important consequences. Not only did it allow communists like the Argentinian doctor Ernesto 'Che' Guevara, and Castro's brother, Raúl, to become central figures in Fidel Castro's revolution, but it would give an opening, once Batista was ousted, to the small, but disciplined and highly organised Communist Party of Cuba.

Castro's second attempt at overthrowing the Batista regime began with a disastrous landing of eighty-two fighters from the 26 July Movement from a leaky yacht, *Grandma*, on 2 December 1956. Ambushed by the Cuban Army, only seventeen men escaped to start guerrilla operations. From this inauspicious beginning, Castro took full advantage of the widespread hatred of the Batista regime, and used his own undoubted skills in both guerrilla war and, perhaps more importantly, in propaganda and publicity, to build his revolution. Within a year, the 26 July Movement was fighting in three separate areas of Cuba. Furthermore, it was clear that the Cuban Army had no real stomach for the fight, with, for example, a Cuban Marine commander joining the Movement in July 1958, along with men and equipment. By the end of that year, the guerrillas launched an offensive that led to Batista fleeing Cuba, followed, on 8 January 1959, by Castro's triumphant entry into Havana.

Consolidating the revolution

The defeat of Batista marked the end of one era for Cuba, and the beginning of a new era, the precise outline of which was far from clear. Castro's movement had won a guerrilla and political war, but now the anti-Batista alliance that was the 26 July Movement had to win its peace, and consolidate, then define its revolution. The constant was the personality of Castro himself. Although it was, at first, far from clear just what Castro was proposing for Cuba, the figure of Castro dominated. From the outset, it was this which worried US politicians and planners most. Following his meeting with Castro in April 1959, the US Vice-President, Richard Nixon, reported that:

> The one fact we can be sure of is that Fidel Castro has those indefinable qualities which make him a leader of men. Whatever we may think of him, he is going to be a great factor in the development of Cuba and very possibly in Latin American affairs generally.[2]

This was a highly perspicacious remark by Nixon, although it is less well-known than his other comment about Castro that the Cuban leader was 'either incredibly naïve about Communism or under Communist discipline'.[3] In fact, it is difficult to make any decision about just when Castro decided to follow a Communist route. His own pronouncements are of little help as he subsequently claimed that he had been a Marxist-Leninist from the outset. Yet there was evidence that at the beginning of his period in power he was a social reformer and a Cuban patriot, but also someone who was wary of Communist influence, despite 'formally declaring that he was a communist' on 16 January 1959.[4] In a similar vein, Castro did not immediately seek aid from the Soviet bloc, but, for example, bought weapons from Belgium, and in September 1959, approached the United Kingdom government with a request to buy seventeen of the RAF's latest fighter aircraft, the Hawker Hunter. This latter request was refused at the behest of the US government. But it was clear that Castro had the ability to exploit his own charismatic personality in a way that was reminiscent of Mussolini. Like the Italian *Duce*, Castro saw himself as the 'Maximum Leader'. Like Mussolini too, Castro had the ability to indulge in long public speeches which roamed back and forth between history, politics, and exhortations to patriotic struggle. Castro called his public speeches to huge crowds of supporters 'direct democracy', just as Mussolini had called his speeches 'dialogues'. Castro had one advantage over the *Duce*, however, in that Cuba's position as one of the wealthiest country in Latin America, and its closeness to the USA, meant that there were far more television sets per head of the Cuban population than in any other Latin American country, and Castro used this to extend his 'direct democracy', and 'through them Castro turned the country aflame'.[5]

If Castro was unclear about the future of his revolution, two of his closest allies were not. Che Guevara and Raúl Castro were Communists, and were central to military and para-military developments in 1959 that would enable the regime to survive internal opposition, CIA plotting, and invasion. Both men were of the opinion that the transition to a full Communist revolution was necessary, 'that only an extreme solution could be victorious: either a dictatorship of the proletariat or the ruin of the Revolution'.[6] That transition to a dictatorship was necessary not only because of opposition within Cuba, including from members of the 26 July Movement, but also from external threats from the USA. In addition to maintaining popular enthusiasm for the Castro government by continued continuing social and land reform, Che and Raúl Castro stressed the need for the reform and development of loyal military and security forces.

Learning lessons

Two events greatly influenced the creation of new, Castro-supporting, military and security forces. One was a coup, witnessed at first hand by Che Guevara, in Guatemala in 1954, the other was the 'Matos affair' in Cuba in October 1959. The 1954 Guatemala coup was central not only to the establishment of the Castro militia and the strengthening of the Cuban regime, but, for different reasons, was central to the CIA's decision to support an invasion of Cuba by exiles. The CIA and the USA learnt the wrong lesson from Guatemala, while the Castro regime took the correct lessons from the affair.

Guatemala's economy, like those of most Latin American countries, was dominated by US business interests. In Guatemala's case the United Fruit Company had extensive land holdings, and wielded significant economic and political influence. In the late 1940s, Guatemalan politics entered a reformist period, with successive governments attempting to institute land reform, undertake development projects to make Guatemala more competitive, and boost the living standards of its population. The victor in the 1950 presidential election was the former defence minister, Colonel Jacobo Árbenz, who sought to maintain the advances that had been made. His reformist government was faced by increasing opposition from large landowners and American business interests which lobbied strongly in Washington for action against Árbenz whom they portrayed as a communist. In the USA, President Eisenhower took office in 1953, after having campaigned on a strongly anti-Communist ticket. The CIA was keen to boost it status, extend its remit and role, and convince the US Administration that when it came to combatting Communism, it could achieve more than diplomacy or overt military action.

The CIA saw the opportunity to oust Árbenz as one that was both necessary and too good an opportunity to miss, for 'success in some low-profile endeavor against the only Communist-influenced state in the New World seemed valuable to the Agency in building up credit with the new administration'[7] in Washington. In Guatemala, the Árbenz government realised that they faced a serious threat from opponents and the US government. Unfortunately for Árbenz, the workers and peasants of Guatemala were, unlike those of Cuba, not the inheritors of a long history of rebellion. Further, although Árbenz was both an ex-army officer and former minister of defence, the officer corps of the Guatemalan Army was becoming increasingly alienated from the President. Aware that his government was unlikely to be able to rely on the army in a coup attempt, or armed rebellion, Árbenz attempted to create a loyal militia to counter the army and protect the government. But he acted too late. In fact, the establishment of the pro-government militia was seen by the Army's officer corps as being further evidence that Árbenz was firmly under the control of the handful of communists in his government. The CIA and the US administration responded by attempting to blockade Guatemala and prevent arms shipments to the country. The Guatemalan Army issued Árbenz with an ultimatum to sack the communists in his government, but 'the unyielding President replied that he would fight to the last man among his worker and peasant supporters'[8] in the militia. But that militia was still forming, had almost no training, little popular support, and few weapons. On 18 June 1954, a mere 200 CIA-backed rebels crossed the border from Honduras into Guatemala, advanced a few miles then halted. Meanwhile, a handful of CIA-flown aircraft attacked against no air opposition, while CIA radio stations began a massive propaganda bombardment of the country. Within a few weeks, the Árbenz government had collapsed through a lack of self-confidence, the ineffectual nature of its new militia, and the CIA's deployment of a small number of aircraft, a token ground force, and a propaganda offensive. It was a notable success for the CIA, but the ease with which it had engineered the overthrow of Árbenz not only made the Agency over-confident in its abilities, it also provided a stark, first-hand warning for Che Guevara. In a letter to his mother in Argentina, Guevara wrote of Árbenz, 'he did not consider that an armed people is invincible, despite the recent examples of Korea and Indochina. He could have armed the people but he chose not to, and this is the result'.[9] Che's analysis of the wars in Korea and Indochina might have been questionable, but he was, in all probability, more insightful when it came to the Guatemalan crisis, and, in future, the situation in Cuba in the aftermath of Castro's revolution. For Che, Guatemala strongly suggested 'the need for mobilizing a whole people against external attack as well as for the early purge of an inherited conservative officer corps while there was still time. In the future, Fidel Castro would prove to be his apt pupil.'[10] Interestingly, Che was also impressed by the effectiveness, and the psychological impact, of the small number of fighter-bombers the CIA deployed in their overthrow of Árbenz. All these Guatemalan lessons were well learnt by Che Guevara, and would be put into practice by the Castro regime.

In Cuba in October 1959, the Matos crisis accelerated military and security moves by the Castro government. Major Húber Matos was a well-known and popular fighter from the early days of the anti-Batista struggle and had been appointed by Castro to be Army Chief in Camaguey Province. Matos became increasingly concerned about the growth of influence of Communists in the Cuban government and he and most of his officers resigned in protest. His resignation resulted in his arrest, and a show trial were he was accused of conspiring against the revolution. The Matos trial was a clear sign that the Castro government was clearly embedded on the path to becoming a Communist regime, while for Castro and his circle, it conformed the need to establish a militia, while thoroughly purging the regular armed forces, not only of any remaining Batista era personnel, but also of 26 July Movement personnel who objected to Communism.

A militia to defend the revolution

The official founding of the Cuban National Revolutionary Militia (MNR) took place amid a climate of suspicion and fear of outside intervention, heightened by the first Cuban exile 'air raid' on Havana on the 21 October, when a B25 'Mitchell' bomber, flying from Florida, dropped thousands of anti-Castro leaflets on the city. Enthusiastic ground fire led to the deaths of two, with forty-five people being injured. 'Castro immediately went to the Havana television centre and 'banned all night flights to Cuba, suspended habeas corpus once more and announced a plan to gather a volunteer army of workers'.[11] The new MNR was to be recruited through factories, sugar and tobacco plantations, Communist Party organisations, and from student bodies. It was under the overall control of Raúl Castro as head of the Revolutionary Armed Forces (FAR), with two other loyalists, Major Sergio del Vale, and Captain Rogelio Acevedo, in operational command. In addition to the beginnings of the MNR, the Castro secret police, the 'G2', under one of Castro's original comrades, Ramiro Valdés, was expanded, and the regular army was purged further and began to receive ideological as well as military training. By December 1959, the Castro government had become a para-militarised regime clearly modelled on the 'People's democracies' of the Soviet bloc. On 17 December, Castro made another speech in which he predicted that in the new year Cubans would have to 'defend the Revolution with weapons in their hands [and…] that workers in bars, servants in private houses, should denounce to the police all remarks against the revolution; [and] all ordinary men should become soldiers of the Revolution'[12] in the MNR. To aid the police, the G2 and the regime in identifying 'counter-revolutionaries', the MNR was given a plain-clothes arm – the Committees for the Defence of the Revolution (CDR) – organised to provide informants in every street and work place in Cuba. The CDR would come to play not only a security role and a support for the MNR, but also engaged in regime propaganda efforts and formed 'a significant link between Fidel and the people'.[13]

By the beginning of 1960, therefore, the Castro regime had taken significant steps to establish, consolidate and protect what was increasingly a Communist state. A series of show trials took place in February, with 104 'counter-revolutionaries' sentenced, *habeas corpus* having been finally suspended two months earlier. The MNR was well on the way to having 150,000 militia men and women, who received eight hours training a week, and could be called up for full-time tours of duty. The commanding officer of the MNR in each province of Cuba was usually the head of the G2 in that province, and the militia was ready to defend the revolution.

Sabotage, infiltration, and the Escambray – the MNR wins its first battles

The Castro regime's development of its security and defence apparatus was not just to consolidate and embed the revolution. The militiamen and women of the MNR faced armed resistance throughout 1960, including threats from inside and outside the island, culminating in a major MNR operation during the winter of 1960-61. Despite its militia status, and despite US intelligence sources having a low opinion of the fighting capabilities of the MNR, the force grew in size and confidence and extended its role throughout its first year in existence. Its activities enabled the regime to gradually strangle internal armed resistance, something which pushed CIA planners towards a significant landing by Cuban exiles, as opposed to a strategy of supporting guerrilla activity, sabotage and propaganda. The very success of the MNR helped create the strategic conditions that led to the Bay of Pigs invasion.

The fall of Batista led immediately to many of those who had been clearly identified with the regime leaving for exile in the USA, other Latin American countries, or Spain. As it became clear that the Castro regime was increasingly influenced by Communists, so more Cubans headed for exile, including many who had fought against Batista. By the beginning of 1961, as many as 100,000 Cubans had gone into exile.[14] The exile communities provided the impetus for anti-Castro activities, and a recruiting ground for the CIA, which was keen to support covert activity against the regime. Guerrilla groups also formed inside Cuba, which the CIA wanted to supply with arms and equipment. Using Cuban exiles, the CIA trained infiltrators in resistance warfare techniques, and used Cuban air crews to drop men and supplies, or US and Cuban crews to infiltrate supplies and personnel by boat. All of this proved remarkably difficult, but was the CIA's first choice strategy when it came to undermining the new Cuban regime.

José 'Pepe' Regalado went into exile in Florida in April 1959, and joined one of the very first anti-Castro groups, the 'Anti-Communist Revolutionary Crusade'. He then went to Guatemala, where he and other early exiles were trained by the CIA in infiltration and guerrilla warfare techniques. He was part of one of the very first teams infiltrated into Cuba by the CIA. The team's role was to provide leadership and skills for an already existing resistance group which had little of either. Regalado's description of his team provides an account of the training the CIA could give to support the anti-Castro forces:

> We were told the first team to go into Cuba would be the one going to Matanzas. It included: team leader Jorge Rojas; telegraphy operator Jorge Gutérrez Izaguirre, who was nicknamed El Sheriff; Jorge Recarey in armaments; Antonio Abel Pérez Martín in psychological warfare and propaganda; and myself in intelligence. We left Key West aboard two boats: one was called the Wasp, and it was painted all black and was about thirty-four feet long. It was captained by Kikío Llansó. Also aboard was Rolando Martínez, the most courageous Cuban I have ever known. The other ship was commanded by Captain Villa, a Spaniard.[15]

It took four attempts to infiltrate this guerrilla cadre into Cuba by boat, something that was typical for both boat and air infiltration. The CIA had difficulties with acquiring enough boats of suitable size and endurance with reliable crews, and the Cuban MNR were increasingly to be found guarding likely landing spots, with small, machine-gun armed sections covering inlets and river mouths. Regalado's team eventually, after various mishaps, met up with the guerrilla band they had been sent to aid. It turned out to be made up of sixteen teenagers and young men in their early twenties, hiding out in a camp that was far from secure. Regalado taught them escape and evasion techniques, and then the CIA-trained men told the group that they had to disband 'and get out, because they were dead men there'.[16] The cadre then dispersed into the nearby town of Colón, two of the men taking a taxi there. The night time taxi ride was interesting in that it showed that anti-Castro saboteurs were at work: 'it seemed as if it was daytime from all the fires in the cane fields and factories, set ablaze by the saboteurs'.[17]

Despite the poor state of the guerrilla group that Regalado and his group disbanded, sabotage and terror attacks were frequent during this period.

US national intelligence attempted to monitor levels of sabotage, and provided a list of 'examples' for the period from October 1960 until April 1961:

1) Approximately 300,000 tons of sugar cane destroyed in 800 different fires.
2) Approximately 150 other fires, including the burning of 42 tobacco warehouses, two paper plants, 1 sugar refinery, two dairies, four stores, twenty-one Communist homes.
3) Approximately 110 bombings, including Communist Party offices, Havana power station, two stores, railroad terminal, bus terminal, militia barracks, railroad train.
4) Approximately 200 nuisance bombs in Havana Province.
5) Derailment of six trains, destruction of microwave cable and station, and destruction of numerous transformers.[18]

The Cuban MNR was to the fore in attempting to stem these attacks, providing static guards for key installations, as well as being the main force deployed in the attempt to wipe out guerrilla groups. Just how many anti-Castro guerrillas there were in the countryside is uncertain. One Cuban Army officer, José Ramón Fernández, who had served in the Batista army, was imprisoned for conspiring against the Batista regime, and went on to become a General under the Castro regime, estimated that there were 'more than five thousand bandits in small bands in various places'.[19] The CIA estimated that prior to the Bay of Pigs landings there were up to 7,000 insurgents in Cuba. However, as the CIA Inspector General's Survey of the Cuban Operations (the Kirkpatrick Report) noted in October 1961, those 7,000 were in 'individual groups [that] are small and very inadequately armed'.[20] A CIA summary dated 12 April 1961 gave further details of the nature of organised anti-Castro resistance:

On the latest estimate there are nearly 7,000 insurgents responsive to some degree of control through agents with whom communications [i.e., with the CIA and exiles] are currently active. About 3,000 of these are in Havana itself, over 2,000 in Oriente, about 700 in Las Villas in central Cuba. For the most part, the individual groups are small and inadequately armed.[21]

Despite this, the activities of the guerrilla bands, individuals, and small terror group in the towns, were having an effect on the security of the regime.

The period was characterised by 'rumours of invasion, emergencies, conspira-cies, and acts of violence. Militiamen had often to be kept from work, thereby adding to economic difficulties. Exile sources believed that 1,330 had been shot by the government by October 1960, and by March even more'.[22] The impact of the activity of the Castro police, security and militia forces reduced the numbers of guerrillas in groups Cuba to around 1,200, plus 1,000 individuals by March 1961',[23] showing that regime was winning the war against guerrillas, sabotage and terror.

Both sides in the low-level conflict sought to increase their capacity to combat · their enemies. The CIA redoubled its efforts to get supplies and arms to the guerrillas, but it continued to face real problems in successfully landing men, and, even more so, supplies, by sea. Air drops proved particularly difficult, to the extent that American CIA pilots who were not, at this stage, on operational duty over Cuba began to doubt the Cuban exile pilots' accounts of air dropping supplies. In fact, the CIA's own records show that 'the total amount of supplies put into Cuba by air and boat operation amounted to about 93,000 pounds (46.5 tons) ... enough to equip 1,250 men'.[24] The Castro government also had its difficulties in supplying its growing militia and re-equipping its army and air force. A major arms shipment from Belgium arrived in Havana harbour in March 1960, aboard the French cargo ship, *La Coubre*, and while it was being unloaded a number of explosions killed up to 100 dock workers, and injured many more people. Sabotage was strongly suspected, although it was just as likely that the explosions were a result of an accident. Castro took full advantage of the disaster, blaming the US during another of his major speeches at the funeral of those killed. The mass funeral was attended by large numbers of militia, for whom the seventy-six tons of small arms and ammunition aboard the *La Coubre* had been intended. Other shipments of arms were blocked by US diplomatic efforts, with, for example, a ship being detained in Hamburg before it got underway for Cuba. Castro turned, perhaps inevitably, to the Eastern Bloc countries for weapons, including anti-aircraft guns, tanks, assault guns, small arms, and aircraft.

The first Soviet tanks arrived in October 1960, and the Cuban army began a crash-programme of trying to train crews as quickly as possible. One of the army officers chosen for the new armoured units was Néstor López Cuba, who later recalled that, 'everything we learned in the morning from the Soviet instructors we had to teach at night to the rest of the *compañeros*'.[25] It was not just members of Cuba's regular army who were trained to use the Soviet equipment, as members of the MNR were also trained on Soviet anti-aircraft guns, and artillery. Finally, Cubans were selected to go to the Soviet Union to train on the Mig-15 jet fighter. Time was working in Castro's favour, but there were still significant pockets of guerrilla activity that had to be tackled, most pressingly in the Escambray Mountains.

The Escambray region of Cuba is a forested and mountainous district some 2,500 square miles in extent, providing good terrain for classic guerrilla operations. It was here that the largest groups of anti-Castro guerrillas operated, and had some support among small farmers, anti-Communists, and Catholics. The danger for Castro was that the Escambray could become a centre for wider operations against the government and that it would be a safe haven for anti-Communists, and an area that the CIA-backed exiles could use to supply the guerrillas. The extent of the Escambray meant that only the militia men and women of the MNR could hope to defeat the guerrillas there. What they lacked in training, or, in some cases, in morale, the militia made up for by sheer weight of numbers. During the winter of 1960–61, the regime used the MNR to mount a major offensive in the Escambray. This was the militia's first sustained action and provided much needed field and combat experience.

At the beginning of the campaign, some 40,000 MNR were mobilised in Havana, in forty battalions of around 1,000 men each. They were reinforced by local militia, and by regular units of the Cuban armed forces, but the brunt of the two month operation was borne by the MNR. The government's tactics took advantage of the numbers available to them, and the MNR would cordon off areas which were then combed through, forcing the guerrillas to fight or try and break through the perimeter. Viktor Dreke, a Castro loyalist and an officer in the *Lucha Contra Bandidos* (Struggle Against the Bandits) units of the MNR later went out of his way to claim that captured rebels were treated well, but the fighting was vicious, and the few guerrillas who were captured were, in all probability, shot out of hand.[26] Despite the two-month-long offensive, some guerrillas did manage to survive, although their effectiveness was greatly impaired. Che Guevara estimated that there were still around 200 active guerrillas in the Escambray in early 1961,[27] and, in fact, it was not until 1965 that the last resistance there was eliminated. Despite its limitations, the MNR had a number of factors in its favour. It was largely recruited from 'lower income peasants and urban workers' who were the regime's primary support base; it was receiving more training and increased flows of equipment as Eastern Bloc support increased; it was a large force of at least 200,000; and its cadres were 'well organized, well equipped, and trained units [were] emerging'.[28]

By the end of 1960, the economic position in Cuba was very poor. Attempts to remove the country from the grip of US business led to confusion, disorganisation and falling production. The US also closed its doors to Cuban sugar, forcing the regime to find new markets. However, in other respects, time was on the Castro regime's side. In addition to opponents who chose exile rather than remain in Cuba, the regime was quick to arrest both real and suspected opposition, so that 'conditions in Cuban prisons from 1960 onwards once again, as under Batista or Machado, beggar description'.[29] The Communist Party, the police, G2, and the MNR's intelligence and informers' organisation, the Committees for the Defence of the Revolution, were increasingly effective. In addition, the re-building of the regular armed forces was underway with the help of the Soviet Union and the Eastern Bloc countries, and on 1 January 1961, there was a big parade in Havana to showcase the latest Soviet military hardware in the hands of the Cuban Army and the MNR. There was still armed resistance, sabotage and terrorism, but the Castro regime used this opposition to its advantage, justifying its increasingly arbitrary security policy as necessary in the face of counter-revolution backed by the USA. That security policy was increasingly successful, and not just in the Escambray. As well as that fighting, the winter of 1960–61 saw Rogelio González Corzo of the *Movimiento de Recuperación Revolucionaria* (the Movement to Recover the Revolution, MRR, founded by Manuel Artime) lead 'a powerful campaign of sabotage and terrorism in Havana; many bombs were laid, letter boxes blown up, water mains destroyed, sugar and tobacco plantations set aflame'.[30] However, this activity led to another security crackdown using all the regime's forces, including the MNR, and Corzo, along with other MRR activists, were arrested and executed. For the anti-Castro resistance inside Cuba, and outside, in Florida and Guatemala, along with their CIA sponsors, time was running out. This was appreciated by the Agency, which noted, in an internal memo, that: 'we estimate that time is against us. The Castro regime is steadily consolidating its control over Cuba'.[31]

The Bay of Pigs – the MNR save the Castro regime
The CIA and the Cuban exiles; plans and people

CIA planning to bring down the Castro regime underwent significant changes in a relatively short period of time. Those changes were driven by the realisation that time was on Castro's side, and that his various security and defence policies were stabilising and strengthening the regime. The strategic initiative was with Castro, not the CIA planners, nor the Cuban exiles. The progress of the CIA's and the exiles' preparations for overthrowing the Castro regime was hampered by a number of difficulties, some of which, such as maintaining secrecy among a large number of exiles, were inevitable. Worse, political considerations, at the highest level in US policy making, impacted on the eventual choice of an invasion of Cuba to such an extent that success was highly unlikely. These political considerations, seen by many who were involved with the exile movement as a fatal weakness, were compounded by misreadings of the Castro government's determination to resist. In particular, there was a mis-reading of the willingness of the Cuban militia, the MNR, to defend the Castro regime.

In March 1960, President Eisenhower asked the CIA to organize the various groups of Cuban exiles into a force that could be used to destabilise, and eventually bring down, the Castro regime. The operation was put in charge of Richard Bissell, the CIA's Deputy Director for Plans. As the Agency's head of covert operations, he was a veteran of the Guatemalan coup of 1954, and the man most responsible for the driving the successful U-2 spy plane programme. To run the covert operation against Cuba, Bissel assembled the same team of men who had been successful in 1954 against Árbenz. It was unsurprising, therefore, that Bissell and his team had high expectations that a similar strategy to that employed in Guatemala in 1954 would also work against Cuba. This was, in all probability, the first mistake made by the CIA in its 'Program of Covert Action Against the Castro Regime'. The initial planning by the CIA envisaged supporting exiles willing to be infiltrated back into Cuba as trained guerrilla fighters. After the first few dozen volunteers were trained at various US military training areas, it was decided to move almost all training to Guatemala. Exiles were then trained by the CIA in Guatemala with the full co-operation of the Guatemalan government under President Miguel Ydígoras Fuentes, the successor to Carlos Castillo Armas who was assassinated in 1957. Locating the training in Guatemala was seen as a necessity, as action against the Castro regime had to be covered by plausible deniability on the part of the US government. All guerrilla action would be presented as being the independent work of Cuban exiles. The almost obsessive political insistence on deniability would hamper the programme from the outset and would be one of the factors that led directly to the failure of the invasion. Worse, very few observers were taken in by US government claims to have had nothing to do with the exiles' efforts to overthrow Castro.

The exiles' army was led by José 'Pepe' Peréz San Román, a US-trained Cuban army officer who had been imprisoned by the Batista regime, readmitted to the Cuban army after Castro's revolution, but imprisoned and exiled after he helped fellow officers to escape from Cuba. His second-in-command was another ex-Cuban Army officer, Erneido Oliva González, who had lost his commission after the revolution. The political leader in the exile military, and a major figure in the exile movement, was Dr. Manuel Francisco Artime, who had fought with Castro against Batista, and had held a government post after the revolution.[32] Strongly Catholic, like many Cubans, he went into exile in Florida after the Matos affair when it was apparent that the Castro government was transforming rapidly into a communist regime. In addition to the military element, the CIA strove to create a unified political front for the exiles. This task was particularly difficult as there were numerous political groupings, perhaps as many as two dozen, operating among the exile community, ranging from former Batista supporters to ex comrades of Castro. The political front eventually took shape as the *Frente Revolucionario Democratio* (FRD), although its control over what was nominally its own armed forces was minimal.

As the difficulties of infiltrating sufficient numbers of exile fighters into Cuba by boat or air became more pronounced, largely because of the effective deployment of the MNR at likely landing sites, and the Castro security forces became more repressive and more effective in their operations, so it was clear that the original CIA concept would have to change if there was any chance of overthrowing Castro. Planning moved towards the idea of an amphibious landing on Cuba, supported by air strikes to completely destroy Cuba's air force and provide close air support for the exiles.

As the number of exiles training in Guatemala continued to grow, so the CIA developed its new plan of landing a heavily armed, air-supported, force on Cuba. The plan that was settled on by the Agency was known as the 'Trinidad Plan', and took its name from the coastal town which was to be the main objective of the attacking force. This plan was the Agency's preferred option, and in addition to the tactical advantages of a landing at Trinidad, it was also believed that the area was the most anti-Castro and that it would provide a large number of volunteers for any force landed. More realistically, there was the option of taking to the Escambray and fighting a guerrilla war from there. However, by the beginning of 1961, even this was less of an option after the MNR's successful drive against existing guerrilla groups. Whatever the merits of the Trinidad Plan, it was all academic for when the newly elected US President, John F. Kennedy was shown the plan he cancelled it, saying that the whole operation was too 'noisy' and would make it impossible for the US to deny involvement. The CIA planners were sent away and told to come up with a new plan within 36 hours. This plan was for the landings that would be known as the Bay of Pigs invasion.

The new plan envisaged extensive air raids in the days prior to the landings, the aim of which was to totally destroy Castro's air force. The Cuban exiles, known as 'Brigade 2506' and consisting of 1,511 infantry, paratroops and tank crew, along with 300 support troops,[33] were to be landed on three beaches (in addition to a small diversionary feint at the eastern end of Cuba). They would then secure a beachhead that would enable the FRD 'provisional government' to land and, if necessary, call for open support from the USA. All this would be supported by extensive radio propaganda broadcast, as in the 1954 Guatemalan coup, from Swan Island. The belief was that the Brigade would be well enough armed and supplied to stop any attacks by the Cuban militia and army, especially as the hinterland was largely swamp, crossed by two main roads that formed the only avenue by which to attack the beachhead. Both members of Brigade 2506, and the CIA, believed that these events would deal a destabilizing blow to the regime, that large numbers of MNR militia would cross over to the Brigade, or desert, and that, backed by the propaganda offensive, and the possible assassination of Castro, the regime would fall. Almost all of this proved to be unfounded.

Castro prepares to defend the Revolution

For Castro, one thing was clear, and that was the US was at some point going to attempt a major assault on his regime, using exiles, or as Castro saw them, 'mercenaries'. The CIA had not been able to maintain any real security when it came to recruiting and training the exiles. As early as August 1960, the Castro government knew that Cubans were being trained in Miami.[34] Security became even less effective once the men began training in Guatemala, with local newspapers reporting on the presence of the Cubans, and, eventually, the New York Times published a front page article about the training on 10 January 1961.[35] Not only were the Cuban security, military and militia continually strengthened, the offensive in the Escambray carried through, but dispositions were made to counter any attempted invasion, or major infiltration of guerrillas.

In preparing for the defence of the island, the MNR came into its own, thanks to both the territorial nature of its organisation, and the size of the force. The MNR had an alarm, and trip-wire function. For example, given the suitability of the Escambray for guerrilla operations, and the appreciation that not all the guerrilla groups had been destroyed in the winter of 1960-1961, it was necessary to prevent successful reinforcement by sea. There were few places on the cost to the south of the Escambray Mountains were boat infiltration could be carried out, largely at the mouths of rivers. As a result the MNR made sure that all such spots were 'guarded by militia posts armed with machine guns. A small group landing at such a point by shuttling from a larger vessel in small boats would probably receive heavy casualties'.[36] Each of these posts were manned by militia units numbering between 100 and 200. The deterrence effect of such small groups of machine gun-armed MNR played a not insignificant role in the defeat of the landings when they came.

In addition to taking advantage of the large numbers of militia, drawing upon local members of the force in rotation to defend key areas, the MNR also received training on Eastern Bloc equipment as it became available. By the time of the Bay of Pigs invasion, Cuba had received between 30 and 40,000 tons of military equipment from the Eastern Bloc,[37] worth around $30 million. This equipment was for the 32,000 personnel of the Cuban army, and the 200,000 of the MNR. The army was still being reorganised and trained and was too small to absorb all the new equipment. As a result the MNR militia were given basic training to use the Soviet field guns, and Czech-made anti-aircraft guns. The typical method of training was that the small number of Soviet and Czech military advisers would train groups of Cubans who would then go on to train Army and MNR personnel on equipment that they had only just become familiar with.

The final, and crucial, element in the Castro regime's defensive preparations related to the small Cuban air force. Again, the Guatemalan example was in the minds of Cuban planners. Then, a small number of CIA-manned aircraft had proved crucial, more so than the feeble ground invasion. The awareness of the importance of control of the air lay behind Cuba's purchase of anti-aircraft artillery from the Eastern Bloc, the attempted purchase of Hawker Hunter fighters from the UK, and the dispersal and defence of the operational aircraft that Cuba did have. The Cuban air force, the *Fuerza Aérea Revolucionaria* (FAC), possessed a range of fixed-wing trainer, fighter-bomber, bomber and transport aircraft. Castro's air force inherited ten P-47s, two P-51s, five FB.11 Sea Furies, two Grumman Avengers, six B-26Cs, five T-33 jet trainers, seven Texans, a T-28, two C-47s, one C-46, one Catalina, and one C-54.[38] In addition, there were a handful of helicopters and some Piper liaison aircraft. However, most of these aircraft were non-operational, and there was a shortage of pilots, with only twelve available, and not all qualified to fly all types. The out of service aircraft, including all the P-47s and the P-51s, were grouped together in threes as decoys, while the operational aircraft were dispersed around the island, camouflaged, and protected by anti-aircraft artillery. With his forces ready and waiting, training continuing, new supplies of weapons, and more advisors on the way, Castro and his regime waited for the invasion.

Invasion

Three days before the opening of the invasion, the CIA planners gave the officers of Brigade 2506 the first briefing on the invasion plan. At this point, the Brigade was at its jump-off base – 'Base Trampoline' – at Puerto Cabezas, Nicaragua. The plan involved a diversionary landing by 160 men under the command of Nino Diaz, on the eastern end of the island, in Oriente province, some thirty miles from the US base of Guantanamo in the early hours of 14 April. The following day, air strikes by Brigade B-26B bombers would destroy the *Fuerza Aérea Revolucionaria* on the ground. CIA spy plane flights had, it was believed, identified all Castro's aircraft, and Brigade B-26Bs, painted in FAR colours, would both neutralise the danger to the invasion from the air, and allow the US government to claim that the attacks were the work of FAR pilots rebelling against the Castro regime. The air strikes would take place over two days, D-2 and D-1, and would be followed, on 17 April, by landings on three beaches. The main landing was to be at Blue Beach at Playa Girón, with a supporting landing some five miles west and into the inlet headed by Playa Larga – Red Beach. In addition there would be a smaller landing to the east of Girón – Green Beach. The landings would enable a substantial beach head to be secured, the approaches, through swampland, could only made along three roads from the interior, each of which would be cut by Brigade paratroops, and attacked by Brigade B-26s, unhindered by Castro's air force, which would have been destroyed on the ground. That was the outline of the plan.

The MNR had its first success in relation to the intended diversionary landing. The feint by the men under Higinio 'Nino' Diaz, a former officer in the 26 July Movement, was intended to draw Castro's forces away from the real landings. The diversion was an important element for the Brigade, but as the men approached their beach on the night of 14 April, D-3, militiamen were spotted on and near the beach itself. Diaz called off the landing and the landing party returned to their motor cruiser and sailed away from the shore to wait until the following night. But the same happened again on the 15 April. The MNR's role as a point defence force had an impact before a shot was fired.

The following day, 15 April, saw the first of the Brigade's air raids. The issue of the air strikes prior to the landings has been, since the events of April 1961, highly contentious. For the CIA planners, the original intention of large scale raids by B-26s would have greatly enhanced the prospects of the Brigade:

> The plan was to carry out a series of large air strikes from D-2 until D Day, with two air strikes per day – one at dawn and the other at dusk – using as many aircraft as possible, with those on D Day dedicated to attacking targets around the landing area and providing close air support. It was planned to deploy at least two B-26s to Playa Girón airfield to support plausible deniability regarding US responsibility for the attacks, and also to protect the invading Brigade.[39]

With his air force gone, Castro's troops would have been exposed to Brigade air attacks, some flying from the captured air strip at Playa Girón. Events during the battle would show just how devastating such close support missions could be, but political decisions, taken at the last minute, watered down the scale of the air strikes to a fatal degree. For many in the Brigade, and the CIA officers involved, the blame for the reduced air element lay at the feet of President Kennedy, who still clung to the threadbare hope that the US could deny any direct responsibility. In the event, eight B-26Bs were launched from Nicaragua, each carrying two 500lb demolition bombs, ten 200lb fragmentation bombs, plus eight rockets, in addition to each aircraft's powerful .50cal machine gun armament.[40] The result was that, 'while the attack did inflict considerable damage, Castro actually still had four or five fighters, two, or possibly three "Sea Furies" and two jet T-33s, as well as two B-26 bombers'.[41] These aircraft would prove to be fatal to the entire invasion.

The day following the first of the Brigade's air raids, Castro addressed a large rally of MNR and supporters at the funeral of those killed in the air raids. This was an important speech in which Castro declared, for the first time, that Cuba was a Socialist state, and, mixing a powerful appeal to patriotism and socialism, called on Cubans to resist 'the mercenaries':

> Comrades, workers, and peasants. This is the Socialist and Democratic Revolution of the humble, with the humble, for the humble … This attack of yesterday was the prelude to an aggression of mercenaries. All units must now go to their battalions … Let us form battalions and dispose ourselves to sally out facing the enemy, with the National Anthem … with the cry of 'To the fight' ['*Al combate*'], with the conviction that to die for our country is to live and that to live in chains is to live under the yoke of infamy and insult … *Patria o Muerte, venceremos.*[42]

In the following few days, hundreds of members of the MNR would die in the fierce fighting that followed the Brigade landings. Castro did not just limit himself to rallying his followers, however, as the air raids triggered a huge security operation in which the G2, the police and militia rounded up and detained tens of thousands of real, and imagined, opponents. Just how many people were arrested is unclear, but it was probably between 100,000 and 200,000 people – 'between the raids on 15 April and the evening of 17 April, perhaps 100,000 were arrested … including most of the CIA's 2,500 agents and their 20,000 suspected counter-revolutionary sympathisers'.[43] Others give higher figures, with one estimate being of 'no fewer than half a million people … detained all over the island'.[44] Whatever the number, the round-up had removed, in one stroke, any real chance of the landings sparking off any kind of widespread resistance; something that did not, in fact, feature in the CIA's planning to any real extent.

The first of Castro's followers to be killed in action were a patrol of MNR. In the early hours of 17 April, militia stationed at Playa Larga (Red Beach), saw lights briefly flashing offshore. Thinking that the lights came from a fishing boat trying to find its way to the beach, an MNR jeep headed down to the beach and turned its headlights on to guide the fishing boat. In fact, the lights came from a malfunctioning marker light being brought ashore by men of one of the Brigade's frogmen teams, who were to guide the landing craft in. With the team was Gray Lynch, one of the two CIA officers with the invasion force. He described what happened next:

> On the edge of Playa Girón, a militia outpost had seen the light. Two militia, in a jeep, started down the beach road, from our left. At this point we were forty yards from the shore, and everyone but me was out of the raft in knee-deep water, preparing to go ashore.
>
> When we spotted the jeep coming towards us, I told everyone to get down low in the water behind the raft, while I stretched flat on the raft with the BAR pointing at the beach. The jeep came on, then braked to a halt directly in front of us. It backed up and turned. Its headlights were shining straight into our faces. There was no doubt the militiamen had seen us. Before the jeep had finished its turn, I poured half a magazine into it, but the damn jeep's lights were still on.
>
> As I was finishing off my first magazine, the frogmen had moved out from behind the raft, and they were also pouring fire into the jeep. Two BARs and four Thompson submachine guns were plowing a solid sheet of tracer bullets into the vehicle. I was on my third magazine before the jeep's lights finally went out.[45]

Despite the weight of fire, only one militiaman was killed, and the MNR had fulfilled its early warning/trip wire role. The Brigade's frogmen reached the beach and placed the lights to guide in the landing craft. Just as they finished the task, more MNR militia, alerted by the firing opened fire on the frogmen from half-built holiday houses close to the beach. One of the Brigade's frogmen, Andy Pruna, remembered, 'we opened up almost automatically with our BARs and we really gave them hell … we knocked out perhaps as many as twenty in a few minutes and the rest ran away and left their weapons'.[46] This may have been only token resistance, but, more importantly, militia manning a microwave transmitter were able to inform Havana that landings were taking place, something that also happened as the landings took place at Blue Beach.

At 3.15am, Castro was informed that the awaited landings were taking place, and immediately placed his remaining air force on alert. Castro also appointed a Cuban Army officer, Major José Fernández as overall field commander, with Flavio Bravo given the command of militia forces. One assessment of their subsequent performances was that Fernández 'showed himself much of the coolest of Castro's officers in the following days, though little was made of him in heroic myth afterwards. He certainly seemed infinitely more competent as a commander than "Major" Flavio Bravo, the young Communist contemporary of Castro's at the university'.[47] Castro also ordered the full mobilisation of the MNR, with the Matanzas militia, specifically Battalions 26, 211, 219, 225, and 227, being sent to the landing area, along with armour and anti-aircraft units. These would be joined later by ten other MNR battalions from La Habana and Las Villas,[48] to form the main element of Castro's defence. The first battalion to be moved into action was Battalion 339, with 528 effectives, including three mortar batteries. The battalion had been fighting in the Escambray since January, and was ordered to move from its billet at the Central Australia sugar mill, to the landings eighteen miles away at Playa Larga. The commander of Battalion 339, Captain Ramón Cordero Reyes, sent two companies of his militia ahead of his main force. This advanced group arrived near Playa Larga just before daylight, where the 2 Battalion of Brigade 2506 was partially ashore.

The two companies of Battalion 339 ran straight into heavy automatic fire from the 2nd Battalion of the Brigade, supported by. 50-cal and. 30-cal fire from a Brigade catamaran that had brought the frogman team into the beach. Landed infantrymen who were slowly disembarking from one of the Brigade's ships, the *Barbara J*, also drove off other vehicles, at least one of which contained civilians, the first civilians to die in the assault. As the remainder of Battalion 339 arrived, they were attacked from behind by one of the heavily armed parachute units. Caught between the paratroopers and the men of the 2nd Battalion, the MNR battalion collapsed. 'Captain Cordero Reyes managed to escape in a jeep to Central Australia, and, arriving around 9.00 a.m., said that his unit was either killed, wounded or dispersed. When asked which forces were left between the enemy and Central Australia, he replied: "There's nothing."'[49]

Of the 528 effectives of the militia battalion, only around fifty escaped in any sort of order from this first action at Playa Larga, which was a result of the better training and equipment of the 2 Battalion.[50] At Playa Girón, the landings were also contested by militia, who were beaten off by the .50-cal machine guns on the Brigade's ships, particularly the *Blagar*, which then landed men from the Brigade by landing craft. The 4 and 6 Battalion of the Brigade would land here, as would the 3 Battalion, which had been ear-marked for the Green Beach landings to the east. That was called off when it was realised that Castro still had aircraft. The Brigade captured around 150 MNR personnel and some civilians at Playa Girón, and the Brigade's political leader, Dr Manuel Francisco Artime, went to question one of the militia who had been wounded – a 12-year-old boy.

> I went to see this boy and he asked why we had come to fight against them. And I told him that we had come to liberate the country from Russian control, from the communist regime. The boy replied: 'I am a Communist'. I started explaining to him what communism meant, what it meant to lose your liberty; that he was only a little part of the big machine, that it was a regime that would destroy anybody who opposed its policies; and when I finished the boy said to me: 'I think you believe what you say, but my teachers and my father tell me different. I believe them. You are mistaken.'[51]

'This incident made me very sad,' Artime said. Despite this encounter, some fifty prisoners, militia and civilians, did volunteer to aid the Brigade at Girón, but the Brigade's commander, 'Pepe' San Román, admitted that captured MNR militia 'did not want to fight with Castro but they were frightened of us'.[52] In fact, if their actions were anything to go by, many of the militia did want to fight for the Castro regime, and the CIA's belief, shared by the exiles, that a successful landing would lead to mass desertions from the MNR, was unfounded.

The MNR were, then, the first troops to engage with the Brigade on the landing beaches, and although they were beaten back and were unable to prevent the establishment of beachheads at Playa Larga and Playa Girón on D-Day, 17 April, the air arm of the regime made a decisive intervention early on the same day. Although left with only a handful of operational T-33s, Hawker Sea Furies, and two B-26 bombers, this was enough to seriously damage the attacking forces who were without effective air cover. Although the Brigade was informed that Castro still had an air strike capacity, there was not enough time to either finish landing all men and equipment, or to withdraw ships and landing craft out of Cuban waters. At first light, two Sea Furies, and a B-26 took off for the short flight to the landing beaches, they were followed by one of the T-33s. The aircraft attacked Brigade ships with rockets, bombs and cannon fire, and off Red Beach, the *Houston*, still carrying the 5 Battalion, under Montero Duque, a single squad of the 2 Battalion, along with trucks, jeeps and the Brigade's field hospital. The ship was holed by a rocket and the captain was forced to run it aground away from the landing beach. As the 5 Battalion abandoned the ship, attempting to make their way to the swamps, they were attacked again from the air. Most of them made it ashore, but with little of their weaponry, and under the ineffectual command of Duque, they would have no further impact on events. Meanwhile, off Blue Beach, Castro's aircraft hit the *Río Escondido*, which was loaded with aviation fuel, and ten days' worth of ammunition for the Brigade along with medical supplies and the radio truck that should have been the communications hub for the entire Brigade. The ship was abandoned, and exploded shortly afterwards. The. 50-cal anti-aircraft guns on Brigade ships, did, however, put up enough defensive fire to deter at least two FAL aircraft from pressing home attacks, as well as shooting down a Sea Fury and a B-26. But the damage was done. Not only had vital supplies been lost, but the Brigade's other major ships left the beaches, taking all hope of effective re-supply away with them.

Despite the air attacks, most of the Brigade was put ashore, but minus key support equipment, and, crucially, the necessary reserves of ammunition to sustain the landings. The next stage of the battle involved waves of MNR militia, Cuban police and Army being thrown against the Brigade's beach head. Castro was aware that he had to crush the landing as quickly as possible if the Brigade was not to establish its 'provisional government' on Cuban soil. There was little scope for tactical finesse, as there was only one major approach to each beach, with each road flanked by swampland. It was on these narrow fronts that the militia would have to advance.

Castro's first advance – the destruction of a Militia battalion
Castro's first ground assault came in the mid-afternoon on 17 April. The road that led north-south between Central Australia and Playa Larga (Red Beach) passed through the small town of Pálpite, which was held by militia from the MNR's *Escuela de Responsables de Milicias* (the militia training school). They were the advance guard of Castro's force, as the MNR Battalion 339 had already been engaged and dispersed earlier in the day by men from the Brigade's 2 Battalion as they secured their beach head.[53] The Brigade's commander, 'Pepe' San Román, headquarted at Blue Beach, had reinforced Oliva's 2 Battalion with two of the Brigade's five M41 'Walker Bulldog' tanks, two trucks with ammunition, and men from the 4 and 6 Battalion. Although this force was small, with each of the Brigade's 'Battalions' only numbering around 175 men each, they were heavily armed. In addition to the tanks' 76mm guns, Oliva's force was equipped with recoilless rifles, bazookas, mortars and .30 and .50-cal machine

guns. Once the militia from the *Escuela de Responsables de Milicias* in Pálpite was reinforced by more militia, travelling in trucks and buses, the whole force set off, along the road, towards Playa Larga. No reconnaissance was made, and the column simply drove down the road, closely packed together. They failed to spot the Brigade's troops and tanks waiting in defensive positions. Máximo Leonardo Cruz, a Brigade company commander, leading three squads of twelve men each, plus a reinforced squad with a 75mm and a 57mm recoilless rifles and .50-cal machine guns was in position in the path of the MNR advance. Cruz called up Oliva's tanks, trucks and mortars, who arrived shortly before Castro's militia blundered into the Brigade. Cruz described what happened next:

> 'When they [the MNR] were about five hundred yards from us they stopped,' Cruz said, 'and they started putting up their mortars and getting their weapons prepared. They didn't send any forward observers to see where we were and they didn't know our positions. When I saw that they had all their weapons ready, I gave the order to open fire. I had to do it because they were getting organized there. When I gave the order to fire, you could see them flying up in the air. I threw everything at them with the three shells of the 75 I had left, with the 57, with the machine guns and all the weapons we had there. In ten or fifteen minutes there was a big mound of dead men all over the road.'[54]

Worse was to come for the militia who survived this onslaught, as two of the Brigade's B-26s chose that moment to arrive over the battlefield. The two aircraft made repeated passes over the remains of the burning column, using bombs, rockets and their batteries of nose-mounted .50-cal to finish off the militia unit – 'when it was over, only a handful of the 968 men of the 339th [sic] were left to creep away an bury themselves under the mud and water of the mangrove swamps'.[55] As Cruz remarked *'No quedó ni el gato* (not even the cat was alive)'.[56] However, both of the Brigade's attack aircraft were then intercepted by a FAR Sea Fury and a T-33. One of the B-26s was brought down immediately, while the other was damaged and would subsequently be lost at sea, with both crewmen.

While this action was playing itself out, Castro arrived at the Central Australia mill to direct operations in person. Accompanying the 'Maximum Leader' were substantial reinforcements of militia and regular army. Castro later enumerated his reinforcements: 'we had a tank company [five T34/85s], four batteries of

112mm howitzers [*sic.*, in fact they were 122mm Soviet howitzers], eight anti-aircraft batteries and a battery of 37 mm. cannons, a company of bazookas and a special combat column and a battery of mortars'.[57] In addition, there was a battery of six 85mm field guns.[58] Castro moved the headquarters to Pálpite, and began to prepare for a night attack against the Brigade. Any night attack is difficult, and although Castro chose veterans of the Rebel Army to spearhead the attack, they would be supported by militia.

Night battle – the Rotunda

The night battle of the Rotunda was to be the fiercest fighting of the Bay of Pigs. From captured prisoners, the Brigade learnt that Castro was massing troops for a night-time thrust down the road to Playa Larga aiming to break the Red Beach bridgehead. Oliva received further reinforcement from San Román at Blue Beach, consisting of three more M-41s and more mortars. Oliva had time to position all his forces at the two sets of crossroads which formed the road entrance to Playa Larga, and gave the feature the name of the Rotunda. Castro's choice of a night attack was, in part, a reflection of his need to destroy the Brigade's bridgeheads before conditions on the ground enabled the exiles to land their political leaders and call for overt US support. But, as the ambush and destruction of the MNR earlier had shown, few of Castro's forces were well-trained enough to carry out a night assault.

Castro's night attack began with a bombardment of what was believed to be the Brigade's positions by the recently received Soviet 122mm howitzers. Once again, limited training of both regular and militia gunners limited the effectiveness of the bombardment: 'the 122mm guns of Castro's forces opened fire against the beach at 7.30 p.m., initially with very poor efficiency, with their shells falling close to the positions of the 81mm mortars, but then they started landing to the south until falling into the sea. At 0.30 a.m., the artillery fire ceased',[59] Around 1200 rounds were fired, but inaccurate, uncorrected gunnery, and the narrow and shallow positions of the Brigade meant that the exiles had suffered only 'eight or nine dead and thirty wounded'.[60]

The attack was led by General El Gallego Fernández, the head of the militia training school, *Escuela de Responsables de Milicias* at Matanzas. Militia from the 1 and 3 Companies of the training school spearheaded the assault, supported by a M20 'super bazooka' rocket launcher company. They were followed by four T34/85 tanks (with another acting as a radio relay at Pálpite) and the

Columna 1 Especial de Combate. Despite the strength of this force, it was forced into a narrow frontage on and near the road, some 75 feet in width, by the marshes on both sides. The dug-in defenders waited until the first militia were close before opening heavy fire, killing around fifteen men immediately. The militia went to ground, but the T34 (and, perhaps a JS-III) advanced on the road junction,[61] forcing the lightly armoured M-41s back into Playa Larga. The commander of the Castro tank unit, Néstor López Cuba, was in the lead T-34 as the tanks tried to break into Playa Larga. The defenders hit the tank with all the weapons they had, and losing a track, it slid off the road. Cuba was subsequently injured by shrapnel after transferring to another T-34. That tank, too, was disabled by an M-41 which rammed it, while another T-34 was destroyed by bazooka fire. By 12.20am the initial tank fighting was over, and the attackers' route into Playa Larga was partially blocked by the damaged and destroyed T-34s. At 3am, the first infantry attack was mounted by a wave of MNR militia, to be met by heavy small-arms, machine-gun, and mortar fire. The MNR continued to attack in poorly-coordinated waves. The pressure of numbers, and the knowledge that ammunition was running out, led to Oliva ordering the use of white phosphorus mortar bombs: "'The shouting of the enemy at that moment was just like hell," he said. "Everything was on fire. They were completely demoralized because that *fósforo blanco* really burns the skin. It was like a curtain, completely covered with *fósforo blanco*. The tanks and the mortars saved us"'.[62] Despite the horror of the white phosphorous mortar bombs, men and tanks still tried to break into Playa Larga in small groups. Not long after the use of phosphorous, Oliva was talking to the crew of one of his M-41s, which had a problem with its 76mm gun. At that moment, another T-34 appeared, apparently unaware that it was in the Brigade's lines. The driver got out of the tank and came towards Oliva and his M-41. Only at the last moment did he realise his mistake, but it was too late and the M-41 hit the T-34 from a range of only 25 yards.

By 5.30am, Castro's forces had pulled back from the chaos of the Rotunda. Less than 400 men of the Brigade had held off waves of infantry and militia attacks, supported by armour. A captured Castro tank driver told Oliva that '2,100 men – three hundred regular soldiers, 1,600 militia, and two hundred policemen – plus twenty tanks, including Sherman and Stalin tanks' had taken part in the night's fighting.[63] It may be that some 500 of Castro's forces were killed, with over 1,000 wounded, during the Rotunda battle, while 200 were, temporarily, taken prisoner. However, although the Brigade's casualties were comparatively light, they had expended most of their ammunition, were exhausted, and could expect no further reinforcement. The decision was made to abandon the Playa Larga beachhead and retire to Blue Beach at Girón.

The frontal assaults carried out by Castro's army, police and the MNR were costly and failed to take the beachhead by force of arms, but the earlier destruction and dispersal of the Brigade's ships and supplies ensured that the beachhead was no longer tenable for the Brigade. Even had the Brigade been re-supplied at Red Beach, it would not have been able to hold out for longer against the numbers available to the regime. By the morning after the Rotunda battle, Castro's forces had been reinforced by more tanks, howitzers, mortars, anti-aircraft guns, and Battalion 111 of the MNR. The supply of arms and equipment from the Eastern Bloc, and the availability of large numbers of militia were strong cards in Castro's defence deck.

Militia advance on Blue Beach, Playa Girón
At the Girón beachhead, the successful air attacks against the Brigade's ships, which sank the *Rio Escondido*, had led to the withdrawal of the remaining ships and landing craft. Not only would the Brigade not be re-supplied by sea (although some air drops were carried out), the men ashore lost the additional fire support provided by the. 50-cal and 75mm recoilless rifles mounted on the ships. The initiative was with Castro's forces, and MNR from Battalion 111 were, with armour support, able to drive back Brigade paratroops covering the road between Covadonga and San Blas. But more militia, from Battalion 117, also supported by tanks, were unable to force the paratroops beyond San Blas, where they had joined up with Brigade infantry from the 4 Battalion. By the morning of 18 April, the scene was set for the final drive to crush the Brigade in their Blue Beach positions.

Castro's forces were now in a position to advance down the coastal road from Playa Larga to the Brigade's beachhead at Girón, as well as to continue the advance from San Blas against the beachhead. The remains of the Brigade – the men of the 2 Battalion from Playa Larga, and the 6 and 3 Battalion, plus the M-41s and some of the 1 Battalion paratroopers – would be facing an attack on two fronts by large forces, with little real hope of any substantial resupply.

At daylight on 18 April, the Castro troops resumed their attack on Playa Larga, not realising that the Brigade had evacuated their positions in the night after the Rotunda fighting. By 8am, the discovery that Playa Larga was empty of Brigade forces was made, and Castro ordered a rapid advance down the coast road towards Girón. At mid-day, General Fernández had a column of MNR militia and armour ready. He ordered militia Battalion 123 to advance down the coast road in supporting formations for six SU-100 Soviet heavy assault guns, and with air defence provided by two batteries of anti-aircraft machine guns. But before the advance could begin, Castro informed Fernández that the 'mercenaries' were on the run, and ordered a rapid advance to take Girón before 6pm.[64] Accordingly, Fernández issued new orders for the militia battalion to accompany the assault guns in buses and lorries, with the anti-aircraft machine guns taking up the rear of the column towed by trucks. The long column set out on the road to Girón. A little later, six Brigade B-26s took off from Puerto Cabezas in Nicaragua for what would be the final totally successful air support mission flown by the aircraft. By this time, many of the Cuban exile aircrew were too exhausted to continue flying, so three CIA pilots, former members of the Alabama Air National Guard, also took part. One of these was Connie Seigrist who described later what happened to the MNR and armour column late that afternoon:

> We six aircraft departed Puerto Cabezas and arrived over the Bay of Pigs about an hour before dark. We spread, armed our switches, and test fired our guns when the coast was coming in sight. My air-craft carried eight 225lb fragmentation bombs, eight fragmentation rockets, and fully armed fourteen forward firing .50 cal guns. Some others carried napalm. As we were coming over the coast I could see a convoy of vehicles coming from inland down the only road toward the beach. I knew our invading troops did not have enough ground equipment to form a convoy plus no blue stripes [air recognition sign] were visible. I set the intervalometer to release all bombs equally spaced within four seconds. When lined up on the lead tank I started my dive. When in range I released the bombs and simultaneously held down on my firing trigger while flying down the whole convoy.[65]

On the ground, the militia of Battalion 123, and their supporting armour, were engulfed by the bombs, rockets,. 50-cal fire and napalm. A seven-mile stretch of the Castro column was destroyed, the Brigade's six B-26s' 'raked it repeatedly from end to end. They worked as a team, and methodically turned the section into flaming rubble and fleeing troops'.[66] The B-26s left the attack zone just in time, as two of Castro's T-33s arrived over the burning column of militia buses and trucks. Just how many of Battalion 123 escaped the attack is unclear, but the Battalion was effectively destroyed, and the attack on Playa Girón had to be postponed until the morning of the 19 April.

19 April, the defeat of the invasion

The MNR had suffered heavy casualties in the fighting with the Brigade and from air attack, with two battalions destroyed. The final day's fighting would also see militia heavily engaged. During the night of 18/19, Castro's artillery pounded the remaining Brigade beachhead, and the destroyed Battalion 123 was replaced by a police battalion. For the Brigade, the only support came from the air. Three, partially successful, re-supply drops made by the exiles' C-54 Skymasters, with a lone C-46 Commando managing to land at the Girón airstrip with 850 pounds of supplies. Shortly after the C-46 landed, two Brigade B-26s bombed tanks and trucks approaching Girón from San Blas. However, two other B-26s were shot down by Castro's T-33s and ground fire, with a third being damaged. This was the last air support the Brigade would receive. Castro's ground forces, however, continued to receive support by the T-33s, Sea Furies and a B-26.

Shortly after first light, the final Brigade B-26 air attack on the three battalions of militia, advancing on the San Blas-Girón road, disorganised this large force, and gave the defending Brigade commander, Del Valle, an opportunity:

> He organized a counterattack with his paratroops and the Third Battalion. Standing on top of one of his two tanks, De Valle signaled for the attack. The men moved forward under a heavy artillery barrage, some walking dazedly, others running, but all going forward. To the forward observers, watching through binoculars, it was like a picture: the lines of men, the bright blue sky and the early morning sun, the puffs of smoke and earth rising from the craters, the flash of small arms fire and the blue uniforms of the enemy ... It was a gallant, forlorn, even foolhardy attack – and yet it was succeeding. Castro's vastly superior forces broke and ran.[67]

But it was the swansong of the Brigade, as the men of the Third Battalion faltered, then began a disorganised retreat, leaving the paratroops and the two tanks to continue the defence. By late morning, the MNR battalions had regrouped, and led by tanks, they dislodged the last Brigade defenders on the road to Girón, but only after two T-34s and an SU-100 were destroyed by a Brigade M-41 and mortar fire.

By 2pm, the remains of the Brigade were all on and around the beach at Playa Girón, with little ammunition, and none for their mortars. Some of the men tried to reach US destroyers waiting off shore to evacuate the Brigade. The Brigade's leaders refused to be evacuated, and Oliva gathered a small force of his men, plus one of the M-41s, to make a last stand, against militia of the MNR. Oliva said that his force was attacked 'by planes ... at the same time, they were fired on by ground troops of [MNR] Batallón 326, which damaged the track of the tank with a bazooka, leaving it unserviceable, and the troops disbanded and escaped to the swamps, being the last force of the Brigade to fight'.[68] The MNR had fired the last shots of the battle of the Bay of Pigs, just as they had fired the first.

Aftermath

For the USA and its Cuban exile allies of Brigade 2506 the invasion at the Bay of Pigs 'intended to overthrow Castro ... succeeded in helping him to strengthen his regime internally and enhance his image internationally as David defeating Goliath'.[69] Central to Castro's success in that apparently unequal struggle was Castro's militia, the MNR, which was in the forefront of consolidating and securing the revolution prior to the invasion, and in its frontline role during the Bay of Pigs. Without the MNR, matters might have gone very differently for the Castro regime. After the defeat of the invasion, the regime continued to strengthen its military position, with increased flows of weapons, training and support from the Soviet Union and its Eastern Bloc allies. The Cuban Armed Forces were fully reorganised in the aftermath of the Bay of Pigs. Although that reorganisation involved the disbandment of the MNR, the militia principle continued, with 'the more professional and loyal militia members transferred to the regular Army; the others ... reorganized into the Popular Defense Forces, a new military reserve organization'.[70] In such a highly ideological, para-militarised society as Communist Cuba, there was still an important place for a militia.

Chapter 8
Amateurs in the Age of the Professional

This brief history of the amateur soldier covers 164 years of militia and volunteer service in North America and Europe, from the French Wars in the late eighteenth and early nineteenth-century to the Cold War in the early 1960s. Throughout that period, the professional soldier dominated, yet there was always room for, and sometimes a desperate need for, the amateur soldier in his various guises. Although the amateurs rallied for different regimes and politics, for Monarchies, Republics and communist Cuba, as well as fascism and anarchism, there were, nonetheless, similarities in the nature of these amateur soldiers.

Of the actions covered here, the two where militias made a winning difference to the battle were those of the battle of Châteauguay in 1813, and the Bay of Pigs in 1961. At Châteauguay, and the subsequent battle of Crysler's Farm, militias were to the fore in stopping what was probably the most dangerous of the US's offensives against British North America in the War of 1812. At Châteauguay, some 339 Canadians, including about two dozen Indians, stopped 3,564 Americans, largely regulars, in a woodland battle that saw some US officers throw away their swords. The defenders were a combination of Canadian Fencibles, Voltigeurs, Select Embodied Militia, and Sedentary Militia, supported by a number of Abenaki and Nipissing warriors, with a reserve, of 600 Select Embodied Militia. On the part of the British and the *Canadiens*, their strengths were that they had constructed successive fieldworks in a strong position, part flanked by a stream; they were fighting in defence of their homeland; and they were exceptionally well led. Their commanding officer was the experienced professional, Lieutenant Colonel Charles-Michel d'Irumberry de Salaberry, who was supported by two aggressive, confident officers of militia, Captain Jean-Baptiste Brugière and Captain Charles Daly. The combination of effective, experienced leadership, and the motivation provided by the defence of homeland, brought a country-saving victory.

The case of the Cuban militia, the MNR, at the Bay of Pigs, has a similarity with the defence at Châteauguay, in that the Cubans were defending their homeland, but also an ideology. This was the 'freedom' motive that Jock Haswell spoke about in his history of 'Citizen Armies'.[1] It is difficult to make any conclusions about leadership at the Bay of Pigs, for although the invaders were defeated, the ground fighting was marked by some very heavy casualties taken by the militia of the MNR, and little in the way of tactical finesse. Nonetheless, from the very first attempts at landing by the men of the invading Brigade 2506, the MNR was central to the defence of Castro's Cuba.

If Châteauguay showed the potential of well-led amateurs, the siege of the Alcázar reinforced the value of leadership and discipline. The besieging Republican militias, from a variety of leftist causes, proved incapable of defeating a very hard-pressed rebel defence. Attempts by the Republican government, and loyal regular army officers, to impose discipline, were defeated by anarchist and revolutionary socialist militias, who thereby threw away the advantages they had. Conversely, the small group of rebel Falangist militiamen who had taken refuge in the Alcázar, made a disproportionate contribution to the successful defence of the fortress, in part because they put themselves under the leadership of a regular army officer, Captain Emilio Vela Hidalgo, who was also a Falangist.

Although the amateur soldier has been most in evidence in defence of his homeland, some have engaged in aggressive, offensive war. In this book, the two examples are US militia and volunteers in the War of 1812 and in the Spanish-American War of 1898. The performance of the US militias in the War of 1812 was mixed, and the perennial constitutional questions of where, when, for how long, and at whose behest, came to the fore. These issues were also there in the run-up to the Spanish-American War, but the enthusiasm for the pursuit of that war, the first of the US's overseas wars, meant that there was no shortage of men clamouring to take part, including the amateur elite, the 1 US Cavalry Volunteers, the 'Rough Riders'. Yet, these amateurs and other National Guard and Volunteer units, very nearly did not see active service, as initial planning by the federal government and the War Department had left them out of the offensive equation.

The 1898 tensions between the amateur soldiers of the US, the US War Department and the US Army, is just one example of the 'love-hate' relationship that has characterised that between governments and the amateur soldier. In what might be called the 'Anglo' model, enthusiastic amateurs, in the USA, England and Britain, repeatedly pushed their governments into accepting their demands to organise, and recognising their role in the military scheme of affairs. In different contexts, militias have been the preferred political option in societies and states in the process of collapse, such as in Spain, 1936–39, or, in Cuba, to consolidate the emergence of a new regime. In the case of Castro's Cuba, it was the insight of Che Guevara that pushed forward the establishment of the MNR, in a largely top-down formation of an amateur army.

By their very nature, amateur forces tended to have a much more direct involvement with the societies they came from. The professional was far more likely to be barracked with his fellows, or to be sent abroad, and, even when billeted on civilians, as was frequently the case up until the nineteenth-century, he was rarely billeted in his own locality. The professional soldier's life was lived apart from the society he came from, and he was often feared or scorned. But the amateur was the citizen in arms, even if only for a few weeks' embodiment and training, or an annual camp, or weekly drill. This aspect of the amateur soldier explains the frequent reluctance of governments to encourage the bottom-up formation of militia, while, at the same time, governments often needed militias to support national defence. The potential dangers, for government, can be seen in the militia mutinies in England in 1795, which illustrated how the wartime soldier still saw his interests through the lens of the civilian. Yet those mutinies were limited, and were put down with the aid of other volunteers. By contrast with the 1795 mutinies, the Volunteer soldier of the Victorian period in Britain became an integral part of the transformed, industrialised, society of its lifetime, and the grey or green-clad Volunteer was a familiar figure. Very few of those Volunteers saw active service, but, when it came, they, like the other amateurs in this book took their place in the firing line.

Notes

Chapter 1

1. Goldsworthy, Adrian, *Roman Warfare* (Cassell, London, 2000) p.107.
2. Ibid., p.108.
3. Haswell, Jock, *Citizen Armies* (Peter Davies Ltd., London, 1973).
4. Ibid., pp.13–14.
5. Ibid., p.12.
6. Ibid., pp.11–12.
7. Von Clausewitz, Carl, *On War* (Penguin Books, Harmondsworth, 1968 edition), p.119.
8. Orr, David R., Truesdale, David, *'Ulster Will Fight ...'; Home Rule and the Ulster Volunteer Force, 1886–1922* (Helion & Company, Solihull, 2016), p.vii.
9. One of the best accounts, in English, of the Freikorps, remains Nigel H. Jones' *Hitler's Heralds; the Story of the Freikorps, 1918–1923* (John Murray, London, 1987). It includes a fairly complete list of all Freikorps units, pp.249–265.
10. Quoted in Michael A. Ledeen, *The First Duce; D'Annunzio at Fiume* (The John Hopkins University Press, Baltimore, 1977), p.43.
11. A contemporary view of the Stockton Volunteers, quoted in Winifred Stokes' 'Investigating the history of local volunteer regiments: the Stockton Volunteers and the French invasion threat of 1798–1808, *The Local Historian*, vol. 37, No: 1, February 2007, p.27.
12. Cullen, Stephen Michael, *In Search of the Real Dad's Army; the Home Guard and the Defence of the United Kingdom* (Pen & Sword Military, Barnsley, 2011), p.55.
13. Ibid., p.169.
14. Bruce, Phillip, *Second to None; the Story of the Hong Kong Volunteers* (Oxford University Press, Oxford, 1991), p.220.
15. Graves, Donald E., *Field of Glory; the Battle of Crysler's Farm, 1813* (Robin Brass Studio, Toronto, 1999), p.273.

Chapter 2

1. Burke, Edmund, *Reflections on the Revolution in France* (Penguin Books edition, with an introduction by Conor Cruise O'Brien, Harmondsworth, 1969), p.9.
2. Longmate, Norman, *Island Fortress, the Defence of Great Britain, 1603–1945* (Pimlico, London, 2001), p.212.

3. Rule, John, *Outside the Law: Studies in Crime and Order, 1650–1850* (University of Exeter, Exeter Papers in Economic History, 1982), p.vi.
4. Longmate, *Island Fortress*, p.214.
5. Nelson, Ivan, F., *The Irish Militia, 1793–1802; Ireland's Forgotten Army* (Four Courts Press, Dublin, 2007), p.41.
6. Ibid., p.42.
7. Ibid., p.26.
8. Longmate, *Island Fortress*, p.225.
9. Ibid., p.226.
10. Cousins, Geoffrey, *The Defenders; A History of the British Volunteer* (Frederick Muller, London, 1968), p.78.
11. Longmate, *Island Fortress*, p.230.
12. Ibid., p.234.
13. Ibid., p.235–236.
14. Ibid., p.236.
15. Ibid., p.238.
16. Cousins, *The Defenders*, p.55.
17. See Chapter 3, 'The War of 1812', below for an account of the importance of the Militia model as a democratic force in both the USA and Canada.
18. Cookson, J.E., 'Service without Politics? Army, Militia and Volunteers in Britain during the American and French Revolutionary Wars', *War in History*, 2003, volume 10, number 4, p.388.
19. Norfolk, R.W.S., *Militia, Yeomanry and Volunteer Forces of the East Riding, 1689–1908* (East Yorkshire Local History Society, Beverley, 1965), p.9.
20. Nelson, *The Irish Militia*, pp.55–63.
21. Wells, Roger, 'The Militia Mutinies of 1795', in John Rule (ed.) *Outside the Law: Studies in Crime and Order, 1650–1850* (Exeter Papers in Economic History, University of Exeter, 1982), p.42.
22. Ibid., p.52.
23. Ibid., p.53.
24. Ibid., p.59.
25. Ibid., p.63.
26. Nelson, *The Irish Militia*, p.76.
27. Jackson, Thomas, *Narrative of the Eventful Life of Thomas Jackson, Militiaman and Coldstream Sergeant, 1803–15* (first published, 1847, and Helion & Company, Solihull, 2018, with notes and commentary by Eamonn O'Keeffe).
28. Ibid., p.16.
29. O'Keeffe, Ibid., note 8, p.19.
30. Ibid., p.17.
31. Ibid., pp.17–18.

32. Jackson entitled his chapter on the assault on Bergen-op-Zoom, 'The Disastrous Attack and Storming of Bergen-op-Zoom', and in a fine piece of writing conveyed the chaos and terror of the fighting which led to the amputation of his leg. Ibid., pp.61–88.

33. Ibid., p.26.

34. Ibid., p.26.

35. Ibid., p.27.

36. Ibid., pp.26–27.

37. Ibid., p.27.

38. Ibid., p.36, note 40.

39. Steppler, Glenn A., *Britons To Arms! The Story of the British Volunteer Soldier and the Volunteer Tradition in Leicestershire and Rutland* (Budding Books, Stroud, 1997), p.xi.

40. Reid, Stuart, & Chappell, Paul, *King George's Army 1740–1793: (2)* (Osprey, London, 1995), p.42.

41. Ibid., p.43.

42. Norfolk, R.W.S., *Militia, Yeomanry and Volunteer Forces of the East Riding*, p.44.

43. Sargeaunt, B.E., *The Royal Manx Fencibles* (Gale and Polden Ltd., Aldershot, 1947), p.46.

44. Norfolk, R.W.S., *Militia, Yeomanry and Volunteer Forces of the East Riding*, p.19.

45. Ibid., p.24.

46. Ibid., p.25.

47. Ibid., pp.48–52.

48. H.T. Dickinson, 'Popular Loyalism in Britain in the 1790s', quoted by J.E.Cookson, 'Service without Politics?' p.393.

49. Cookson, ibid., p.397.

50. Quoted in, Steppler, Glenn A., *Britons To Arms!*, p.14.

51. Cullen, Stephen M., *In Search of the Real Dad's Army; the Home Guard and the Defence of the United Kingdom* (Pen & Sword, Barnsley, 2011), pp.11–12, 16–18.

52. Steppler, *Britons To Arms!*, p.15.

53. Ibid., p.20.

54. Ibid., p.20.

55. See Chapter 4, 'The Rifle Volunteers: The 'wonder of the age', the Victorian amateur soldier', below.

56. See Chapter 3, 'The War of 1812; War, society and politics – militias in the United States and Canada, 1812–1815', below.

Chapter 3

1. Skeen, C. Edward, *Citizen Soldiers in the War of 1812* (The University Press of Kentucky, Lexington, 1999), p.1.

2. Shea, William L., 'Militia', in Gallaly, Alan (ed.), *Colonial Wars of North America, 1512–1763; an encyclopedia* (Garland Publishing, New York, 1996), p.440.

3. Dederer, John M., 'War and Society in Colonial America', in Gallaly, Alan (ed.), *Colonial Wars of North America*, p.775.

4. Sulte, Benjamin, 'The Captains of Militia', *The Canadian Historical Review*, vol. 1, no: 3, September, 1920, pp.243–244.

5. Ibid., p.241.

6. Reid, Stuart, *North America 1753–63; British Redcoat versus French Fusilier* (Osprey Publishing, Oxford, 2016), p.76.

7. Ibid., p.76.

8. Skeen, *Citizen Soldiers*, p.4.

9. Estimates for the number of Loyalists who rallied to the Crown vary, but between 30,000 and 50,000 Americans served in the various Provincial Corps, some of whom were given regular status. Many more served in Loyalist militia units. Katcher, Philip, *The American Provincial Corps, 1775–84* (Osprey Publishing, 1973).

10. Skeen, *Citizen Soldiers*, p.4.

11. Benn, Carl, *The War of 1812* (Osprey Publishing, Oxford, 2002), p.18.

12. Ibid., p.26.

13. Skeen, *Citizen Soldiers*, p.2.

14. Rammage, Stuart A., *The Militia Stood Alone; Malcolm's Mills, 6 November, 1814* (Valley Publishing, Summerland, BC, 2000), p.54.

15. The upper figure is given by Benn (2002), p.27; the lower by Skeen (1999), p.12.

16. Skeen, *Citizen Soldiers*, p.6.

17. Ibid., p.38.

18. Chartrand, René, *British Forces in North America, 1793–1815* (Osprey Publishing, Oxford, 1998), p.9.

19. For a list of British regiments and corps in Canada during the war, see Ibid., pp.9/10.

20. Chartrand, *British Forces in North America*, p.35.

21. Quoted by Chartrand, Ibid., p.35.

22. Facey-Crowther, David, R., 'Militiamen and Volunteers: The New Brunswick Militia 1787–1871', *Acadiensis*, vol. 20, no: 1 (Autumn 1990), p.151.

23. Ibid., p.152.

24. Ibid., p.155.

25. Chartrand, *British Forces in North America*, p.38.

26. Ibid., p.40.

27. Skeen, *Citizen Soldiers*, p.82.

28. Ibid., p.82.

29. Tupper, Ferdinand Brock (ed) *The Life and Correspondence of Major-General Sir Isaac Brock, K.B.* (Simpkin, Marshall, and Co., London, 1847 edition), p.246.

30. Darnell, Elias, *A Journal Containing an Accurate and Interesting Account of the Hardships, Sufferings, Battles, Defeat and Captivity of Those Heroic Kentucky Volunteers and Regulars, Commanded by General Winchester, in the Years 1812–1813*, in *Massacre on the River Raisin* (Leonaur Publishing, 2013, first published, 1814).

31. Ibid., p.108.

32. Atherton, William, *Narrative of the Suffering and Defeat of the North-West Army Under General Winchester*, in *Massacre on the River Raisin*, (Leonaur Publishing, 2013, first published, 1814), pp.22/3.

33. Ibid., pp.28/9.

34. Darnell, *A Journal*, p.113.

35. Ibid., p.113.

36. Contemporaries used two spellings of the British officer's name, Proctor and Procter, the latter is used here.

37. Atherton, *Narrative*, p.30.

38. Ibid., p.35.

39. Cruikshank, E.A., *Harrison and Procter: The River Raisin* (Leonaur Publishing, 2013; first published, 1912), p.193.

40. Ibid., p.194.

41. Darnell, *A Journal*, pp.111/2.

42. Skeen, *Citizen Soldiers*, p.96.

43. Quoted in Skeen, *Citizen Soldiers*, p.98.

44. Ibid., p.99.

45. Benn, *The War of 1812*, p.35.

46. Van Rensselaer in his report to General Dearborn, quoted in Skeen, *Citizen Soldiers*, p.99.

47. Ibid., p.101.

48. Ibid., p.105.

49. Graves, Donald E., *Field of Glory; The Battle of Crysler's Farm, 1813* (Robin Brass Studio, Toronto, 1999), p.93.

50. Ibid., p.92.

51. Ibid., p.97.

52. Benn, *The War of 1812*, p.45.

53. O'Sullivan, quoted in Graves, *Field of Glory*, pp.100/01.

54. Ibid., p.102.

55. Ibid., p.105.

56. O'Sullivan, quoted in Graves, *Field of Glory*, p.107.

57. Skeen, *Citizen Soldiers*, p.115.

58. Benn, *The War of 1812*, p.56.

59. Ibid., p.59.

60. Quoted in, Rammage, *The Militia Stood Alone*, p.27.

61. Quoted in Ibid., p.92.

62. Ibid., p.105.

Chapter 4

1. Perhaps the best contemporary account of the experience of Militia service before regular army active service, is Jackson, Thomas, *Narrative of the Eventful Life of Thomas Jackson;*

10

Militiaman and Coldstream Sergeant, 1803–15 (Helion & Company Limited, Solihull, 2018. New edition with introduction, notes and commentary by Eamonn O'Keeffe).

2. Steppler, Glen, *Britons to Arms! The Story of the British Volunteer Soldier* (Budding Books, Stroud, 1997), p.20.

3. Beckett, Ian F.W., *Riflemen Form; a Study of the Rifle Volunteer Movement, 1859–1908* (Pen & Sword, Barnsley, 2007 edition), p.9.

4. Ibid. p.9.

5. Sondhaus, Lawrence, *Naval Warfare, 1815–1914* (Routledge, London, 2001), p.74.

6. Beckett, *Riflemen Form*, p.20.

7. Cousins, Geoffrey, *The Defenders; A History of the British Volunteer* (Frederick Muller, London, 1968), p.103.

8. Mackenzie, S.P., *The Home Guard; a military and political history* (Oxford University Press, Oxford, 1995), p.7.

9. Steppler, *Britons to Arms!*, p.31.

10. Beckett, Ian, F.W., *The Amateur Military Tradition, 1558–1945* (Manchester University Press, Manchester, 1991), p.164.

11. Cunningham, Hugh, *The Volunteer Force; A Social and Political History, 1859–1908* (Archon Books, Hamden, CT, 1975), pp.104/05.

12. Mathias, Peter, *The First Industrial Nation; an Economic History of Britain, 1700–1914* (Methuen, London, 1969), p.449.

13. The discussion in this chapter is focused on the Volunteer Movement in Britain. The Volunteer Movement in Ireland possessed particular features, related to political-religious divisions; any treatment of which would require a further chapter.

14. Beckett, *The Amateur Military Tradition*, p.178.

15. Cousins, *The Defenders*, p.113.

16. Beckett, *The Amateur Military Tradition*, p.178.

17. Cousins, *The Defenders*, p.111.

18. Grierson, J.M, *Records of the Scottish Volunteer Force, 1859–1908* (1909, reprinted, Uckfield, The Naval & Military Press Ltd., 2004), p.368. This remains the most complete account of the Volunteer Movement in Scotland, and is complete with essential statistics relating to the force, along with excellent colour plates of Scottish Volunteer uniforms by Grierson. For Wales, the multi-volume *History of the Welsh Militia and Volunteer Corps, 1757–1908*, by Bryn Owen, is indispensable.

19. Lord Kingsburgh (Colonel, the Right Hon. Sir J.H.A. Macdonald, KCB), quoted in Grierson, J.M, *Records*, pp.12–13.

20. Cousins, *The Defenders*, p.122.

21. Ibid. p.135.

22. Cunningham, *The Volunteer Force*, pp.104–109.

23. Ibid., p.103.

24. Beckett, *The Amateur Military Tradition*, p.169.

25. Grierson, *Records*, p.52.

26. Cunningham, *The Volunteer Force*, p.114.

27. Beckett, *The Amateur Military Tradition*, p.174.

28. Steppler, *Britons to Arms!*, p.36.

29. Beckett, *The Amateur Military Tradition*, p.177.

30. Cunningham, *The Volunteer Force*, p.119.

31. Ibid., p.123.

32. Steppler, *Britons to Arms!*, p.34.

33. Cunningham, *The Volunteer Force*, p.10.

34. Busk, Hans, *Rifle Volunteers; How to Organize and Drill Them* (1859, reprinted, Uckfield, The Naval & Military Press Ltd, no date), p.29.

35. Steppler, *Britons to Arms!*, p.38.

36. Grierson, *Records*, pp.68–9.

37. Beckett, *The Amateur Military Tradition*, p.183.

38. Cousins, *The Defenders*, p.116.

39. Beckett, *The Amateur Military Tradition*, p.181.

40. Grierson, *Records*, p.82.

41. Beckett, *The Amateur Military Tradition*, p.184.

42. Mackinnon, Major-General H.W., *The Journal of the C.I.V. in South Africa* (John Murray, London, 1901), pp.118–119.

43. Malmassari, Paul, *Armoured Trains; an Illustrated Encyclopaedia 1825–2016* (Seaforth Publishing, Barnsley, 2016), p.233.

44. *Leicester Daily Mercury*, 7 August, 1879, quoted in Steppler, *Britons to Arms!*, p.99.

45. Belfield, Eversley, *The Boer War* (Leo Cooper, London, 1993), p.7.

46. Mackinnon, *The Journal*, pp.1–2.

47. Ibid., p.252.

48. Childers, Erskine, *In the Ranks of the CIV; a narrative and diary of personal experiences with the CIV battery* (Honourable Artillery Company) in South Africa (Smith, Elder & Co, London, 1901)

49. Ibid., p.28.

50. Mackinnon, *The Journal*, pp.3–4.

51. Ibid., pp.221–223.

52. Childers, *In the Ranks*, p.88.

53. Ibid., p.104.

54. Ibid., p.149.

55. Ibid., p.167.

56. Mackinnon, *The Journal*, p.104.

57. Ibid., p.252.

58. Ibid., p.92.

59. Ibid., pp.112–113.

60. Ibid., pp.108–109.

61. Childers, *In the Ranks*, pp.300–301.

Chapter 5

1. Hill, Richard, *War at Sea in the Ironclad Age* (Cassell, London, 2002), p.97.

2. Miller, Nathan, *Theodore Roosevelt, A Life* (William Morrow & Co Inc, New York, 1992), p.234.

3. Ibid., p.250.

4. Ibid., p.244.

5. Sondhaus, Lawrence, *Naval Warfare, 1815–1914* (Routledge, London, 2001), p.173.

6. Quoted in Cosmas, Graham A., *An Army for Empire; the United States Army in the Spanish-American War* (Texas A&M University Press, College Station, 1998 edition), p.66.

7. Ibid., p.9.

8. Ibid., p.2.

9. Ibid., p.6.

10. Quotes, Ibid., p.82.

11. Quoted, Ibid., p.70.

12. Post, Charles Johnson, *The Little War of Private Post; the Spanish-American War seen up close* (University of Nebraska Press, Lincoln, 1999 edition), pp.4/5.

13. Cosmas, *An Army for Empire*, p.87.

14. Roosevelt, Theodore, The Rough Riders (Dover Publications, New York, 2006 edition), p.14.

15. Ibid., p.73.

16. William Allen White of Kansas, quoted in Freidel, Frank, *The Splendid Little War* (Little and Brown, Boston, 1958), p.33.

17. Roosevelt, *The Rough Riders*, p.13.

18. Miller, *Theodore Roosevelt*, p.312. Later, in 1906, as President, Roosevelt was responsible for the dismissal from the all-black 25th Infantry Regiment of 167 men over the Brownsville incident in Texas. They were dismissed 'without honor' and some of their white officers believed it was a case of injustice rooted in racism. Roosevelt's biographer notes that, 'in the case of equal rights for black Americans, he vacillated – and so did his policies;' Miller, p.466.

19. Post, *The Little War of Private Post*, p.36.

20. Ibid., p.38.

21. Cosmas, *An Army for Empire*, p.142.

22. Cosmas, Graham, & Gjernes, Marylou, 'Introduction to the Bison Books edition' of Post, *The Little War of Private Post*, p.vi.

23. M.B. Stewart, quoted in Freidel, *The Splendid Little War*, p.36.

24. Post, *The Little War of Private Post*, p.8.

25. Ibid., p.10.

26. Ibid., p.22.

27. Cosmas, *An Army for Empire*, p.171.

28. Ibid., p.180.

29. Parker, John H., *The Gatlings at Santiago; the History of the Gatling Gun Detachment, U.S. Fifth Army Corps, During the Spanish-American War, Cuba, 1898* (Leonaur edition, no place of publication, 2009).

30. Post, *The Little War of Private Post*, pp.109–110.

31. Ibid., p.111.

32. Ibid., p.115.

33. Ibid., p.115.

34. Roosevelt, *The Rough Riders*, p.49.

35. Ibid., pp.49–50.

36. Cosmas, *An Army for Empire*, p.209.

37. Roosevelt, *The Rough Riders*, p.64.

38. Parker, *The Gatlings*, p.105.

39. Quoted in, Freidel, *The Splendid Little War*, p.119.

40. Cosmas, *An Army for Empire*, p.210.

41. Dwight E. Aultman, quoted in Freidel, *The Splendid Little War*, p.127.

42. Captain Lee, quoted in Freidel, *The Splendid Little War*, p.140

43. Ibid., p.133.

44. Post, *The Little War of Private Post*, p.179.

45. Parker, *The Gatlings*, p.105.

46. Cosmas, *An Army for Empire*, p.217.

47. Parker, *The Gatlings*, p.108.

48. Ibid., p.113.

49. Roosevelt, *The Rough Riders*, pp.75–76.

50. Roosevelt, quoted in Freidel, *The Splendid Little War*, p.160.

51. Post, *The Little War of Private Post*, pp.184–185.

52. Richard Harding Davis, quoted in Freidel, *The Splendid Little War*, p.163.

53. Unnamed Spanish officer, quoted in Freidel, *The Splendid Little War*, p.162.

54. Post, *The Little War of Private Post*, p.195.

55. Cosmas, *An Army for Empire*, p.218.

56. Roosevelt, quoted in Freidel, *The Splendid Little War*, p.175.

57. Secretary of War, Russell Alger, in a telegram to General Shafter, 3 July 1898, quoted in Cosmas, *An Army for Empire*, p.219.

58. Ibid., p.225.

59. General Wheeler, quoted in Freidel, *The Splendid Little War*, pp.255–256.

60. Post, *The Little War of Private Post*, pp.203–204.

61. Parker, *The Gatlings*, p.140.

Chapter 6

1. Thomas, Hugh, *The Spanish Civil War* (Pelican Books, Harmondsworth, 3rd edition, 1977), p.11.

2. Ibid., p.336.

3. Ibid., p.65.
4. Ibid., p.66.
5. Ibid., p.68.
6. Ranzato, Gabriele, *The Spanish Civil War* (The Windrush Press, 1999), p.45.
7. Ramiro Ledesma Ramos, quoted in Thomas, *Spanish Civil War*, p.111.
8. Primo de Rivera, José Antonio, from his preface to the book, *Dictatorship of Primo de Rivera as seen from abroad* (1931), in Hugh Thomas (ed.), *José Antonio Primo de Rivera: selected writings* (Jonathan Cape, London, 1972), p.39.
9. José Antonio Primo de Rivera, quoted in Stanley Payne, *Falange: A History of Spanish Fascism* (Stanford University Press, Stanford, 1961), p.41.
10. Bolin, Luis, *Spain: The Vital Years* (J.B. Lippincourt, Philadelphia, 1967), p.139.
11. Thomas, *Spanish Civil War*, p.328.
12. Cullen Stephen M., 'Leaders and Martyrs: Codreanu, Mosley and José Antonio', *History*, vol. 71, no: 233, October 1986, p.429.
13. Bolin, *Spain: The Vital Years*, p.148.
14. Ibid., p.152.
15. Thomas, *Spanish Civil War*, p.208.
16. Ibid., p.322.
17. Ibid., p.246.
18. Kisch, Richard, *They Shall Not Pass; the Spanish People at war, 1936–9* (Wayland Publishers, London, 1974), p.46.
19. Ibid., p.57.
20. Ibid., p.54.
21. Ibid., p.56.
22. Güner, Fisun, 'Felicia Browne: the only known British woman to die in the Spanish civil war', *The Guardian*, 20 July, 2016, https://www.theguardian.com/lifeandstyle/womens-blog/2016/jul/20/meet-the-only-known-british-woman-to-die-in-the-spanish-civil-war (accessed, 02/03/2018).
23. Fyrth, Jim, & Alexander, Sally (Eds.), *Women's Voices from the Spanish Civil War* (Lawrence & Wishart, London, 1991), pp.257/61.
24. Ibid., p.274.
25. Kisch, *They Shall Not Pass*, p.53.
26. Ibid., p.61.
27. Orwell, George, 'Notes on the Spanish Militias', in, Peter Davies (Ed.), *Orwell in Spain* (Penguin Books, London, 2001), pp.278/9.
28. Ibid., p.279.
29. Kisch, *They Shall Not Pass*, p.60.
30. Orwell, 'Notes on the Spanish Militias', pp.277–289.
31. Ibid., p.287.

32. Hall, Christopher, *Revolutionary Warfare: Spain 1936–37* (Gosling Press, Pontefract, 1996), p.16. The details of the organisation of militias in this chapter are taken from Hall. Christopher hall has written a valuable series of books covering various aspects of the left-wing militias, including *'Disciplina Camaradas'; Four English Volunteers in Spain 1936–39* (Gosling Press, Pontefract, 1994), and *'In Spain with Orwell'; George Orwell and the Independent Labour Party Volunteers in the Spanish Civil War, 1936–1939* (Tippermuir Books Ltd., 2013).

33. Hall, *Revolutionary Warfare*, p.17.

34. Zaloga, Steven J., *Spanish Civil War Tanks* (Osprey Publishing, Oxford, 2010), p.11.

35. Malmassari, Paul, *Armoured Trains; An Illustrated Encyclopaedia 1825–2016* (Seaforth Publishing, Barnsley, 2016), p.438.

36. Ibid., p.439.

37. Thomas, *Spanish Civil War*, p.313.

38. Ibid., pp.371–372.

39. Cardozo, Harold G., *The March of A Nation; My Year of Spain's Civil War* (Right Book Club edition, London, 1937), p.19.

40. Beevor, Antony, *The Battle for Spain; The Spanish Civil War 1936–1939* (Weidenfeld & Nicolson, London, 2006), p.198.

41. Ibid., p.198.

42. Cardozo, *The March of A Nation*, p.58.

43. Payne, *Falange*, p.144.

44. Ibid., p.121.

45. Thomas, *Spanish Civil War*, p.506.

46. Payne, *Falange*, p.45.

47. Thomas, *Spanish Civil War*, p.279.

48. Cardozo, *The March of A Nation*, p.38.

49. This section is built on the work on Cecil Eby, whose *The Siege of the Alcázar; Toledo: July to September 1936* (The Bodley Head, London, 1965) is the best single account in English.

50. Eby, *The Siege of the Alcázar*, pp.15–16.

51. Ibid., p.30.

52. Ibid., p.56.

53. Ibid., p.134.

54. Ibid., p.152.

55. 'Pedro Villaescusa Bonilla, Jefe de la Falange en El Alcázar', http://www.fnff.es/Pedro_Villaescusa_Bonilla_Jefe_de_la_Falange_en_El-Alcazar_1 (accessed, 5 January, 2018). Also, Eby, *The Siege of the Alcázar*, p.203.

56. Ibid., p.236.

57. Thomas, *Spanish Civil War*, p.413.

58. Eby, *The Siege of the Alcázar*, p.214.

59. Peirats, José, *Anarchists in the Spanish Revolution* (Freedom Press, London, 1990), p.159.

60. Ibid., p.160.
61. Payne, *Falange*, p.143.
62. Ibid., p.144.
63. Sagarra, Pablo, González y Lucas Molina, Óscar, *Divisionarios; testimento gráfico de los combatientes Españoles de la Wehrmacht* (La esfera de los libros, Madrid, 2012).

Chapter 7

1. Thomas, Hugh, *Cuba: A History* (Penguin Books, London, 2010 edition), p.731.
2. Kornbluh, Peter (ed), *Bay of Pigs Declassified; the Secret CIA Report on the Invasion of Cuba* (The New Press, New York, 1998), p.7.
3. Ibid., p.7.
4. Thomas, *Cuba: A History*, p.731.
5. Ibid., p.750.
6. Ibid., p.805.
7. Higgins, Trumbull, *The Perfect Failure: Kennedy, Eisenhower, and the CIA at the Bay of Pigs* (W.W.Norton, New York, 1987), p.21.
8. Ibid., p.29.
9. Ernesto Che Guevara, in a letter to his mother, dated 4 July, 1954; from Ernesto Che Guevara, *Latin America Diaries* (Ocean Press, Melbourne, 2011), p.93.
10. Higgins, *The Perfect Failure*, p.35.
11. Thomas, *Cuba: A History*, p.841.
12. Ibid., p.850.
13. DIA, *Handbook on the Cuban Armed Forces*, April 1979 (DDB–2680–62–79), p.I-1.
14. Thomas, *Cuba: A History*, p.918.
15. José 'Pepe' Regalado, in Triay, Victor Andres, *Bay of Pigs: An oral history of Brigade 2506* (University Press of Florida, Gainesville, 2001), pp.63/4.
16. Ibid., p.65.
17. Ibid., p.65.
18. Kornbluh, *Bay of Pigs Declassified*, pp.172–3.
19. Waters, Mary-Alice (ed.), *Making History: Interviews with four generals of Cuba's Revolutionary Armed Forces* (Pathfinder, New York, 1999), p.112.
20. Kornbluh, *Bay of Pigs Declassified*, p.51.
21. Kornbluh, *Bay of Pigs Declassified*, p.131.
22. Thomas, *Cuba: A History*, p.914.
23. Kornbluh, *Bay of Pigs Declassified*, p.51.
24. Kornbluh, *Bay of Pigs Declassified*, pp.83–4.
25. Quoted in Waters (ed), *Making History*, p.20.
26. Dreke, Victor (Edited by Mary-Alice Waters), *From the Escambray to the Congo* (Pathfinder, New York, 2002), p.111.
27. Thomas, *Cuba: A History*, p.915.

28. Kornbluh, *Bay of Pigs Declassified* p.170.

29. Thomas, *Cuba: A History,* p.896.

30. Ibid. p.915.

31. Memo dated 11 March, 1961, in Kornbluh, *Bay of Pigs Declassified,* p.119.

32. The leaders of the Cuban exiles involved in the Bay of Pigs operation gave their story in *The Bay of Pigs; The Leaders' Story of Brigade 2506,* by Haynes Johnson with Manuel Artime, José Peréz San Román, Erneido Oliva, and Enrique Ruiz-Williams (W.W. Norton & Company, New York, 1964).

33. Rivas, Santiago, *Playa Girón; The Cuba Exiles' Invasion at the Bay of Pig 1961* (Helion & Company, Solihull, 2016), p.15.

34. Wyden, Peter, *Bay of Pigs: The Untold Story* (Simon & Schuster, New York, 1979), p.45.

35. Ibid., p.46.

36. Kornbluh, *Bay of Pigs Declassified,* p.7.

37. Ibid., p.52.

38. Rivas, *Playa Girón,* p.31.

39. De Quesada, Alejandro, *The Bay of Pigs; Cuba 1961* (Osprey Publishing, Oxford, 2009), p.20.

40. Rivas, *Playa Girón,* p.31.

41. Johnson, *The Bay of Pigs; The Leaders' Story,* p.94.

42. Thomas, *Cuba: A History,* p.921.

43. Ibid., p.927.

44. De Quesada, *The Bay of Pigs; Cuba 1961,* p.23.

45. Lynch, Grayston L., *Decision for Disaster; Betrayal at the Bay of Pigs: a CIA participant challenges the historical record* (Potomac Books, Washington, DC, 2009), p.85.

46. Johnson, *The Bay of Pigs; The Leaders' Story,* p.106.

47. Thomas, *Cuba: A History,* p.925.

48. Rivas, *Playa Girón,* p.25.

49. Ibid., p.41.

50. Ibid., p.41.

51. Johnson, *The Bay of Pigs; The Leaders' Story,* pp.116–117.

52. Ibid., p.116.

53. Johnson (1964), Lynch (2009), and de Quesada (2009) all state that the action that started at around 2.30pm on the 17th involved the destruction of Battalion 339. However, Rivas (2016), citing Cuban sources notes that Battalion 339 had been 'defeated at 9.00am' that morning; Rivas, *Playa Girón,* note 48, p.49.

54. Cruz, quoted in Johnson, *The Bay of Pigs; The Leaders' Story,* p.124.

55. Lynch, *Decision for Disaster,* p.101. Lynch notes in this quotation that it was the 339 Battalion of the MNR, but in an earlier account for the CIA, cited by Rivas (2016), p.49, Lynch said that the MNR were from the *Escuela de Responsables de Milicias.*

56. Cruz, quoted in Johnson, *The Bay of Pigs; The Leaders' Story,* p.125.

57. Castro, Fidel, *Playa Girón; A Victory of the People. Address by Dr. Fidel Castro Ruz, Prime Minister of the Cuban Revolutionary Government at the Special "People's University" TV broadcast, Sunday, April 23, 1961, to inform the people on the invasion of the mercenaries* (Editorial en Marcha, Havana, 1961), p.62.

58. Rivas, *Playa Girón*, p.50.

59. Ibid., pp.50–51.

60. Lynch, *Decision for Disaster*, p.103.

61. Lynch, ibid., says that one of the attacking tanks was a heavy JS-III, as does Johnson, *The Bay of Pigs; The Leaders' Story*, though other most other sources say that only T-34s were involved in this fighting. Lynch, p.103; Johnson, p.135.

62. Oliva, quoted in Johnson, *The Bay of Pigs; The Leaders' Story*, p.135.

63. Ibid., p.137.

64. Rivas, *Playa Girón*, p.56.

65. Connie Seigrist, quoted in Ibid., pp.58–59.

66. Lynch, *Decision for Disaster*, p.126.

67. Johnson, *The Bay of Pigs; The Leaders' Story*, p.157.

68. Rivas, *Playa Girón*, p.65.

69. Kornbluh, *Bay of Pigs Declassified*, p.3

70. DIA, *Handbook on the Cuban Armed Forces*, pp.I-4.

Chapter 8

1. Haswell, Jock, *Citizen Armies* (Peter Davies Ltd, London, 1973), pp.11–12.

Bibliography

Andres, Victor, *Bay of Pigs: An oral history of Brigade 2506* (University Press of Florida, Gainesville, 2001)

Atherton, William, *Narrative of the Suffering and Defeat of the North-West Army Under General Winchester*, in *Massacre on the River Raisin*, (Leonaur Publishing, 2013, no place of publication; first published, 1814)

Beckett, Ian F.W., *Riflemen Form; a Study of the Rifle Volunteer Movement, 1859–1908* (Pen & Sword, Barnsley, 2007 edition)

Beevor, Antony, *The Battle for Spain; The Spanish Civil War 1936–1939* (Weidenfeld & Nicolson, London, 2006)

Belfield, Eversley, *The Boer War* (Leo Cooper, London, 1993)

Benn, Carl, *The War of 1812* (Osprey Publishing, Oxford, 2002)

Bolin, Luis, *Spain: The Vital Years* (J.B. Lippincourt, Philadelphia, 1967)

Bruce, Phillip, *Second to None; the Story of the Hong Kong Volunteers* (Oxford University Press, Oxford, 1991)

Burke, Edmund, *Reflections on the Revolution in France* (Penguin Books edition, with an introduction by Conor Cruise O'Brien, Harmondsworth, 1969)

Busk, Hans, *Rifle Volunteers; How to Organize and Drill Them* (1859, reprinted, Uckfield, The Naval & Military Press Ltd, no date)

Cardozo, Harold G., *The March of A Nation; My Year of Spain's Civil War* (Right Book Club edition, London, 1937)

Castro, Fidel, *Playa Girón; A Victory of the People. Address by Dr. Fidel Castro Ruz, Prime Minister of the Cuban Revolutionary Government at the Special "People's University" TV broadcast, Sunday, April 23, 1961, to inform the people on the invasion of the mercenaries* (Editorial en Marcha, Havana, 1961)

Chartrand, René, *British Forces in North America, 1793–1815* (Osprey Publishing, Oxford, 1998)

Childers, Erskine, *In the Ranks of the CIV; a narrative and diary of personal experiences with the CIV battery (Honourable Artillery Company) in South Africa* (Smith, Elder & Co, London, 1901).

Cookson, J.E., 'Service without Politics? Army, Militia and Volunteers in Britain during the American and French Revolutionary Wars', *War in History*, 2003, volume 10, number 4

Cousins, Geoffrey, *The Defenders; A History of the British Volunteer* (Frederick Muller, London, 1968)

Cruikshank, E.A., *Harrison and Procter: The River Raisin* (Leonaur Publishing, 2013, no place of publication; first published, 1912)

Cullen, Stephen M., *In Search of the Real Dad's Army; the Home Guard and the Defence of the United Kingdom* (Pen & Sword Military, Barnsley, 2011)

Cullen Stephen M., 'Leaders and Martyrs: Codreanu, Mosley and José Antonio', *History*, vol. 71, no: 233, October 1986

Cunningham, Hugh, *The Volunteer Force; A Social and Political History, 1859–1908* (Archon Books, Hamden, CT, 1975)

Cosmas, Graham A., *An Army for Empire; the United States Army in the Spanish-American War* (Texas A&M University Press, College Station, 1998 edition)

Darnell, Elias, *A Journal Containing an Accurate and Interesting Account of the Hardships, Sufferings, Battles, Defeat and Captivity of Those Heroic Kentucky Volunteers and Regulars, Commanded by General Winchester, in the Years 1812–1813, in Massacre on the River Raisin* (Leonaur Publishing, 2013, no place of publication, first published, 1814)

De Quesada, Alejandro, *The Bay of Pigs; Cuba 1961* (Osprey Publishing, Oxford, 2009)

Dederer, John M., 'War and Society in Colonial America', in Gallaly, Alan (ed.), *Colonial Wars of North America*

DIA, *Handbook on the Cuban Armed Forces*, April 1979 (DDB–2680–62–79)

Dreke, Victor (Edited by Mary-Alice Waters), *From the Escambray to the Congo* (Pathfinder, New York, 2002)

Eby, Cecil, *The Siege of the Alcázar; Toledo: July to September 1936* (The Bodley Head, London, 1965)

Facey-Crowther, David, R., 'Militiamen and Volunteers: The New Brunswick Militia 1787–1871', *Acadiensis*, vol. 20, no: 1 (Autumn 1990)

Freidel, Frank, *The Splendid Little War* (Little and Brown, Boston, 1958)

Fyrth, Jim, & Alexander, Sally (Eds.), *Women's Voices from the Spanish Civil War* (Lawrence & Wishart, London, 1991)

Goldsworthy, Adrian, *Roman Warfare* (Cassell, London, 2000)

Graves, Donald E., *Field of Glory; the Battle of Crysler's Farm, 1813* (Robin Brass Studio, Toronto, 1999)

Grierson, J.M, *Records of the Scottish Volunteer Force, 1859–1908* (1909, reprinted, Uckfield, The Naval & Military Press Ltd., 2004)

Guevara, Ernesto 'Che', *Latin America Diaries* (Ocean Press, Melbourne, 2011)

Güner, Fisun, 'Felicia Browne: the only known British woman to die in the Spanish civil war', *The Guardian*, 20 July 2016

Hall, Christopher, 'Disciplina Camaradas'; Four English Volunteers in Spain 1936–39 (Gosling Press, Pontefract, 1994)

Hall, Christopher, *Revolutionary Warfare: Spain 1936–37* (Gosling Press, Pontefract, 1996)

Hall, Christopher, *'In Spain with Orwell'; George Orwell and the Independent Labour Party Volunteers in the Spanish Civil War, 1936–1939* (Tippermuir Books Ltd., no place of publication, 2013)

Haswell, Jock, *Citizen Armies* (Peter Davies Ltd., London, 1973)

Higgins, Trumbull, *The Perfect Failure: Kennedy, Eisenhower, and the CIA at the Bay of Pigs* (W.W.Norton, New York, 1987)

Hill, Richard, *War at Sea in the Ironclad Age* (Cassell, London, 2002)

Jackson, Thomas, *Narrative of the Eventful Life of Thomas Jackson, Militiaman and Coldstream Sergeant, 1803–15* (first published, 1847, and Helion & Company, Solihull, 2018, with notes and commentary by Eamonn O'Keeffe)

Johnson, Haynes, with Manuel Artime, José Peréz San Román, Erneido Oliva, and Enrique Ruiz-Williams, *The Bay of Pigs; The Leaders' Story of Brigade 2506* (W.W. Norton & Company, New York, 1964)

Jones, Nigel H., *Hitler's Heralds; the Story of the Freikorps, 1918–1923* (John Murray, London, 1987)

Katcher, Philip, *The American Provincial Corps, 1775–84* (Osprey Publishing, 1973)

Kisch, Richard, *They Shall Not Pass; the Spanish People at war, 1936–9* (Wayland Publishers, London, 1974)

Kornbluh, Peter (ed), *Bay of Pigs Declassified; the Secret CIA Report on the Invasion of Cuba* (The New Press, New York, 1998)

Ledeen, Michael A., *The First Duce; D'Annunzio at Fiume* (The John Hopkins University Press, Baltimore, 1977)

Longmate, Norman, *Island Fortress, the Defence of Great Britain, 1603–1945* (Pimlico, London, 2001)

Lynch, Grayston L., *Decision for Disaster; Betrayal at the Bay of Pigs: a CIA participant challenges the historical record* (Potomac Books, Washington, DC, 2009)

Mackenzie, S.P., *The Home Guard; a military and political history* (Oxford University Press, Oxford, 1995)

Mackinnon, Major-General H.W., *The Journal of the C.I.V. in South Africa* (John Murray, London, 1901)

Malmassari, Paul, *Armoured Trains; an Illustrated Encyclopaedia 1825–2016* (Seaforth Publishing, Barnsley, 2016)

Mathias, Peter, *The First Industrial Nation; an Economic History of Britain, 1700–1914* (Methuen, London, 1969)

Miller, Nathan, *Theodore Roosevelt, A Life* (William Morrow & Co Inc, New York, 1992)

Nelson, Ivan, F., *The Irish Militia, 1793–1802; Ireland's Forgotten Army* (Four Courts Press, Dublin, 2007)

Norfolk, R.W.S., *Militia, Yeomanry and Volunteer Forces of the East Riding, 1689–1908* (East Yorkshire Local History Society, Beverley, 1965)

Orr, David R., Truesdale, David, *'Ulster Will Fight ...'; Home Rule and the Ulster Volunteer Force, 1886–1922* (Helion & Company, Solihull, 2016)

Orwell, George, 'Notes on the Spanish Militias', in, Peter Davies (Ed.), *Orwell in Spain* (Penguin Books, London, 2001)

Parker, John H., *The Gatlings at Santiago; the History of the Gatling Gun Detachment, U.S. Fifth Army Corps, During the Spanish-American War, Cuba, 1898* (Leonaur edition, no place of publication, 2009)

Payne, Stanley, *Falange: A History of Spanish Fascism* (Stanford University Press, Stanford, 1961)

Peirats, José, *Anarchists in the Spanish Revolution* (Freedom Press, London, 1990)

Post, Charles Johnson, *The Little War of Private Post; the Spanish-American War seen up close* (University of Nebraska Press, Lincoln, 1999 edition)

Rammage, Stuart A., *The Militia Stood Alone; Malcolm's Mills, 6 November, 1814* (Valley Publishing, Summerland, BC, 2000)

Ranzato, Gabriele, *The Spanish Civil War* (The Windrush Press, 1999)

Rivas, Santiago, *Playa Girón; The Cuba Exiles' Invasion at the Bay of Pigs 1961* (Helion & Company, Solihull, 2016)

Reid, Stuart, & Chappell, Paul, *King George's Army 1740–1793*: (2) (Osprey, London, 1995)

Reid, Stuart, *North America 1753–63; British Redcoat versus French Fusilier* (Osprey Publishing, Oxford, 2016)

Roosevelt, Theodore, *The Rough Riders* (Dover Publications, New York, 2006 edition)

Sagarra, Pablo, González y Lucas Molina, Óscar, *Divisionarios; testimento gráfico de los combatientes Españoles de la Wehrmacht* (La esfera de los libros, Madrid, 2012)

Sargeaunt, B.E., *The Royal Manx Fencibles* (Gale and Polden Ltd., Aldershot, 1947)

Shea, William L., 'Militia', in Gallaly, Alan (ed.), *Colonial Wars of North America, 1512–1763; an encyclopedia* (Garland Publishing, New York, 1996)

Skeen, C. Edward, *Citizen Soldiers in the War of 1812* (The University Press of Kentucky, Lexington, 1999)

Sondhaus, Lawrence, *Naval Warfare, 1815–1914* (Routledge, London, 2001)

Steppler, Glenn A., *Britons To Arms! The Story of the British Volunteer Soldier and the Volunteer Tradition in Leicestershire and Rutland* (Budding Books, Stroud, 1997)

Stokes, Winifred, 'Investigating the history of local volunteer regiments: the Stockton Volunteers and the French invasion threat of 1798–1808, *The Local Historian*, vol. 37, No: 1, February 2007

Sulte, Benjamin, 'The Captains of Militia', *The Canadian Historical Review*, vol. 1, no: 3, September, 1920, pp.243–244

Thomas, Hugh, *Cuba: A History* (Penguin Books, London, 2010 edition)

Thomas, Hugh (ed.), *José Antonio Primo de Rivera: selected writings* (Jonathan Cape, London, 1972)

Thomas, Hugh, *The Spanish Civil War* (Pelican Books, Harmondsworth, 3rd edition, 1977)

Tupper, Ferdinand Brock (ed) *The Life and Correspondence of Major-General Sir Isaac Brock, K.B.* (Simpkin, Marshall, and Co., London, 1847 edition)

Von Clausewitz, Carl, *On War* (Penguin Books, Harmondsworth, 1968 edition)

Waters, Mary-Alice (ed.), *Making History: Interviews with four generals of Cuba's Revolutionary Armed Forces* (Pathfinder, New York, 1999)

Wells, Roger, 'The Militia Mutinies of 1795', in John Rule (ed.) *Outside the Law: Studies in Crime and Order, 1650–1850* (Exeter Papers in Economic History, University of Exeter, 1982)

Wyden, Peter, *Bay of Pigs: The Untold Story* (Simon & Schuster, New York, 1979)

Zaloga, Steven J., *Spanish Civil War Tanks* (Osprey Publishing, Oxford, 2010)

Index